SOCIAL WORKERS COUNT

Social Workers Count

NUMBERS AND SOCIAL ISSUES

Michael Anthony Lewis

OXFORD
UNIVERSITY PRESS

Oxford University Press is a department of the University of Oxford. It furthers
the University's objective of excellence in research, scholarship, and education
by publishing worldwide. Oxford is a registered trade mark of Oxford University
Press in the UK and certain other countries.

Published in the United States of America by Oxford University Press
198 Madison Avenue, New York, NY 10016, United States of America.

Library of Congress Cataloging-in-Publication Data
Names: Lewis, Michael Anthony, 1965- author.
Title: Social workers count : numbers and social issues / by Michael A. Lewis.
Description: New York : Oxford University Press, [2018] | Includes bibliographical
references and index.
Identifiers: LCCN 2018024142 (print) | LCCN 2018039615 (ebook) |
ISBN 9780190467142 (updf) | ISBN 9780190467159 (epub) |
ISBN 9780190467135 (pbk. : alk. paper)
Subjects: LCSH: Social service—Economic aspects. | Mathematics.
Classification: LCC HV41 (ebook) | LCC HV41.L47 2018 (print) |
DDC 361.301/51—dc23
LC record available at https://lccn.loc.gov/2018024142

9 8 7 6 5 4 3 2 1

Printed by WebCom, Inc., Canada

For Tomomi;

May she always appreciate SAM

Contents

Preface

THIS BOOK HAS one main objective: to sensitize social work students, as well as professional social workers, to the relevance of mathematics to our field. I'll do this by connecting math to a variety of social issues, especially policy-related ones. Along the way, I hope to teach (or reteach) readers some basic mathematics. Examples of issues we'll focus on are the measurement of poverty, adjusting the levels of social welfare benefits for inflation, the relationship between probability theory and determining whether the adult caretakers in a family have abused or neglected their children, estimating the effectiveness of a parenting skills training program, using math to assess the financial security of a household, using math to determine the fairness of an allocation of scarce resources, the relationship between math and politics, and a host of others. Given the small role mathematics currently plays in the training of social workers, I should say a few words about why I think such a book is warranted.

Both the National Association of Social Workers (NASW) and the Council on Social Work Education (CSWE) stipulate that social workers have an obligation to advocate for social policies that promote equity and social justice. Such advocacy requires social workers to take part in policy discussions/debates. We aren't the only ones, however, involved in such discussions: business professionals, policy analysts, economists, and other social scientists take part as well. A good number of policy debates, as well as social and economic discussions more generally, have quantitative dimensions. Arguably, members of the previously mentioned professions and disciplines are better prepared to handle these dimensions than are many social workers. The problem this poses is that our proposals for promoting equity and social justice may not be taken seriously if we don't show a basic understanding of the quantitative dimensions of the issues at hand. This book is an attempt to *begin* to address this situation.

I emphasize "begin" because I want to make it clear that I don't expect to turn readers into mathematicians. In fact, I'm not a mathematician but a quantitative social scientist who also has training in social work. If readers, especially those who don't consider themselves "numbers people," come away from the book with more of an appreciation of the mathematical aspects of social issues, I'll consider it a success.

Social work instructors who are reading this might wonder where such a book fits into the curriculum. I suspect it would best serve as a supplementary text for required (or elective) courses in social policy. It could also be used as a supplement for courses in social administration. Valerie Ringland, mentioned in the Acknowledgments, was a doctoral student much more recently than I was. She feels the book could be useful to social work students, including doctoral ones, who are required to study statistics but have forgotten the basic mathematical concepts on which this subject is based.

At this point, let me say a word about style. First, something about the distinction between *numerals* and *numbers*. The symbols "II," "2," "two," and "dos" all refer to the same thing. The thing they refer to or stand for is an idea of "twoness." That thing is a *number*. The symbols, which are all different ways of referring to twoness, are called *numerals*. Of course, there are numerals that refer to other numbers as well. The distinction between numerals and numbers is given a lot of attention in more philosophical or theoretical treatments of mathematics. But, with apologies to philosophers and mathematicians, I won't care much about that in this book. That is, I may say "number" when, technically, I should probably say "numeral" or vice versa. For what I want to accomplish, such a "mistake" simply doesn't matter.

The second thing I should say about style has to do with writing. I've deliberately adopted an informal and conversational tone. That is, I've chosen to write the book as if I'm having a conversation with the reader. This isn't to everyone's taste, so I apologize to those who don't like this sort of thing. All I can say in defense is that I believe such a tone might be less intimidating and more accessible to those, like I assume many readers will be, who are a bit "math phobic."

Even though the intended audience of this book is social workers, social and health scientists who want a gentle overview of basic mathematics—as well as how it's related to social issues—could also benefit. However, they would have to tolerate frequent references to social work.

The prerequisites for this book are modest. Anyone who has met the requirements for admission into a master's degree program in social work or a similar discipline/profession is prepared to read it. In fact, I suspect anyone who has completed high school mathematics is.

Acknowledgments

I FIRST THOUGHT of writing this book over a decade ago and ran the idea by an editor at a university publisher. She thought it was interesting but felt there wasn't a market for such a book. Upon hearing this, I gave up.

A few years ago, I emailed two colleagues about the anxiety and discomfort many social workers have when it comes to math. As we went back and forth online, I told them about the book idea I'd given up on. But then something surprising happened: both of them encouraged me to write it. Their view was that the world of social work had changed and that there might be a market for such a project now. The fact that I'm writing these lines suggests that perhaps they were right. So I want to start by thanking these two colleagues for inspiring me to get back to the book: Kristin Ferguson and James Mandiberg. Kristin also read part of the manuscript and was a continuing source of encouragement throughout the whole process.

Several others also read parts of the manuscript; although I take full responsibility for any mistakes that remain, I'm sure their input made the book a better one. These helpful eyes came from Peter Westfall, Shiro Horiuchi, Jessica Bovo, Patricia Dempsey, Alexis Kuerbis, Michael P. Marder, Maria Rodriguez, Valerie Ringland, and Samuel Arbesman.

Two other people I should thank are Dana Bliss and Andrew Dominello of Oxford University Press. Their patience and encouragement during the writing of this book made a long and tedious process much less so than it could've been.

Last, but certainly not least, I want to thank my "roommate" Eri Noguchi. For over 25 years, we've talked about social work, politics, economics, mathematics, statistics, and a host of other topics. When I had ideas about what to include in the book, she was the first person I'd run them by. I'm sure the book is much better for my having done so. I also have Eri to thank for the title, *Social Workers Count*.

1

ARGUMENTS AND SOCIAL ISSUES

POLICY DEBATES, AS well as debates about social issues more generally, involve arguments. Consider the minimum wage. Some contend that minimum wage laws are good because they assure that people will be paid enough to meet their needs. Others counter that such laws are bad because they cause unemployment, especially among low-skilled workers.

Here's another example. While recently[1] reading the online edition of a newspaper, I came across a story about President Trump's desire to restrict legal immigration. He claims that doing so would increase wages for American workers, especially low-wage workers. The article goes on to discuss the fact that many, though not all, economists are skeptical about Trump's position. They argue that immigration restrictions aren't likely to help American workers. This is because even if the flow of immigrants is slowed, employers will probably replace immigrants with automation instead of native-born workers.

Although arguments play an important role in discussions of social issues, our training as social workers doesn't expose us to much material about the nature, construction, and evaluation of arguments. This chapter is a small attempt to rectify this situation.

ARGUMENTS

When you hear the word "argument," you might think of the heated conversations many of us have over Thanksgiving dinners. However, these Thanksgiving dinner conversations may or may not be examples of what I have in mind when we use that term in this book. To understand what an argument is, you first need to understand what a *statement* is.

A statement is a sentence that can either be true or false but not both. For example, "the US poverty rate decreased between 2010 and 2014" is a statement. If we had trustworthy data on the poverty rates in 2010 and 2014, we could compare them and determine whether this statement is true or false.[2] Also, it should be clear that if it's true that the poverty rate decreased between 2010 and 2014, then it can't also be false that this rate decreased between those two years.

An argument is a collection of statements, one of which is called the *conclusion* and the other(s) the *premise(s)*. Premises are statements which support or provide reasons for believing that the conclusion of an argument is true. Consider the following example:

> *Premise*: The US poverty rate in 2010 was 15.8%, and in 2014 it was 15.3%.
> *Conclusion*: Therefore, the US poverty rate decreased between 2010
>   and 2014.

It's probably easy to see that the premise of this argument is meant to convince the argument's audience that the conclusion is true.

How do we determine whether the premises of an argument provide good reasons for believing that its conclusion is true? In other words, how do we evaluate the quality of an argument? The answer to this question depends on the type of argument we have in mind, and there are two major types of arguments—*deductive* arguments and *inductive* arguments.

A deductive argument is one which claims that its conclusion *must* be true if its premises are true. Here is an example:

> *Premise 1*: Any kid residing in a family of four whose annual income is less
>   than $23,850 per year is poor.
> *Premise 2*: Timothy is a kid residing in a family whose annual income is less
>   than $23,850 per year.
> *Conclusion*: Therefore, Timothy is poor.

If it's really true that any kid residing in a family of four whose annual income is less than $23,850 per year is poor, and Timothy is such a kid, then it *must* be true that Timothy is poor. That is, the statement after the word "conclusion" *has to be* true if the two premises are true. Whenever granting the truth of the premises of a deductive argument guarantees the truth of its conclusion, we have what's called a *valid* deductive argument.[3] Why could I use phrases like "must be" and "has to be" in the first few sentences of this paragraph? The answer to this question depends on understanding the concept of *contradiction*.

A contradiction is a statement which posits that something is true and, *at the same time*, that it's not true. The statement "Anne is suffering from clinical depression, and Anne is not suffering from clinical depression" is an example of a contradiction. Contradictions are always regarded as false because the rules of logic tell us that no statement can be both true and not true at the same time. Thus, contradictions are to be avoided when one is making an argument.

Here's how the idea of contradiction applies to the argument about Timothy. If premises 1 and 2 of that argument are true, but we deny that the conclusion is true, this amounts to a contradiction. We would be saying that Timothy resides in a family of four whose annual income is less than $23,850 per year, that anyone residing in such a family is poor, but that Timothy is not poor. This is the same as saying that Timothy is poor and simultaneously that he's not poor.

Now consider the following argument:

Premise 1: Anyone who works hard will be very rich.
Premise 2: Diane is very rich.
Conclusion: Therefore, Diane works hard.

Think carefully about this argument. Suppose by "works hard" we mean doing something of value to an employer for at least 10 hours a day in return for a wage or salary. By "very rich" we mean having an income of more than a million dollars per year. Many people might disagree with the first premise, but, for the sake of discussion, let's assume it's true. Let's also assume that the second premise is true. The fact that these two claims are true doesn't mean the conclusion of the argument must be true.

To see this, imagine that Diane spends 16 hours a day watching some of her favorite shows on television and that she's not being paid a wage or salary for this. Also, assume that during the eight hours left in the day she sleeps. Suppose, however, that Diane is the daughter of a wealthy family, and they've set her up to receive more than a million dollars per year in income. This shows that it's logically possible for Diane to be rich, for it to be true that anyone who works hard will be very rich, and for Diane *not* to be spending her time working hard. That is, if we

grant the truth of the two premises of this argument but deny the truth of its conclusion, we haven't asserted a contradiction.

What we have here is an attempt at (or claim of) a deductive argument, but that
attempt hasn't been successful. The conclusion of the argument doesn't have to
be true, assuming its premises are true. Such unsuccessful attempts at deductive
arguments are called *invalid* deductive arguments.

Now think about this argument:

Premise 1: Any kid whose first name begins with the letter "T" is poor.
Premise 2: Timothy is a kid whose first name begins with the letter "T."
Conclusion: Therefore, Timothy is poor.

This argument is very similar to the previous one about Timothy. A moment's
reflection should convince you that if premises 1 and 2 are true, then the conclusion of the argument must be true as well. But you might've noticed that the first
premise of this argument looks kind of "fishy." That is, you might doubt that just
having a first name beginning with the letter "T" is enough to make you poor.

So, suppose we assume that premise 1 of this second argument is actually false.
It would still be the case that *if* that premise (along with premise 2) were true, the
conclusion of the argument would have to be true as well. If granting the truth of
the premises of a deductive argument (regardless of whether they're actually true)
means its conclusion must also be accepted as true, we still have an example of a
valid deductive argument. In other words, what makes a deductive argument valid
is not having premises which are actually true. Validity is about what conclusion
must be drawn if we assume the argument's premises are true. Conclusions of
valid deductive arguments are sometimes said to *follow from* the premises of such
arguments.

Let's go back now to the first argument about Timothy, reproduced here:

Premise 1: Any kid residing in a family of four whose annual income is less
    than $23,850 per year is poor.
Premise 2: Timothy is a kid residing in a family whose annual income is less
    than $23,850 per year.
Conclusion: Therefore, Timothy is poor.

The first premise of this argument probably seems plausible. Whether it's true
would depend on how we determine whether someone is poor, a topic we'll discuss in a later chapter. But let's say we know for a fact that premise 1 of that argument is true, as well as premise 2. It would then follow that the conclusion of
the argument must be true as well. Here, we would have a case of a valid deductive

argument with a very important feature: the premises of the argument are *known to be true*. Such an argument is called a *sound* argument. If one is presented with a sound argument, then the premises (or premise) of that argument constitute good reasons for believing that its conclusion is true.

So, if you're faced with someone attempting to make a deductive argument and you want to see if it "holds water," you can do the following:

1. *Try to determine if the argument is valid.* You can do this by assuming that its premises are true, assuming that its conclusion is false, and seeing if this leads you to a contradiction. If so, the argument is valid.
2. *Try to determine if the premises of the argument are actually true.* There is no step-by-step procedure for doing this. You'll have to rely on your experience, reading you've done, studies you've been involved in, and the like.
3. If you've shown that the argument is valid and believe it to be sound, then you have good reasons for assuming that the conclusion of the argument is true.

We stated earlier that the other major type of argument is inductive. An inductive argument is one where the conclusion isn't claimed to follow from its premises. Instead, the premises are thought to provide evidence in favor of the argument. What we mean by "in favor of" is that the premises are meant to convince the target audience of the argument that the conclusion is true even though there is a recognition that the conclusion doesn't follow from the premises.

Consider the following argument:

Premise 1: Most people who abuse their children were themselves abused when they were children.
Premise 2: John abuses his child.
Conclusion: Therefore, John was abused when he was a child.

If you read this argument carefully, you'll see that it's possible for both premises to be true while the conclusion is false. That is, just because John abuses his kid and most of those who abuse their children were themselves abused as kids, doesn't necessarily mean that John was abused as a kid. There are clearly people who abuse their kids but who weren't themselves abused, and John might be one of them.

So, this argument clearly isn't a successful deductive argument. But the one who makes it may not at all intend it to be. They may, instead, intend to make an inductive argument. That is, they're not claiming that the conclusion follows from the premises but that the premises provide evidence or good reasons for believing that the conclusion is true. They might claim that the truth of the premises makes it more likely than not that the conclusion is true. The phrase "more likely than not" isn't very clear. The notion of "likely" has to do with probability, a topic we'll cover in a later chapter. But I suspect you already have an intuitive idea of what probability means, so let's think of "more likely than not" as a probability greater than 50%.

When it comes to inductive arguments, deciding whether premises provide good reasons for believing the conclusions of such arguments is trickier than with deductive ones. Science is an area which, arguably, specializes in the construction and evaluation of inductive arguments. What constitutes good reasons for believing in the conclusion of an argument among scientists largely comes down to whether one has data to support that conclusion. Consider something like global climate change.

Most climatologists think the world is in the midst of a warming trend and that human activities related to carbon emissions is largely to blame. They base this in part on theories from chemistry and physics about how carbon, as well as other greenhouse gases, interacts with sunlight. But these theories have been confirmed by a lot of data. Also, climate scientists have observed how carbon emissions and the global average temperature have both been trending upward in the past hundred years or so. Let's state this argument more schematically:

Premise 1: Average global temperature has been trending upward over the past 100 years or so.
Premise 2: Carbon emissions from human activities have been trending upward over the past 100 years or so.
Premise 3: Theories from chemistry and physics predict that increases in carbon emissions should increase global average temperature.
Premise 4: These theories have been confirmed by experimental data.
Conclusion: The observed increase in average global temperature is caused by the increase in carbon emissions.

Climate scientists realize that the truth of these four premises doesn't guarantee the truth of the conclusion of this argument. The reason the conclusion could be false, even if the four premises are true, is that theories from chemistry and physics predict that other things in addition to increases in human-induced carbon emissions *could* cause an increase in average global temperature. If one of these things were also occurring along with the human-induced increase in carbon emissions, as well as the increase in average global temperature, this other factor may be the cause of the temperature increase instead of the culprit being human activity. But, as far as I can tell from what I've read about the topic, climate scientists do think the premises in the preceding argument are true and that this makes the conclusion of the argument more likely than not. In fact, the "more likely than not phrase" may not be strong enough here. I suspect climate scientists don't think the probability of the truth of the conclusion is just a little more than 50% but considerably larger than that value.

There is another issue that must be considered in the evaluation of arguments, whether deductive or inductive. Take a look at the following statement:

"Blacks in the United States are more oppressed than are whites."

It should be clear that this statement could serve as a premise or conclusion of an argument. It should also be clear that, in order to evaluate whether it's true, we would need to know what the terms "blacks," "whites," and "oppressed" mean.[4] What makes a person black or white? Biologists tell us that it's not in the genes. Sociologists tell us that a person's race is a social construction. But who does the constructing? Do people define their races for themselves, do others define them, or does a person's race result from some combination of self- and other-imposed definitions?

What about oppression? Most people might agree that some categories of people are oppressed. Those who are forced to work without receiving a wage are typically called slaves, and we suspect most would agree that slaves are oppressed. But are wage workers in capitalism oppressed? Marxists, as well as others with a similar political orientation, might say "yes." "Free market" Libertarians are likely to say "no." Who's right?

Social scientists tell us that blacks have higher poverty rates and lower wages, on average, than whites. Does this *mean* that blacks are more oppressed than whites? In other words, is it *by definition* the case that if a group has a higher poverty rate and lower average wage than another group, then that first group is more oppressed than is that other group? We suspect some would not agree with this definition of oppression. But, in order to decide whether the preceding statement is true or false, we would need to agree on some definition of oppression. For how else could we decide whether blacks in the United States are more oppressed than are whites?

My intention here isn't to settle questions of what makes people black, white, or oppressed. Instead, I'm trying to show the importance of definitions by highlighting how evaluating the *truth value* (whether or not a statement is true) of statements depends on some level of agreement about the meanings of key concepts used in them.

DIFFERENT TYPES OF STATEMENTS USED IN ARGUMENTS

We said earlier that an argument is made up of statements. This section is about different types of statements that are used in arguments. One is called a *negation*. If p is a statement, the negation of p is *not p* or *it's not the case that p*. For example, suppose we have the statement "black children are more likely to end up in foster care than white children." The negation of this would be "it's not the case that black children are more likely to end up in foster care than white children" or "black children are not more likely to end up in foster care than white."

The rules of logic tell us that if a statement is true, its negation is false, and, if a statement is false, its negation is true. So, if the statement "black children are more likely to end up in foster care than white children" is true, then the statement "it's not the case that black children are more likely to end up in foster care than white children" must be false.

Another type of statement found in arguments is called a *conjunction*. These are also called *and* statements. If p is a statement and q is a different one, then *p and q* would be the conjunction of these two statements. A conjunction is true when the two statements comprising it are both true and false otherwise.[5]

For example, here's the conjunction "nonprofit social service agencies rely on private contributions and nonprofit social service agencies rely on public funding." This statement would be true if it's actually the case that nonprofit agencies rely on both private contributions and public funding and would be false otherwise.

To understand another type of statement, suppose a social worker says that a client they're working with is "either receiving benefits from the Temporary Assistance for Needy Families (TANF) program[6] or they're receiving them from the Supplemental Nutrition Assistance Program (SNAP)." This statement would be ambiguous since it could mean one of two different things. It could mean that the client is receiving either TANF benefits or SNAP benefits but not both. Or it could mean that the client is receiving TANF benefits, SNAP benefits, or both TANF and SNAP benefits. Mathematicians call "or" in the "either/or but not both case" the *exclusive or*. The "or" in the "either/or including the possibility of both case" is called the *inclusive or*. When mathematicians use the term "or" they typically mean it in its inclusive sense, and whenever I use the term in this book, I'll mean it this way, too, unless I specifically say otherwise.

The inclusive or is the basis of another type of statement frequently found in arguments—a *disjunction,* also called an *or* statement. It takes the form *p or q,* where p and q are any two statements. In order for a disjunction to be true, at least *p* or *q* must be true. Thus, a disjunction is only false if both the statements making it up are false.

For example, consider the earlier statement "my client is either receiving benefits from TANF or they're receiving benefits from SNAP." This is made up of the following two statements: (1) "my client is receiving benefits from TANF" and (2) "they're receiving benefits from SNAP." In order for the disjunction made up of each of these statements to be true, at least one of them must be true. That is, this disjunction would be false only if the clients being referred to were neither receiving TANF nor SNAP benefits.

To see another type of statement which comes up in arguments, suppose a social worker made the following claim: "if a family of four in the United States has an income less than \$23,850 per year, then that family is struggling to survive." This is an example of what mathematicians call a *conditional* or *if* statement. More generally, it can be written as *if p, then q*, where *p* and *q* are any two statements of interest. According to the rules of logic, a conditional statement is always true unless the statement coming directly after "if" is true but the one coming directly after "then" isn't true. So, the claim "if a family of four in the United States has an income less than \$23,850 per year, then that family is struggling to survive" would only be false if there is a family of four somewhere in the United States with an income less than \$23,850 per year and which is *not* struggling to survive. And, going back to a point we made earlier, we would need to agree on what it means to be "struggling to survive" to assess the truth value of this particular conditional expression.

Sometimes the statement that comes after "if" in a conditional statement is called a *sufficient condition*. It's sufficient in the following sense. If the overall conditional statement is true, and we know that the statement after "if" is true, then it *must* be the case that the statement after "then" is also true. In other words, the truthfulness of the statement after "if" is enough, all by itself, to guarantee the truthfulness of the statement after "then." However, the statement after "then" can still be true even if the statement after "if" isn't.

In our example, suppose it's true that "if a family of four in the United States has an income less than \$23,850 per year, then that family is struggling to survive." We then encounter a family whose income is less than \$23,850 per year. Then we know immediately that the family must be struggling to survive. However, this doesn't necessarily mean that a family's income *must* fall below \$23,850 per year in order for that family to be struggling to survive. A family with an income of \$23,851 per year and one with an income of \$30,000 per year, as well as families with other income levels might be struggling to survive, too.

The statement that comes after "then" in a conditional statement is sometimes called a *necessary condition*. It's necessary in the following sense. If the overall conditional statement is true, the statement after "then" *must* be true in order for the statement after "if" to be true. Yet the truthfulness of the statement after "then" isn't enough (isn't sufficient) to guarantee the truthfulness of the statement after "if."

Take a look again at the statement "if a family of four in the United States has an income less than $23,850 per year, then that family is struggling to survive." "That family is struggling to survive" is a necessary condition because, in order for a family of four to have an income of less than $23,850 per year, that family must be struggling to survive. In other words, there simply can't be a family of four with an income less than $23,850 per year who isn't also struggling to survive. Yet being a family of four who is struggling to survive doesn't mean that family must also have an income of less than $23,850 per year. There could be a family of four struggling to survive but who has an income of $300,000 per year, well above $23,850 per year. This could be because one of that family's members has a very bad gambling habit and so, month after month, they lose much of this very high income.

Many people find the necessary and sufficient condition language a bit confusing. It may help to think of a necessary condition as something that must happen in order for something else to happen; however, it happening alone isn't enough to make that other thing happen. A sufficient condition is one where it happening *alone* is enough to make something else happen; but that other thing could still happen even if the sufficient condition didn't happen. Here is another example.

Suppose the following conditional statement is true: "if a person is hired as a professional social worker, then they have at least an undergraduate degree in social work." In this case, "a person is hired as a professional social worker" is a sufficient condition for them having at least an undergraduate degree in social work. That is, having been hired as a professional social worker is enough for it to be true that you also have at least an undergraduate degree in social work. But this isn't a necessary condition because a person can have at least an undergraduate degree in social work without having been hired as a professional social worker. There are unemployed people with at least an undergraduate degree in social work, although, hopefully, not too many of them.

The statement "they have at least an undergraduate degree in social work" is a necessary condition. That is, assuming the overall conditional statement is true, in order for a person to be hired as a professional social worker, they must have at least an undergraduate degree in social work. But this statement isn't a sufficient condition because having at least an undergraduate degree in social work isn't enough, by itself, to get you hired as a professional social worker. You also need good references, to perform well on a job interview, to "know" someone, and so on.

Having gone over some of the types of statements that come up in various kinds of arguments, we'll use a classic social policy argument as further illustration of the relevance of these issues to social workers. In 1971 and again in 1993 (an updated version), a book entitled *Regulating the Poor: The Functions of Public Welfare* was published. The authors of this work are political scientist Frances Fox Piven and social worker-sociologist Richard A. Cloward.[7] In this book, these authors propose the following.

Capitalism is an economic system that is prone to periods of mass unemployment. This is due to "cyclical" phenomena like depressions, panics, recessions, and the like, as well as large-scale changes in how goods and services are produced (for example, more machines and fewer people producing things). Mass unemployment results in people being freed from social control, since our workplaces are important institutions which regulate our behavior, and this can lead to people becoming unruly. This unruliness can take the form of crime or more politicized actions, such as civil disobedience. According to Piven and Cloward, it's during these periods of social unrest when new social welfare programs are introduced or currently existing ones are expanded.

After the introduction of new, or the expansion of preexisting, social welfare programs, social unrest will eventually subside. Once unrest does subside, political authorities will begin to "reform" social welfare. According to Piven and Cloward, such efforts at reform are really attempts to decrease social welfare rolls in order to funnel a supply of cheap labor to employers.

Piven and Cloward's account has generated a great deal of controversy among social policy experts, but I won't get into the details of that debate here. Instead, I'll cast the part of their argument that's been most contentious into terms we've been discussing in this chapter. Then we'll go over what one would need to show in order to challenge this part of Piven and Cloward's argument.

Part of what Piven and Cloward are contending is that social unrest is a necessary but not sufficient condition for initiation or expansion of social welfare programs. Given the earlier discussion about how statements of necessary conditions are related to "if" statements, this is the same as saying "if a new social welfare program has been initiated or an existing one has been expanded, then this has been preceded or accompanied by social unrest." In other words, they're saying that in order for there to be initiation of a new or expansion of an existing social welfare program, there *must* be social unrest. But social unrest alone isn't enough for there to be initiation or expansion. This is because, instead of social unrest leading to initiation or expansion of social welfare programs, it might just lead to those engaging in such unrest being jailed or killed by political authorities.

If someone were interested in discrediting or at least raising questions about this view, they would need to come up with at least one instance when a new social welfare program was initiated, or a preexisting one was expanded, but where this didn't follow or wasn't accompanied by a period of social unrest. If such an instance could be found, then we'd have what's called a *counterexample* to Piven and Cloward's argument. In general, a counterexample can be thought of as an instance of something which was assumed to be impossible.

As another illustration of a counterexample, consider a social worker who contends that it's impossible for someone to save enough money to put a down payment on a house if this person is a recipient of public assistance. The minute we find a recipient of public assistance who saved up enough money to put a down payment on a house, we'd have a counterexample to this prediction.

PROOF AND ARGUMENT

Let's use the US federal minimum wage to introduce the topic of this section. At the time of this writing, that wage is currently $7.25 per hour. We suspect that many social workers, along with many who'd identify as politically progressive, would support an increase in the minimum wage. Many economists, along with many who'd identify as politically conservative, would probably oppose such an increase.[8] The reason many economists would oppose increasing the minimum wage is because they believe it would cause an increase in unemployment. Many economists believe an increase in the minimum wage would result in an increase in unemployment because a number of studies have found that increases in the minimum wage have also been associated with increases in unemployment. Let's recast this argument into the premise–conclusion format we've repeatedly used in this chapter:

Premise 1: A number of studies on the minimum wage have found that increases in it have been accompanied by increases in unemployment.
Conclusion: Therefore, if we were to increase the minimum wage, this would result in an increase in unemployment.

Now imagine a politician who opposes a minimum wage increase and who's talking to another one who supports such an increase.[9] The supporter asks the opponent why they're against the policy. The opponent responds by saying, "I'm against it because a minimum wage increase would also lead to an increase in unemployment." The supporter fires back, "how do you know that would happen"? The opponent responds, "I know because a number of studies have proven that increases in the minimum wage always cause increases in unemployment." Now here's a question: based on many economists' argument, presented earlier, is the politician correct? That is, do we have a proof that increasing the minimum wage will cause an increase in unemployment? To see why the answer to this question is "no," you need to understand what a proof is.

For our purposes, a *proof* is a step-by-step procedure which shows that a certain statement must be true if certain other statements are assumed to be true. The statement which the procedure shows must be true is often called a *theorem*.[10] Now look carefully at what we just said—a proof is a procedure for showing that a certain statement *must* be true if certain other statements are true. We've used this language before. We used it when talking about deductive arguments. This is no accident—a proof is really a kind of deductive argument. The theorem being proven is the conclusion of such an argument. The other statements used in proving the theorem can be thought of as the premises of the proof. The key point is that, in a proof, the theorem or conclusion follows from the premises. That is, the theorem simply *has to be true* if the premises are true. Now let's go back to the economists' argument about the effect of minimum wage increases on unemployment.

Here is that argument again:

Premise 1: A number of studies on the minimum wage have found that
    increases in it have been accompanied by increases in unemployment.
Conclusion: Therefore, if we were to increase the minimum wage, this would
    result in an increase in unemployment.

In order for this to be a proof, the conclusion would have to follow from the premise. That is, if it's true that a number of studies show that increases in the minimum wage have been accompanied by increases in unemployment, it must also be true that increasing the minimum wage at some point in the future would result in an increase in unemployment. Yet this conclusion clearly doesn't follow from its premise.

For one thing, the premise refers to increased unemployment "accompanying" (or being associated with) an increase in the minimum wage. The conclusion, however, refers to increased unemployment "resulting" from a higher minimum wage. This notion of "result" seems to suggest a causal relationship. But two things that are associated may or may not be causally related. We'll come back to this issue in a later chapter on statistics.

Let's assume for the time being that both the premise and conclusion do refer to a causal relationship between minimum wage and unemployment increases. Even then, the economists' argument still wouldn't be a proof. It might be that in every study which showed that a higher minimum wage causes higher unemployment, the minimum wage was increased by at least $600 per hour. Maybe the next increase would only be $1 per hour. Just because, in the past, $600 per hour increases in the minimum wage led to higher unemployment, that doesn't mean that a $1 per hour increase must do so as well. Now, obviously, these earlier studies didn't only look at minimum wage increases of at least $600 per hour. But that's beside the point. To show that the economists' argument isn't a proof, all we need to show is that it's possible for the premise of that argument to be true and its conclusion to be false—the at least $600 per hour versus $1 per hour possibility does exactly that.

Not only is it logically possible for the conclusion of this argument to be false even if its premise is true. There is, arguably, a good reason for believing this conclusion is false. Other studies have shown that increases in the minimum wage haven't been accompanied by increases in unemployment.[11] It should be said, though, that these studies also don't prove that increases in the minimum wage *don't* increase unemployment.

The reason we don't have proofs of the unemployment effects of the minimum wage, one way or the other, is because arguments about the effects of minimum wage increases on unemployment are inductive not deductive arguments. Remember that inductive arguments aren't about conclusions following from premises. All we can hope for is that there are good reasons for believing in the veracity of certain conclusions.

We've been discussing the distinction between proofs and inductive arguments in relation to the minimum wage debate. But this issue can arise in discussions of many topics of interests to social workers. Studies that have found, say, evidence that receipt of public assistance is accompanied by increases in "out of wedlock births," that increases in poverty rates are accompanied by increases in the rate of children entering foster care,[12] that availability of Head Start improves students' performance in school, and the like can be the basis of inductive arguments promoting specific policy prescriptions. The degree to which findings from such studies provide good reasons for certain policy conclusions would depend on the quantity and quality of the studies in question. The main point here is that studies like those just referred to typically don't prove anything, if "prove" is being used the way it is in mathematics.

FALLACIES

Imagine we're in a social policy class discussing the effects of welfare (also known as Aid to Families with Dependent Children [AFDC] or, in revised form, TANF). While doing so, we get to a contention made by the influential political scientist Charles Murray.[13] That contention stated that welfare is an example of a perverse social policy because it causes an increase in poverty (instead of a decrease, as was intended). Almost immediately a student raises their hand and asks if Charles Murray is white. The instructor answers "yes." In response, the student says "Charles Murray is wrong about the effect of welfare on poverty; he's just a rich white man who doesn't like welfare because he doesn't want to pay taxes to support it."

Let's reframe this student's response as the following argument:

Premise: Charles Murray is a rich white man who doesn't want to pay taxes to support welfare.
Conclusion: Therefore, Charles Murray is wrong about his view of the effect of welfare on poverty.

This argument would be a "textbook case" of a particular kind of fallacy. A *fallacy*, in general, is an error or mistake in reasoning. The fallacy here is called the *personal attack* fallacy.[14] The best way to characterize this type of fallacy is to say that it amounts to attacking or criticizing the person (or people, organization, group, etc.) who's made an argument instead of the substance of their argument.

Charles Murray may or may not be a rich white man who doesn't want to pay taxes to support welfare. Let's assume, for the sake of discussion, that the premise of this student's argument is true. Even so, this has no bearing whatsoever on whether his contention about the effect of welfare on poverty is true. That is, Murray's income, race, and what he wants to pay taxes to support is completely irrelevant to the question of the effect of welfare on poverty. I'm not saying that Murray's race, income, and the like has no relevance to anything—I'm simply saying that it is no relevance to the question at hand. If we were psychologists trying to determine the effect of one's income, race, and the like on one's social policy views, then these attributes of Murray would be quite relevant. But that isn't the question here.

Here is another example of the personal attack fallacy. Consider a black person who concludes that affirmative action is good social policy. After being asked by a white person why they think so, the black person says they believe this because the policy has improved the well-being of blacks in America. Immediately the white person says to the black one, "you're just saying that because you're a black person and you benefit from affirmative action."

It may be true that the black person benefits from affirmative action. But pointing this out isn't really addressing this person's argument. If the white person wants to challenge the black one's argument, they'd be better off challenging the premise of that argument. That is, a better tactic would be to question whether affirmative action has indeed improved the well-being of blacks, generally speaking, in America. This would require (1) coming to some agreement on what would indicate an improvement in the well-being of blacks in America and (2) looking at the best available data to determine if such improvement has occurred. Simply pointing out the race of the person making the argument and stating that they benefit from affirmative action is simply a personal attack that has nothing to do with the argument in question.

Of course, personal attack fallacies within the context of the affirmative action debate can cut both ways. In the years I've been teaching, I've come across students who've "rebutted" opponents of affirmative action by calling them racists or stating that they oppose affirmative action because of their white privilege. By now you should see the problem. An opponent of affirmative action may be a racist or may enjoy white privilege but whether either of these things is true has nothing to do with the question of whether affirmative action has merit as social policy.

Another common fallacy is known as the *false cause* fallacy. This occurs when someone assumes that just because one event preceded a second event, the first event must have caused the second one. For example, a family might recently have fallen into poverty. Afterward, that family might also end up with a kid in foster care. The poverty came before the entry into foster care, but assuming this necessarily means the foster care entry was caused by the impoverishment is an error in reasoning. A social worker might find that a client became clinically depressed after the loss of a job, but assuming this necessarily means the job loss caused the clinical depression would be a fallacy. The manager of a social service agency might conclude that noticeable improvement in parenting skill occurring subsequent to a parenting skill course necessarily means this improvement was caused by the course—this would also be an instance of the false cause fallacy.

Yet another fallacy you might sometimes see is the *appeal to accomplishment* fallacy. This occurs when someone assumes that a statement is true simply because of the accomplishments of the person, organization, or the like who's asserted the statement. Here's an example.

Two social work students are discussing whether foster care improves the well-being of neglected kids or whether such kids would be better off remaining with their parents/caretakers. One student asserts that kids would be better off in foster care. The second one asks why the first student believes this. The first student responds by saying "because Maria Gonzalez, a professor of social work at one of the best schools of social work in the country and who's won millions of dollars in federal grants, has stated that children are better off in foster care." This is fallacious reasoning because the fact that Maria Gonzalez has attained these high-level accomplishments, in and of itself, has nothing to do with whether or not neglected kids are better off in foster care. The best way to do this would be to agree on what constitutes being better off and then to gather the best available data for determining foster care's effect on neglected children.

The next fallacy is one I've frequently come across in classes, professional meetings, and the world of political debate. We'll call it the *hasty denial of cause* fallacy. To understand it, assume there are two events called A and B. Suppose someone has predicted that event A is a cause of event B. Someone else observes the world, sees event A occur, doesn't see event B follow, and concludes, because of this, that event A isn't a cause of event B. Here is a more concrete example.

Suppose event A is an income tax increase and event B is an increase in the number of people moving out of the jurisdiction where the tax increase has occurred. Jack contends that income tax increases cause people to leave jurisdictions to avoid paying higher taxes. Jill observes that the town of Sussex raised income taxes and that, after this occurred, there was no evidence of an increase in movement out of the jurisdiction. She concludes, on this basis, that increasing income taxes isn't a cause of people moving to avoid paying them.

Now it's true that Jack's prediction was somewhat imprecise and that Jill has found evidence that's inconsistent with it. Jack is, arguably, now under pressure to revise or perhaps discard his view about the effect of income tax increases on migration. But Jill's fallacy is concluding that there are no circumstances under which an increase in the income tax could cause people to move to avoid paying them. Perhaps income tax increases do cause people to move to avoid paying them but only if they result in tax levels falling beyond a certain threshold. Maybe the tax level after the increase observed by Jill didn't reach that threshold, and this is why she didn't see an increase in migration. Or maybe the level of income tax is one cause, among many, of where people choose to live. Some of these causes, like income tax increases, result in people migrating from the jurisdiction. Others, like high-quality schools, offset migration out of the jurisdiction by resulting in people staying put. Perhaps the income tax increase was accompanied by an improvement in schools, and this is why Jill observed no change in migration. This second possibility may be a little harder to see, so the following physical analogy may help.

Suppose someone contends that the force of gravity pulls things toward the surface of the earth. Someone else notices a plane during take-off and concludes that gravity isn't a cause of things being pulled toward the surface of the earth. This, of course, is a fallacy because gravity isn't the only physical force acting on airplanes, and some of these other forces can offset the effects of gravity. The occurrence of plane crashes, however, is a stark and tragic reminder that the force of gravity is still operating.

There are a number of things covered in logic texts that we didn't discuss in this chapter. But that stands to reason, since this isn't a book on logic. We covered the topics we did because these are the ones which come up most frequently in discussions and debates about social issues. Having covered these more relevant matters, we'll turn, in the next chapter, to another foundation area relevant to the rest of this book—basic mathematical concepts.

NOTES

1. By "recently" I mean around the time I'm writing these lines, early August of 2017.

2. This definition of "statement" is the one used in *crisp* or *classical logic*. In crisp logic, a statement is either true or false—that is, it's not somewhat true, partially true, 55% true, or anything like that. The branch of logic which focuses on partial truth is called *fuzzy logic*. The discussion of logic in this book deals only with classical logic.

3. Strictly speaking, logic—sometimes called *formal logic*—focuses on the validity of deductive arguments that are valid because of the form of those arguments. By the "form" of an argument, I mean the relationship between the premise(s) and conclusion of an argument regardless of what the argument is specifically about. For example, suppose "p" and "q" are statements. The rules of logic tell us that if the premises "if p, then q" and "p" is true, then "q" is also true. This is the case regardless of what "p" and "q" stand for. In contrast to the form, the content of an argument is specifically what the argument is about. The argument in this passage concerning "poverty" is about the definition of that term, as well as whether Timothy's family's income meets that definition. So, the conclusion of this argument isn't based on the formal relationships between premises and conclusion but, instead, on their content. In this chapter, when I discuss the validity of a deductive argument, I'll allow for validity based on either form or content.

4. We'd even need to know what the term "United States" means, but I'll focus only on the terms "blacks," "whites," and "oppressed" to make the point.

5. There are ways to use conjunctions with more than two statements, but I won't spend any time on those.

6. This is a program that mainly provides cash benefits to low-income women with young children. It's more commonly called "welfare," although that term is used more broadly by social policy experts to refer to a variety of benefits that governments provide to citizens/residents.

7. At this writing, Piven is still alive, but Cloward is no longer with us.

8. Just to be clear, I'm not saying that all social workers are politically progressive and all economists are conservative. That just wouldn't be true. But it might be (I suspect it is) the case that the percentage of social workers who label themselves politically progressive is greater than the percentage of economists who do so, and the percentage of economists who label themselves conservative is greater than the percentage of social workers who do so. For those who are rusty regarding percentages, we'll cover them in a later chapter.

9. In this book, we'll use "they," "they're," etc. instead of "he," "she," "hers," etc. in an effort to be gender-neutral.

10. There are other types of statements involved in proofs, such as *lemmas, axioms*, and *corollaries*, but I don't need to get into those for this book.

11. For an overview of research on the effects on the minimum wage, see Schmitt (2013).

12. We'll discuss poverty, as well as other kinds of rates, in a later chapter.

13. Charles Murray is an influential and controversial political scientist, perhaps best known for his book, co-authored with the late Richard Hernstein. See Murray, Charles, and Hernstein (1994).

14. The fallacies we'll discuss are also known by Latin names. For example, this one is also called the *ad hominem* fallacy. *Ad hominem* is Latin for "to the person." We won't use the Latin names in this book. Instead, we'll use the English ones found in Bennett and Briggs (2008).

2

THE MATH YOU NEED TO KNOW

IT'S OFTEN SAID that an area of mathematics called *set theory* is the foundation for all branches of mathematics. For our purposes, set theory can be thought of as the study of groups or collections of things. I discuss set theory in this book for one main reason: concepts from set theory are important for explaining some of the basic ideas in probability and statistics, topics we'll cover in later chapters. But set theory also provides a convenient language for speaking precisely about things which initially seem to have little to do with mathematics. As you read on, I suspect you'll come to see what I mean by this second point.

BASICS OF SET THEORY

A *set* is a group or collection of things. For example, all the people enrolled in the Temporary Assistance for Needy Families (TANF) program on March 27, 2015, can be regarded as a set. Even though a set may be made up of more than one thing, the set itself is considered as a single object. The things which make up a set are called the *members* or *elements* of that set.

To keep matters simple, suppose Jack, Jill, and Cinderella were the only people enrolled in the TANF program on March 27, 2015. Then the set, which I'll call T, with these three as its only members, can be represented like so:

T = {Jack, Jill, Cinderella}

The use of brackets around the members of a given set is one of the most common ways of representing sets; we'll sometimes use this notation in the remainder of the book.

Even though sets often have at least two members, it's possible for a set to have only one element. For example, suppose a social service agency provides services to single parents. Suppose the youngest person served by this agency is named Ellen. Then the set with the youngest person serviced by this agency as its only member could be represented like this:

Y = {Ellen}

Just as a set can have only one member, a set can also have no members. This set is called an *empty set* and is frequently represented as follows:

{}

Assuming no humans residing on Earth were born on Mars and that all clients of social service agencies currently reside on Earth, an example of the empty set would be the set of clients of a given social service agency who were born on Mars.[1]

Consider set T, recipients of TANF, again:

T = {Jack, Jill, and Cinderella}

Suppose both Jack and Jill are white while Cinderella is black. What would the set of black TANF recipients be? It would, of course, be this:

B = {Cinderella}

Notice that the only member of B is also a member of T. This is an example of a *subset*. Generally, a given set is a subset of another one if every member of the first set is also a member of the second one, just as every element of B is also an element of T.

Two sets X and Y are equal if every element of X is also an element of Y and every element of Y is also an element of X. Suppose a social service agency only provides services to poor clients. Then all the people that agency provides services to can be represented as a set. Let's call this set A. All the people this agency provides services to who are poor can also be represented as a set which we'll call Po. Clearly every member of A is also a member of Po, and every element Po is also an element of A. So, these two sets are equal.

Sometimes a set can be a subset of another one but not be equal to it. This was the case with sets B = {Cinderella} and T = {Jack, Jill, Cinderella}. Whenever a given set is a subset of another one but isn't equal to that other set, we have what's called a *proper subset*. So, B is a proper subset of T.

Assuming there is no fraud, all those currently receiving unemployment insurance are unemployed. Those employed in the investment banking industry are obviously not unemployed. So, the set of all those currently receiving unemployment benefits and the set of people working in the investment banking industry have no elements in common. When two or more sets have no members in common, they are called *disjoint sets*.

We've seen that T is the collection of all people on TANF, three of them in our simplified example. Suppose W is the set of all single mothers. We could use these two sets to form another one: the set of all those who are either on TANF, a single mother, or a single mother who is on TANF. This set, which we'll call V, would be the *union* of T and W. Generally, a union of two or more sets is one which is made up of all those elements which are in *at least one* of the sets making up the union. Notice that all the elements of V are in at least one of T or W.

Next we consider the complement of a set. This idea is a bit more complicated than those we've covered so far. Consider the set of all those who are US residents. Some US residents are on TANF, and some are not. Now think of TA as the set of US residents on TANF. Let TA' be the set of US residents *not* on TANF. In the language of set theory, TA' is the complement of TA. In general, the *complement* of set X is all those elements that are members of some larger set but which aren't elements of X.

In the preceding example, the larger set is the set of all US residents. The larger set in the definition of "complement" is called the *universal set*. So, the universal set in our example is the set of all US residents. And the complement of TA' is the set of all those US residents who are not on TANF (that is, who aren't elements of TA).

SETS OF NUMBERS

Having talked a bit about sets in general, let's focus on sets of numbers. We'll deal with such sets quite a bit in this book. The first set of numbers we're exposed to as young children are the *whole* or *natural numbers*. This is the set {0, 1, 2, 3, 4, 5 . . . }. The " . . . " after 5 means that these numbers continue on without end. That is, there is no largest whole or natural number. The natural numbers above 0 are also called *positive numbers*.

Natural numbers come up in discussions of social issues whenever counting is involved. We might need to count the number of people who are poor, the number who receive unemployment benefits, the number who receive food stamps, the number of kids a TANF recipient has, and so on. Assuming people with amputated limbs count as whole persons, the number of poor people, the number of people receiving the social benefits just referred to, and the number of children of a TANF recipient all must be whole numbers. It simply wouldn't make sense to say that one and a half people are living in poverty or that a TANF recipient has two and a half children. In fact, the number of children a TANF recipient has must be a positive number because only people with at least one minor child are allowed to receive TANF.

The next set of numbers we need to discuss are *negative whole numbers*. This is the set of numbers below 0: {−1, −2, −3, −4, −5 . . . }. Again we see the " . . . " to indicate continuing without end. One place where negative numbers come up in discussions of social issues is when we're dealing with deficits of some kind. For example, in a later chapter we'll see that the US federal government collects money from citizens and residents, and it spends money. For the most part, it collects money in taxes and spends it on defense, social welfare benefits, the postal service, and other things.

Nonprofit social service agencies also take in money as well as spend it. They tend to take it in as grants from governments or private donations. And they spend money to provide services which accord with their missions. Individual households also take in money, often as earnings or wages, and spend it to meet their wants and needs. What governments, nonprofit social service agencies, and households have in common is that they can all get into a situation where the amount of money they take in is less than the amount they're spending. When this occurs, these entities experience deficits, and, as we'll see in a later chapter, deficits can be represented as negative whole numbers.

The positive whole numbers, negative whole numbers, and 0 together are called the set of *integers*. That is, integers are elements of the set { . . . −5, −4, −3, −2, −1, 0, 1, 2, 3, 4, 5 . . . }. A visual image of the set of integers is shown in Figure 2.1:

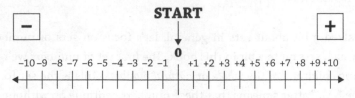

FIGURE 2.1 The Integers (see the website http://passyworldofmathematics.com/arranging-integers-in-order/).

Notice that the numbers to the right of 0 have a "+" next to them, indicating that they're positive integers. Those to the left of 0 have a "–" next to them, indicating that they're negative integers. The arrows on the negative and positive sides represent the fact that the numbers on both sides of 0 continue without end.

Another set of numbers we'll be concerned with in this book is the set of fractions. *Fractions*, for our purposes, can be thought of as numbers written with a line separating them like so: p/q or $\frac{p}{q}$. However, in p/q (or $\frac{p}{q}$), q cannot be 0. When p and q are integers, another term used to refer to fractions is *rational numbers*. The number listed before the line, p, is called the *numerator* of the fraction, whereas q is called the *denominator*.[2]

A *proper fraction* is one where the numerator is less than the denominator. An *improper fraction* is one where the numerator is greater than the denominator. For example, 50/100 would be a proper fraction but 100/50 would be an improper one. Proper fractions will come up a lot in this book when we discuss things such as poverty rates, mortality rates, probabilities, and a host of other issues.

Integers themselves can also be expressed as fractions. All you need to do is place the integer you want to express as a fraction in the numerator and the number 1 in the denominator. For example, the integers 50, 100, and 5,000 can also be expressed as 50/1, 100/1, and 5,000/1. The integers –50, –100, –5,000 can be expressed as –50/1, –100/1, and –5,000/1. The integers expressed as fractions in the previous sentence were all negative. This shows that fractions can assume negative values just as whole numbers can.

Whenever the same integer is in the numerator and denominator of a fraction, that fraction is equal to 1. So, 3/3, 10/10, 2,000,000/2,000,000 are all equal to 1. It's also true that 1 can be expressed as 1/1.

A concept we'll need later in the book is the *absolute value* of a number. The simplest way to think about the absolute value of a number is as the positive version of the number in question. Take the number 5. Since 5 is already positive, the absolute value of 5 is also 5. Now take the number –5. The positive version of –5 is 5; that is, to get the absolute value of a negative number, just drop the negative sign. The symbol for absolute value is "| |." Thus, the absolute value of 5 can be expressed as |–5| = 5.

DECIMAL NUMBERS

Decimal numbers are those with a period (.) between two of the digits making up the number. That period is called the *decimal point*. For example, consider the decimal number 3.5247. The period between 3 and 5 is the decimal point. It'll be important at various points in this book to be able to interpret decimal numbers, so let's go over how it's done. The concept to begin with is place value.

Place value is the idea that the location of a digit tells you something about the value represented by that digit. Let's leave decimal numbers for a moment and consider a number like 824. The digit furthest to the right is located in the ones place. The digit directly to the left of the digit in the ones place is in the tens place. The digit directly to the left of the digit in the tens place is in the hundreds place. The ones' place digit tells us how many ones there are in the overall number, the tens' place digit tells us how many tens there are, and the hundreds' place digit tells us how many hundreds there are. Thus, with 824 we have 4 ones + 2 tens + 8 hundreds. Another way to write this is as follows:

$$100 + 100 + 100 + 100 + 100 + 100 + 100 + 100 + 10 + 10 + 1 + 1 + 1 + 1$$

| 8 HUNDREDS | 2 TENS | 4 ONES |

Even though we haven't gotten to the part of the chapter on addition yet, I suspect you know how to add all these numbers to get a total of 824.

Now consider the number 824,455,723,487,202. Going from right to left, we have the ones', tens', hundreds', thousands', ten thousands', hundred thousands', millions', ten millions', hundred millions', billions', ten billions', hundred billions', trillions', ten trillions', and hundred trillions' places. So, this number is 2 ones + 0 tens + 2 hundreds + 7 thousands + 8 ten thousands + 4 hundred thousands + 3 millions + 2 ten millions + 7 hundred millions + 5 billions + 5 ten billions + 4 hundred billions + 4 trillions + 2 ten trillions + 8 hundred trillions. This is a huge number, far bigger than most of the ones we'll see in this book. But looking at such a big number is a nice way to obtain an understanding of place value.

Getting back to decimal numbers, let's go back to 3.547. The number to the left of the decimal point is the ones' digit we were just talking about. So, by now, you probably know how to interpret any numbers that might appear to the left of that one. The first digit on the right of the decimal point is in the tenths' place, the second is in the hundredths' place, and the third is in the thousandths' place. Going further to the right, we would have the ten thousandths', hundred thousandths', millionths', ten millionths', hundred millionths' places, and so on. So, 3.547 means that we have 3 ones + 5 tenths + 4 hundredths + 7 thousandths. Another way to write 5 tenths is 5/10. We can write 4 hundredths as 4/100 and 7 thousandths as 7/1,000. So, 3.547 can also be written like so:

$$1 + 1 + 1 + 1/10 + 1/10 + 1/10 + 1/10 + 1/10 + 1/100 + 1/100 + 1/100 + 1/100 +$$

$$\underbrace{}_{\text{3 ONES}} \quad \underbrace{}_{\text{5 TENTHS}} \quad \underbrace{}_{\text{4 HUNDREDTHS}}$$

$$1/1000 + 1/1000 + 1/1000 + 1/1000 + 1/1000 + 1/1000 + 1/1000$$

$$\underbrace{}_{\text{7 THOUSANDTHS}}$$

Adding fractions might be something from your elementary school days, so I won't hold it against you if you don't remember how to do it. Instead, I'll cover it later. But another matter about attaching 0s to decimal numbers needs to be cleared up first.

Consider the decimal number .57. We could attach a 0 to the end of this number and not change its value. That is, .57 is the same as .570. One way to see this is to think of .570 as follows:

5 tenths + 7 hundredths + 0 thousandths = .570

If we add no thousandths to 5 tenths and 7 hundredths we get this:

5 tenths + 7 hundredths = .570 = .57

Another way to see that .57 and .570 are the same is to think about decimal numbers a little differently than we have so far. Instead of thinking of .57 as 5 tenths + 7 hundredths, we could think of it as 57 hundredths or 57/100. The number .570 could be thought of as 570 thousandths or 570/1,000. Do you see the pattern? What we're doing is looking at a decimal number and asking how "far out" in place value does it go? Once we figure that out, we can think of the entire decimal number as being that many place values. With .57, the furthest we get is to the hundredths place. So, .57 becomes 57 hundredths or 57/100. With .570, the furthest we get is to the thousandths place; thus, .570 is 570 thousandths or 570/1,000. It can be shown that 57/100 is the same as 570/1,000. It's also true that .57 or 57/100 is the same as .5700 or 5,700/10,000. Again attaching a 0 to the end of a decimal number doesn't change its value no matter how many 0s you attach.

While on the topic of decimal numbers and attaching os to such numbers, we need to say a bit about how whole numbers or integers can be written as decimal numbers. Take the number 15. This number can also be written as 15.0, 15.00, 15.000, 15.0000, and so on. That is, we can add a decimal point and then attach as many os as we want to a number without changing its magnitude.

ARITHMETIC AND NUMBERS

I suspect most of you reading this book will use a calculator or computer to do complicated calculations. So, I'll go into some of the details of how to add, subtract, and perform other operations on different types of numbers but won't "go overboard." Instead, I'll go into just enough detail to refresh your memory about a few basic concepts which we'll need in later chapters.

One of the things we do with numbers is add them. The result of adding two or more numbers is called the *sum* of those numbers. If 60 families served by one agency are poor and 45 different families served by another are also poor, then the sum of poor families served by both agencies is 105, since the sum of 60 and 45 equals 105. That is 60 + 45 = 105.

When we subtract one number from another we get what's called the *difference* between the two numbers. If 105 families served by an agency are poor, and, after six months, 50 of them are no longer poor, there will be a difference of 55 poor families served by the agency since the difference between 105 and 50 equals 55. That is, 105 – 50 = 55.

When two or more positive numbers are added, the result is also positive. Since 6 is positive, 12, which is the sum of 6 + 6, is also positive. When two or more negative numbers are added the result is negative. So, in the expression –6 + –6 = –12, the sum, –12, is a negative number. If a larger number is subtracted from a smaller number, the difference will be a negative number. For example, 5 – 10 = –5 and 10 – 20 = –10.

To add a negative number to a positive number, you do the following. First, change that negative number to a positive number. Next, *subtract* the positive number you just changed from a negative number from the positive number you started with. This may sound confusing but an example should make things clear. Suppose you want to find the sum of 10 + –5. For the first step, change –5 to 5. For step two, subtract 5 from 10 (since 10 is the positive number you started out with). That is, you change 10 + –5 to 10 – 5 = 5. Thus, 5 is the sum of 10 and –5.

If two numbers are multiplied together, the result is called a *product*. You might recall that multiplication is really just a shortened form of addition. Take, for example, the product of $5 \times 10 = 50$. This is the same as adding up ten 5s: $5 + 5 + 5 + 5 + 5 + 5 + 5 + 5 + 5 + 5 = 50$. One of the properties of multiplication is that the order of the numbers being multiplied makes no difference to the product. So, we find that $10 \times 5 = 50$ just as $5 \times 10 = 50$. This also means that $10 \times 5 = 50$ is the same as adding up five 10s: $10 + 10 + 10 + 10 + 10 = 50$.

Even though it's common to use the symbol "$\times$" to refer to multiplication, I won't do so again in this book because I don't want the mathematical symbol "$\times$" to be mistaken for the letter "x." Instead, I'll refer to multiplication using a symbol found widely in computer programming languages: "*." So, instead of writing $5 \times 10 = 50$, I'll write $5 * 10 = 50$.

You might recall that the product of a positive number multiplied by another positive number is also a positive number. The product of a negative number multiplied by another negative number is a positive number. And a positive number multiplied by a negative number is a negative number. Here are some examples. The product of $5 * 5$ is 25, a positive number. The product of $-5 * -5$ is also 25. The product of $-5 * 5$ is -25, a negative number.

If a number is multiplied by itself, this is called *squaring* the number, and the result of squaring a number is called the *square* of the number. For example, $2 * 2 = 4$ so 4 is the square of 2. Another way of saying this is that 4 equals 2 *squared*. The product of $2 * 2$ is also sometimes expressed as 2 to the second *power* or as 2 to the power of 2. This is written as $2^2 = 4$. The little 2 in the upper right of this expression is also called an *exponent*. More generally, in the expression $y = z^x$, x is the *exponent*. The number represented by the letter z is called the *base*. So, in the expression 10^2, "10" is the base and "2" is the exponent.

All the numbers we've discussed so far in this chapter are examples of what mathematicians call real numbers. *Real numbers* also include a set of numbers called *irrational numbers*. Irrational numbers have a relatively technical definition, technicalities we don't need to get into in this book. Just think of them as the numbers in the set of real numbers that are "left over" after considering all the numbers we've discussed so far.

Real numbers can be taken to other integer powers besides the second power, including negative powers. For example, $2 * 2 * 2 = 2^3 = 8$. If a number is taken to a negative power, the result is $1/the\ same\ number\ to\ the\ same\ power\ without\ the\ negative\ sign$. For example, $2^{-3} = 1/2^3 = 1/8$.

Real numbers can also be taken to fractional powers. The only fractional power we'll be concerned with in this book is the 1/2 power. Any number to the 1/2 power is equivalent to the square root of the number, where the notation for square root is "$\sqrt{}$." For example, $4^{1/2} = \sqrt{4} = 2$. Actually, it could also be -2 since $-2 * -2 = 4$. But we'll only be concerned with positive square roots in this book, so whenever you see the square root sign, it'll be referring to the positive square root.

If we divide one number by another one, the result is called a *quotient*. The symbol used for division is "÷." So, in the expression $10 \div 5 = 2$, 2 is the quotient. Another way to symbolize division is by using the same backslash sign we used for fractions: "/." So, $10 \div 5 = 5$ could also be written as $10/5 = 5$. Using this alternative symbol, we've turned the expression $10 \div 5$ into a fraction. Yet another way of symbolizing division is one I'll use a lot later on when we start discussing formulas: $\frac{10}{5}$. As I said earlier, this is another way of symbolizing fractions. So, a fraction is just a different way of expressing division. In a fraction, the numerator is divided by the denominator.

From a conceptual point of view, when a smaller number is divided into a larger one, we can think of the quotient as telling us how many sets of the smaller number can "fit into" the larger one. For example, we can think of $10/5 = 2$ as telling us that two sets of five can fit into 10. As another example, consider 13 divided by 5 or $13/5$. There are two sets of 5 in 13, but this leaves us with 3 leftover. The number 3 is called a *remainder*. In general, whenever a smaller number doesn't divide evenly into a larger one, we're left with a remainder.

Another type of number we ought to say something about is called a pure number. A *pure number* is one that has no unit of measurement associated with it. For example, suppose we ask a parent how many kids they have. The answer we'll get is likely to be something like 1, 2, 3, or more We're not likely to get an answer like 2 lbs of kids, $2 of kids, or 2 years of kids. The first list of numbers (1, 2, 3, etc.) is made up of pure numbers while the second list is not. The second list contains numbers with their associated units of measurement (lbs, $, and years). We'll talk more about measurement and units of measurement in a later chapter.

So far, we've focused on arithmetic with whole numbers. But, as I'm sure you remember from your school days, we can add, subtract, and perform other operations on decimals and fractions, too. Let's start with fractions.

If the fractions you want to add have the same denominator, things are relatively easy. You simply add the numerators as you would any whole numbers, place the resulting sum over the same denominator you started with, and that's your answer. For example, to add $1/10 + 1/10 + 1/10$, you take the sum of $1 + 1 + 1$ which is 3, place 3 over 10 which is $3/10$, and that's your answer.

Subtracting fractions is just as easy when the fractions being subtracted have the same denominator. Suppose you want to obtain the result of $10/27 - 5/27$. First, you would take the difference $10 - 5$ to get 5. Next, you would place the 5 over the 27 to get $5/27$. And that would be your answer. In general, when subtracting fractions with the same denominator, you take the difference (or differences if you're working with more than two fractions) of the numbers in the numerators, place the result over the denominator you started with, and that's your answer.

Adding or subtracting fractions with different denominators is more complicated. Since, as I said earlier, you're likely to do more complicated calculations with a computer or calculator, I'll leave these details for math class. Just realize that fractions with different denominators can be added and subtracted.

Multiplying fractions is easy. You simply multiply the numerators to get the numerator of your product and multiply the denominators to get your product's denominator. So, (5/10) * (27/33) is 135/330.

Suppose you want to divide the fraction 5/10 by 3/9. This can be written as 5/10 ÷ 3/9. The first step is to take the *reciprocal* of the fraction you're dividing into the other one. To take the reciprocal means you "reverse" the positions of the numerator and denominators. Since we're dividing 3/9 into 5/10, we take the reciprocal of 3/9 which is 9/3. The next step is to multiply this reciprocal by the other fraction you started with. So, in our case, we would multiply (5/10) * (9/3), which give us 45/30.

To make things interesting, recall that a fraction itself is another way of representing division. So, 45/30 is the same as 45 ÷ 30. The number 30 goes into 45 one time, leaving us with 15. Recall that the number 15 in this context is called a remainder. Whenever dividing one number into another leaves a remainder, the answer is always some whole number plus a fraction, with the remainder as the numerator of this fraction and the original denominator as its denominator. So, in our case, we would have 45 ÷ 30 = 45/30 = 1 + 15/30. Since 15 is half of 30, we could also write this as 1 + 1/2.

If you enter 45/30 into a computer or calculator, you'll get 1.5. This is the decimal number 1 + 5/10. Since 5 is half of 10, this is also 1 + 1/2. But, again, a fraction is another way of representing division. So, 1/2 = 1 ÷ 2 must equal .5. This *has to be true* if 1 + 1/2 = 1 + 5/10 = 1.5. There is a general principle at work here.

Whenever a larger number is divided into a smaller one (2 being divided into 1, for example), the result will always be a decimal number *with no whole number part*. Notice that 1/2 = .5. It isn't 3.5, 23.5 1,000,000.5—it's just .5.

By this point, it should be clear that fractions and decimal numbers are just two different ways of saying the same thing. For example, .5 and 5/10 are just two different ways of saying 1/2. In fact, any fraction where the numerator is half the denominator is equal to 1/2. So, both 50/100 and 500,000/1,000,000 are also equal to 1/2.

Since decimal numbers are just fractions, it shouldn't be surprising that they can also be added, subtracted, multiplied, and divided. When adding or subtracting decimal numbers, the decimal points in the numbers being added or subtracted, as well as in the answer, should be lined up with one another. Otherwise, adding or subtracting decimals is like adding or subtracting whole numbers. Here is an example involving addition:

```
  .33
+ .21
-----
  .54
```

And here is one involving subtraction:

```
  .33
- .21
-----
  .12
```

Multiplying decimal numbers isn't very different from multiplying whole numbers. The thing to be careful about is to make sure the number of digits to the right of the decimal point in your answer equals the total number of digits behind the decimal points in the numbers being multiplied. An example should make this clear.

Suppose we have to multiply .57 * .33. The number .57 has two digits to the right of the decimal point, while the number .33 also has two digits to the right of its decimal point. Thus, whatever the product ends up being, it has to have 4 digits to the right of its decimal point (because 2 + 2 = 4). Using my computer, I found that .57 * .33 = .1881. Notice that .1881 has 4 digits to the right of the decimal point.

When dividing decimal numbers, it's important to keep straight which number is being divided into which. Actually, this is true when dividing any types of numbers. Suppose we want to divide .57 *by* .33. That is, we want to divide .33 *into* .57. The number being divided **by** some number goes into the numerator of a fraction (remember that fractions are another way of representing division), while the other number goes into its denominator. Since .57 is being divided *by* .33, we end up with .57/.33. The number being divided *into* another number goes into the denominator of a fraction, while the other number goes into the numerator. Thus, since .33 is being divided *into* .57, we get .57/.33. Keeping this in mind is crucial when inputting decimal numbers (or any numbers) into calculators or computers to do division.

INEQUALITIES

It's often necessary to compare the sizes of numbers to one another. Such comparisons can be discussed more efficiently if we're able to use shorthand notation as follows: > (greater than), < (less than), ≥ (greater than or equal to), ≤ (less than or equal to), and ≠ (not equal to). For example, an agency might only be allowed to provide services to people whose incomes are below the poverty line. Suppose the poverty line is $X/year. Then only people with incomes < $X/year would be eligible for the services of this agency.

RATIOS, PROPORTIONS, AND PERCENTAGES

The concept of *ratio* comes up a lot in the mathematics of social issues. It represents a comparison between two quantities. For example, suppose we're interested in how the number of black men stopped and frisked by the police in a given time period compares to the number of white men so stopped. Suppose the number of black men stopped is 100 and the number of white ones stopped is 50. The ratio of black men to white men stopped would be 100: 50. Another way to express this ratio is 100/50. Expressed this second way, it's clear that a ratio is a type of fraction. And recall that a fraction is just another way to represent division. So, to calculate a ratio, you have to divide the number in the numerator by the one in the denominator. Doing that here, we would see that there is a 2 to 1 ratio of black men stopped and frisked to white men stopped and frisked. We could also state this by saying that twice as many or two times as many black men are stopped and frisked as there are white men who are stopped and frisked.

Here is an example of a ratio involving numbers with units of measurement. Suppose the average annual income of non-poor clients served by a social service agency is $50,000 while that of poor ones served is $10,000. Let's write these dollar amounts slightly differently so it's easier to see what happens with the ratio of non-poor to poor clients' average incomes.

That ratio is 50,000 dollars/10,000 dollars. Notice that the numbers in both the numerator and denominator have the same unit of measurement—dollars. A rule of mathematics tells us that when dividing one number into another one where both the numbers have the same unit of measurement, the units of measurement in the numerator and denominator "cancel," and we're left with division of one pure number into another one. Applying that here, 50,000 dollars/ 10,000 dollars = 50,000/10,000 = 5. Notice that "dollars" no longer appears after the first equals sign because the units have cancelled out. So, the average annual income of non-poor clients served by this agency is five times that of the poor clients it serves.

The notion of *proportion* also comes up frequently in discussions of social issues. The demographer Donald T. Rowland states the definition of proportion well—"a ratio in which the denominator includes the numerator."[3] Let's consider an example.

The US government publishes different editions of a volume called *The Statistical Abstract of the United States*. The latest one I could find online is the 2012 edition. These volumes contain a multitude of different types of statistics. Table 348 of the 2012 edition contains estimates of the total number of US residents in jail or prison for the year 2009. That number was 7,225,800. Table 348 also has the estimated number of male residents in jail or prison for that year, which was 5,927,200. The only gender categories the table includes are male and female. Presumably, the federal government hadn't yet heard about gender identities such as *transgender* or *gender nonconforming*. Since an estimated 5,927,200 inmates of correctional institutions were male, it follows, given the government's gender categories, that an estimated 1,298,600 such inmates were female.

Suppose we want the proportion of US inmates in 2009 who were male. What we would do is calculate the ratio of 5,927,200/7,225,800. This ratio is also a proportion because the 7,225,800 inmates is made up of the 5,927,200 males in addition to the 1,298,600 females. To see this, write this proportion as follows: 5,927,200/ (5,927,200 + 1,298,600). Using a computer or calculator, we would find that 5,927,200/(5,927,200 + 1,298,600) comes out to a proportion of about .82.

We'll see proportions over and over again in this book, so it's important to grasp what they are. Again, they're just ratios like $X/(X + Y)$, where X represents some number (with or without units) and $X + Y$ represents the sum of X and Y (with or without units). If X does have units (dollars, euros, or whatever), $X + Y$ must have those same units. The key here is that the denominator includes the numerator. That is, $X + Y$ includes X.

Let's go back for a moment to our male inmate proportion of .82. It should be clear from our earlier discussion that a proportion is also a decimal number. And, based on what we said about decimal numbers, our proportion of .82 can also be written as 82/100. Another name for this number is 82%, which is symbolized as 82%. That is, *percent* means some number divided by 100. So, 83% means 83/100, 45% means 45/100, and 200% means 200/100. The way you get from a proportion to a percent is to multiply that proportion by 100 and attach the percent sign. Thus, .82 * 100 gets us to 82%. You may recall from your earlier school days that a shorthand way of changing a decimal number to a percent is by moving the decimal point two places to the right and placing a "%" sign next the number that results. That's precisely what we did here.

At this point in the book, I've reviewed a lot of mathematics, some of which you may have studied long ago. Given that many (but certainly not all) social workers suffer from "math phobia," you may have found some of the stuff in this chapter challenging. You might also be wondering whether putting yourself through all this was worth it. If you are wondering this, I urge you to keep going. The rest of the book is an attempt to convince you of the relevance of mathematics to a number of issues that social workers are likely to be interested in. By the time you're done, you may be surprised to find that math is more relevant but not as difficult as you'd initially thought.

NOTES

1. It can be proved that there is only one empty set, but we don't need to worry about that in this book.

2. Fractions are sometimes defined in such a way that p and q, in p/q, must be integers. Others define fractions more broadly to include cases where p and q aren't necessarily integers but can be numbers of any type, such as 1.2/1.3. When we discuss fractions in this book, we'll be referring to fractions in which p and q are integers unless otherwise indicated.

3. See Rowland (2014, p. 33).

3

MEASUREMENT AND SOCIAL ISSUES

A PERENNIAL POLICY debate has to do with taxes. Some believe taxes are too high and that they should be reduced to stimulate the economy. Others disagree, but let's stay, for the moment, with those who'd liked to see taxes cut. What do they mean by "stimulate the economy"? Apparently, they have in mind the economy producing more "stuff." This raises the question of how to determine the amount of stuff the economy produces.

Social workers often deal with clients who may be eligible for government assistance of various kinds. Eligibility in such cases is often determined, in part, by whether clients' incomes are below certain levels. This raises the questions of what is income, and how do we determine the size of someone's income?

The issues mentioned in the previous two paragraphs, as well as others we'll touch on in this chapter, have to do with measurement. Let's start things off with a definition.

WHAT IS MEASUREMENT?

Measurement is the assignment of numbers to represent amounts or qualitative aspects of some attribute possessed by objects. The term "objects" is being used broadly to refer to both inanimate as well as animate "things." In the physical realm, we measure things such as weight, distance, speed, and the like. In the social realm, the focus of this book, we measure things such as how much stuff the economy is producing, the average price level, the magnitude of poverty, and so forth. We can also assign numbers—that is, take a measurement—to represent a qualitative attribute such as someone's race or gender identity. Physical scientists might not recognize such numerical assignments as measurement, but we do in the social sciences.[1]

The British statistician David Hand makes a distinction between the *representational* and *pragmatic* or *operational conceptions of measurement*.[2] The representational conception is the one I've been discussing so far. According to it, measurement is about assigning numbers to objects of some kind to represent magnitudes or qualitative features of attributes or traits of those objects. The *operational conception of measurement* has to do with the assignment of numbers to objects, too, but it differs from the representational one in a fundamental way: the assignment of numbers isn't meant to *represent* amounts or qualitative features of objects' traits—instead, the numbers assigned *are* the amounts or qualitative features of those traits. The distinction Hand is making here is subtle but, in his view, critically important. The operational conception relies on a term you'll hear about in your research courses: *operational definitions*.

An operational definition of a concept stipulates the meaning of that concept by stating how a measurement will be done. And since measurement is about assigning numbers to objects, operationally defining a concept amounts to defining it according to the way those numbers will be assigned. Here's an example from physical science.

In their book on Albert Einstein's theory of relativity, Mook and Vargish discuss an operational definition of the concept of *speed*. They remind us that an object's speed is equal to the distance traveled by that object divided by the time taken to travel that distance, or speed = distance/time. So if we wanted to measure the speeds of a set of objects and knew their distances traveled, as well as the times it took to travel those distances, we could measure their speeds using that equation. The numbers we'd end up with, according to the operational conception of measurement, are not representing some underlying trait called speed—these numbers *are* the speeds. That is, according to the operational conception of measurement, the level of some trait of a given object is nothing more or less than the numerical result obtained from applying an operational definition of that trait.

This approach to thinking about measurement arguably has a problematic implication: if there are different ways of operationally defining a trait of some object, and those different methods generate different quantities for *the same object*, then either (1) that object would, *by definition*, have different levels of the trait in question or (2) the different methods, although they claim to be, aren't really measuring the same thing. Since option 1 seems to be a recipe for contradictions, option 2 may be the better one. That is, different ways of operationally defining an attribute are really slightly different attributes. I don't think this problem comes up much in the physical sciences, but I'll leave it to them to decide that. It isn't hard, though, to see how it might arise in policy work.

Consider the issue of poverty. One researcher might operationally define a person to be poor if their income falls below $15,000/year. Another might operationally define someone as poor if their income falls below $25,000/year. Suppose Enrico has an income of $17,000/year. According to the operational conception of measurement and relying on option 1, we'd have to conclude that Enrico is both poor and not poor at the same time since his income is greater than $15,000/year and less than $25,000/year. This is the type of contradiction we want to avoid. If we choose option 2, we'd have to conclude that, although both measures claim to be measures of poverty, they're really measuring slightly different things. This is the case because, by definition, the way something is measured determines what's being measured. So, if we measure something two different ways, we're measuring two different things, although we're using the same word, "poverty," to refer to both of them.

There is something of a debate in the social sciences regarding whether the operational, representative, or some other conception of measurement is the correct one (Hand, 2004). We won't get into that debate in this book because doing so wouldn't really serve our purpose. What we'll do, instead, is look at a number of social scientific practices regarding measurement, focus on the role mathematics plays in those practices, and show how they're related to social issues of concern to social workers.

UNITS OF MEASUREMENT

Many measurements seen in the social realm involve pure numbers. Recall from Chapter 2 that a pure number is one with no units attached to it (that is, no miles, pounds, dollars, etc.). For example, it's pretty common in the social sciences to see gender identity represent numerically.

Suppose we assume that people can identify in four ways: female, male, transgender, or gender nonconforming. If we were involved in a study of the relevance of gender to a given social issue, we might want to assign numbers to people representing their gender identity as follows: 1 = female, 2 = male, 3 = transgender, and 4 = gender nonconforming.

Two things ought to be said about these numbers: (1) they represent qualitative attributes, not amounts of something, and (2) they don't have units attached to them. The number 1 here is just a pure number indicating that someone is female. It's not meant to indicate that a person assigned a 1 contains 1 unit (whatever such a unit might be) of "femaleness."

When a measurement involves units, there are four aspects we need to think about:

1. The "object" being measured
2. The attribute of the object being measured
3. The magnitude or amount of the attribute
4. The "thing" amounts of that attribute are being measured in

Number 4 is referring to the *unit of measurement*. This is probably easiest to see, at first, with a physical measurement.

Suppose someone measures the length of a table and tells us that it's 2 feet long. The object here is the table, the attribute is length, the magnitude is 2, and the unit of measurement is feet.

To take an example from the social realm, suppose a social worker says that a client's income is $50,000 per year. The object here is the social worker's client, the attribute is income, the magnitude is 50,000, and the unit of measurement is US dollars per year.

One of the things to remember about units of measurement is that the same attribute of an object can often be measured in different units. To go back to the table, it was measured in feet, but it could also have been measured in inches, yards, or any other unit for measuring the length of something. Regarding the client's income, it was measured in US dollars per year. But it could also have been measured in euros per year, Japanese yen per year, Canadian dollars per year, and so forth.

Social scientists, including social workers, typically aren't trained to attend to units of measurement the way engineers and physical scientists are. Not receiving such training may render us more prone to make basic mathematical mistakes like the following.

In his book *Street Fighting Mathematics*, physicist Sanjay Mahajan discusses an example similar to the one I'll discuss here. On Knoema, a website cataloguing international data of various kinds, there is a comparison of the net wealth of some of the world's richest individuals to the gross domestic products (GDPs) of certain countries.[3] For example, we're told that, in 2014, Bill Gate's net wealth, at about 76 billion dollars ($76,000,000,000)[4] exceeded the GDP of the Dominican Republic, which was about 60 billion dollars per year ($60,000,000,000 per year). This comparison is problematic.

A person's *net wealth* is equal to the value of what that person *owns* minus the value of what they *owe*. The values of what someone owns and owes can both be measured in a currency unit, like the dollar. A rule from applied mathematics states that measured attributes involving units of measurement can only be added or subtracted if the attributes are measured in the same units. This means that Bill Gates net worth would have to be

Some amount of dollars **owned** − Some amount of dollars **owed**
    = $76,000,000,000

GDP refers to the value of the finished goods[5] produced within the borders of a country over a specified period of time. The term "finished goods" indicates that used goods, such as used cars, aren't considered in calculating GDP. The unit of measurement of GDP is currency/time, and, in the United States, this is typically dollars per year. To see what's wrong with the net wealth versus GDP comparison, we need to take a brief detour into a discussion of how a unit of measurement indicates the type of attribute being measured.

Two terms used throughout the sciences are relevant in this context: *stock* and *flow*. A stock is an attribute which occurs at a *given point* in time. Stocks are typically measured in pure numbers or numbers with some unit of measurement attached, *but time isn't a part of this unit*. Of course, since everything occurs at some point in time, time is relevant to stocks because we must pick some time point to assess the level of a given stock.

A flow is something which occurs *over a period of time*. That is, a flow is something measured in a unit involving an amount of something per time period. Notice here that time is included as part of the unit of measurement of flow variables. An example from social work might be helpful.

Imagine a social service agency that provides services to homeless clients. Suppose that, at 2:30 PM on June 22, 2015, there are 100 people being seen by that agency. The attribute here is the population of homeless people being served by the agency at a given point in time (2:30 PM on June 22, 2015). So, the current population of homeless people being served by this agency is a stock.

Suppose now there is another agency, and we're interested in the "speed" at which this second agency resolves homeless cases, where "resolving a case" refers to having found a shelter for someone, having found housing for them, having helped them find employment, or the like. Imagine we do this by counting the number of cases the agency resolves per day. Suppose we find that the agency regularly resolves 25 cases per day. The attribute here is speed of service, and this is being measured as a count (of resolved cases) per time (day). So, speed of service is a flow.

Now a rule from applied mathematics tells us that only attributes with the same units of measurement can be compared. If you think about it, this makes a lot of sense. If one agency has an overall population of 100 homeless clients *on a given day*, and another provides services to 25 homeless people *per day*, it wouldn't make much sense to say that since 100 is greater than 25, that the first agency is doing more to help the homeless than the second one. These numbers are measuring two very different attributes—on the one hand, how many people on a given day happen to be at a specific location, and, on the other, how many cases each day "flow" through a given location.

It might be easier now to see the problem with the net wealth versus GDP comparison. Net wealth is a stock (measured in currency), while GDP is a flow (measured in currency per unit time). Saying that Gates's net wealth of $76,000,000,000 is greater than the Dominican Republic's GDP of $60,000,000,000 per year makes about as much sense as saying that a homeless agency with 100 people at its site on a given day is helping more people than one which resolves 25 cases per day.

The "Bill Gates's net worth versus poor country's GDP comparison" is trying to get at something important—wealth inequality. It's trying to make a point about the spectacular wealth of someone like Gates relative to the grinding poverty of a place like the Dominican Republic. But if one wants to compare levels of wealth, the thing to do is compare "apples to apples." Comparing a stock attribute to a flow one isn't an apples-to-apples comparison. One way of doing such a comparison would be to compare Bill Gates' net worth to the total net worth of all poor people living in the Dominican Republic. That is, we could calculate the ratio of Bill Gates net worth/Total net worth of all poor people residing the Dominican Republic. Assuming we could obtain the data to make this calculation, we'd end up with a number that we could multiply by 100. We'd then have the size of Bill Gates net worth in comparison to that of all poor people residing in the Dominican Republic.[6]

VALIDITY AND RELIABILITY

Earlier we said *measurement* is the assignment of numbers to represent amounts or the qualitative features of an attribute of a given object. If we're thinking in terms of the representational conception of measurement, there is a question we can ask about any measurement: to what extent do the numbers assigned to represent amounts or qualitative features of some object accurately represent those amounts or features? In other words, to what extent does the procedure used to assign numbers actually measure what's intended? This is the question of what social researchers call the *validity* of a measurement.

Clearly, the more valid a procedure for measuring some attribute, the better. Assuming you want an accurate indication of how much you weigh, you wouldn't want a scale which put you at 10 pounds heavier than you actually are. You might respond that many people would be fine with a scale which told them they're 10 pounds *lighter* than they actually are, but I suspect you see my point. As another example, a social worker genuinely interested in policies to address poverty will want any measure of income to accurately reflect how much income a person or family actually has. As you'll see in a moment, accurate measurement of income isn't as simple as you might think.

Another term, related to measurement, you ought to be familiar with is *reliability*. The reliability of a procedure used to measure some attribute has to do with the degree to which repeated use of that procedure yields consistent findings, *assuming the amount or qualitative nature of the attribute being measured hasn't changed over time*. To see what I'm getting at, consider measuring someone's income.

A common way of measuring income involves the use of a social survey—that is, a researcher may simply ask respondents what their incomes are. Now suppose this first happens at 3 PM on June 24, 2015, and respondents tell the researcher their incomes. A year later, respondents are interviewed again, and, since their incomes haven't changed, they report the same incomes as before. As long as the researcher correctly records and enters—typically into a database—these respondent's incomes, this survey method would be a reliable measure of income.

Even though it may be difficult to see, validity and reliability are distinct concepts. Validity is about the degree to which a measurement procedure allows for the representation of the correct amount or qualitative features of an attribute; reliability is about whether such a method allows one to obtain a consistent finding over time. Let's look at this distinction in relation to our income survey example.

If we follow the survey method and respondents honestly tell the interviewer what their incomes are (and the researcher accurately records and enters them into a database), the method would be valid. If respondent's incomes aren't changing over time and they remain honest, the method would be reliable as well.

Now suppose all respondents decided to lie about their incomes, claiming they earn $10,000 per year less than they really do. The survey method could quite consistently obtain measures of people's incomes that are $10,000 per year too low, giving us a very reliable yet invalid measurement procedure.

MEANING AND MEASUREMENT

In order to measure the magnitude or qualitative features of some attribute, we need to be clear on what we mean by the attribute in question. Take, for example, an attribute like race. As I understand it, according to biologists, there is no such thing as race; yet this hasn't stopped social researchers from conducting countless studies to see if "race" is associated with a host of outcomes. This is because these researchers have determined that race does have a social basis even if it has no biological one. That is, societies have come up with ways of determining the "races" people belong to, and our life chances (as well as, sometimes, our very lives) depend on how we've been racially categorized. Just consider slavery, the old Jim Crow, the New Jim Crow, and the like. Yet race is a "fuzzy" enough concept that most, if not all, of us are hard pressed to precisely define. Is a person's race determined by their skin color, hair texture, who their ancestors are, or what?

A common way of measuring race in the social sciences is assigning numbers to represent people's races. A black person might be assigned the number 1, a white person the number 2, an Asian person the number 3, and so forth. But in order for this method to be valid, this assignment must accurately reflect people's races. And deciding whether it does would require us to answer the questions posed in the last paragraph.

One of the ways social researchers finesse this is by measuring race through self-identification. That is, in surveys or censuses, people are often asked to declare the race they identify with, and, as far as the researcher or census taker is concerned, this becomes that person's race. Then an assignment of numbers, as we've just seen, is used to reflect this self-identification. But this approach has its own problems.

As the history of slavery and oppression referred to earlier indicates, people don't really get to self-identify racially. Had Rosa Parks told the whites on the bus—angry with her because of where she had chosen to sit—that she identified as white, I doubt they would've apologized for the misunderstanding and left her alone.

These complications surrounding the definition and measurement of race have enormous social significance. Almost any social or public health problem you can think of has a racial aspect. Poverty varies by race, certain disease burdens vary by race, unemployment varies by race, educational attainment varies by race, the probability of being imprisoned varies by race, and the list goes on.

To explore this issue further, consider how Blau and Abramovitz, in their highly regarded social policy text, define "social welfare policy": "the principles, activities, or framework for action adopted by government to ensure a socially defined level of individual, family, and community well-being" (Blau and Abramovitz, 2007, p. 20). Paraphrasing a bit, this definition seems to be saying that social welfare policy has to do with things done by some level of government which brings individuals, families, and the community to a specific level of well-being. This seemingly clear definition of social welfare policy is fraught with a number of definitional and measurement questions.

First, is social welfare policy really just about getting individuals, families, and the community to a *specific* level of well-being or to *at least* a specific level? Suppose the specific level of well-being in question were 100 utils.[7] Are Blau and Abramovitz saying that government activities that get individuals, families, and the community to 100 utils would be social welfare policies, but the moment utils exceeded the magnitude of 100, these same activities would cease to qualify as social welfare policies? I seriously doubt this is what they have in mind. So, let's assume that to *at least* a specific level is the correct conception.

A second question which comes up is what is meant by family and community? Some might define the family as a married straight man and woman whose biological kids—if they have biological kids—came after, not before, their marriage. Having read Blau and Abramovitz's book, I doubt this is the view they have in mind. The US Bureau of the Census defines "family" as a group of two or more people residing together who are related by birth, marriage, or adoption. What about community? Does this refer to a geographical community? If so, are we talking about the neighborhood, the city, the state, the country, or what? Does community not refer to geography but to a group of people who share a common identity, regardless of where they live?

A third question has to do with how the well-being of individuals, families, and the community are related to one another. Suppose government adopts principles, activities, or some framework that brings every individual in the nation to at least 100 utils. There are about 300 million people in the United States. If each has been brought to at least 100 utils, that would mean a total of at least 30,000,000,000 utils (300,000,000 * 100 utils = 30,000,000,000 utils). Note here that 300,000,000 is an approximate count of the US population, so it's a pure number; 100 utils is a number with units attached. Notice that the answer, 30,000,000,000 utils, has the same unit of measurement as 100 utils does. What's happened here is an example of the rule of applied mathematics I mentioned earlier: whenever a pure number is multiplied by one with units attached, the final answer will have the same units as the initial one which had units attached.

Now suppose we consider the community as the 300 million US residents. Here is a question: does the 30,000,000,000 utils total that we just calculated mean that the community has attained a level of well-being of at least 30,000,000,000 utils? How does this total of 30,000,000,000 utils relate to the well-being of families? Do we determine how the 300 million residents in the United States cluster into households, use some agreed upon definition of which households are families, add up the amounts of utils in each family, and add these family totals together to get a total across all families? Would the amount of well-being we end up with be the level of family well-being?

If we followed this procedure and used the US Census definition of family, people living alone or those living together but not related by blood, marriage, or adoption wouldn't be families. So their amounts of well-being would have to be left out of our calculation of family well-being. This would mean that individuals and the community would have attained at least 30,000,000,000 utils of well-being, but families would have attained less than this amount.

A fourth question has to do with how to assign numbers to represent magnitudes of well-being and what unit of measurement, if any, should be attached to those numbers. So far, we've been referring to well-being as measured in utils. A util is an imaginary unit of measurement sometimes found in the writings of economists. They know full well that a util isn't really a standard unit of measurement and only use it to conveniently discuss other issues, just as I've been doing. But if we really want to get a handle on whether governments bring individuals, families, and communities to at least some specific level of well-being, we need some way of assigning numbers to represent levels of well-being and determining what, if any, unit of measurement *we can actually observe in the real world* that we might want to associate with such numbers.

An obvious candidate for assigning numbers to represent levels of well-being is income measured in, say, US dollars per year. Or we could use net wealth measured in US dollars. The idea behind using income as a measure of well-being is that income, given the nature of many of the world's economies, allows those who possess it access to the consumption of certain goods and services thought to be necessary for well-being. So, the more income the individual, family, or community possesses the better off that individual, family, or community is. The idea behind using net wealth as a measure of income is that net wealth can be turned into income. For example, if I own a house, I can rent it out. If I own a car, I can drive people around in return for a fee.

But many, including, I suspect, many social workers, would be uncomfortable reducing the measurement of one's level of well-being to how much income or wealth they have. If Jack and Jill both have incomes of $100,000 per year, yet Jack is in perfect health (whatever that means) while Jill lives in chronic pain all over her body, are they really equally well-off? Assuming neither Jack nor Jill like being in chronic pain, I suspect many would respond to this question with an enthusiastic "no." Such a response would suggest that we need a better measure of well-being.

The obvious problem with income or wealth as a measure of well-being is that, rephrasing The Beatles a bit, money can't buy all the things we might need to be well. Let's sidestep this issue and assume, for the sake of discussion, that money is a valid and reliable measure of individual well-being. We would still need to figure out how the well-being of individuals, families, and community are related to one another. That is, we'd have the same problem we had before but with utils now replaced by US dollars per year.

Another issue that would come up, even if we assumed income is a valid and reliable measure of well-being, is the fact that one person's well-being may depend on how well others are doing and not just family members and friends. We may be worse-off just knowing that starvation and homelessness have increased and better-off knowing that they've decreased. This way of being in the world, where your well-being depends on that of others, is sometimes called *altruistic*. So, it would seem that perhaps we should measure Jack's well-being not just by how much income he has coming in but how much Jill has coming in as well.

By now you can probably see what I meant by saying that the definition of social welfare policy is "fraught with a number of definitional and measurement questions." The purpose here isn't to resolve these issues. It's more to help sensitize ourselves to how measurement and, therefore, mathematics are related to something as seemingly qualitative as defining the term "social welfare policy."

MEASUREMENT ERROR

I recently heard on the radio that the US unemployment rate is estimated to be 4.3%. Let's dig a bit into how this number was obtained. Each month, the US government conducts a survey called the Current Population Survey (CPS). This survey focuses on a sample of 60,000 households, which results in about 110,000 people. The sample is selected in such a way that it's representative of the entire US population of eligible workers. That is, the sample is selected to represent that racial, gender, and geographical make-up of the entire US population of eligible workers.

Each month, these 110,000 persons are asked a number of questions related to their employment activities during a specific week in the month called the *reference week*. Based on their responses to these questions, people are classified into one of three categories: employed, unemployment, or not in the labor force.

Employed persons are those who did any work at all for pay or profit during the reference week. This includes part-time workers, temporary workers, and full-time workers. Those who have jobs but did not work during the reference week are also categorized as employed. These are folks who didn't work during the reference week because they were on vacation, ill, had child care problems, were on parental leave, had other family or personal obligations, were involved in a strike, or couldn't work because of bad weather.

Those who, when interviewed, currently don't have a job, have looked for one in the previous four weeks, and are currently available for work are categorized as *unemployed*. Some examples of looking for work include contacting a potential employer about being hired, going to a job interview, contacting friends about a job possibility, and filling out job applications.

Those who are employed and unemployed make up the *labor force*. Putting it slightly more mathematically

Labor force = Number of employed persons + Number of unemployed persons

Those who are neither employed nor unemployed are categorized as *not in the labor force*.

The *unemployment rate* is the number of unemployed persons divided by the labor force or:

$$\text{Unemployment rate} = \frac{\textit{Number of unemployed persons}}{\textit{Labor force}}$$

$$= \frac{\textit{Number of unemployed persons}}{\textit{Number of unemployed persons} + \textit{number of employed persons}}$$

The second version makes it clear—because the numerator is part of the denominator—that the unemployment rate is an example of what in Chapter 2 I called a proportion. The 4.3% unemployment rate mentioned earlier resulted from application of the unemployment rate formula, resulting in .043. This figure was then multiplied by 100 to obtain 4.3%. Now here is a question: do you think the unemployment rate really is 4.3%? The answer to this question, as social researchers would see it, is very likely to be "no." This is the case for two reasons.

Keep in mind that what the government does is select 110,000 people to represent millions more. In other words, it selects a *sample* 110,000 from a *population* of millions.[8] It's very unlikely that dividing the unemployed in the sample by the labor force in the sample will give you exactly the same number as you would get if you could divide the number of unemployed in the entire US population by the labor force in that population. In other words, the 4.3% figure is unlikely to be the same as the true figure for the overall US population.

Whenever a measured quantity based on a sample differs from that quantity in the population we have what's called *sampling error*, since the error stems from the fact that we're using a sample to estimate a quantity of interest in a population.

The other reason our 4.3% figure might diverge from the true population figure has to do with problems associated with surveys. When people respond to surveys, they may deliberately or mistakenly provide inaccurate information. Some who worked during the reference week might say they didn't, or someone who didn't might say they did. When surveys are conducted, it's often necessary to enter collected data into some database or other computerized system. There are ample opportunities for mistakes when this is done. Reporting inaccuracies, data entry errors, and perhaps others enter into our calculated value of 4.3%, rendering it unlikely to equal the true population value.

Sampling errors and the others mentioned together make up what's called *measurement error*. In general, measurement error is any discrepancy between the measured value of some quantity and the true value of that quantity. As social researchers see it, what we've been saying about the unemployment rate applies to all rates which find their way into policy discussions: inflation rates, poverty rates, homicide rates, infant mortality rates, and more. That is, social researchers typically assume that all measured social attributes are estimates of true quantities and that these measured quantities contain some degree of measurement error.

A general way of representing the assumption that all measures of social phenomena are accompanied by measurement error is as follows:

Measured quantity = True quantity + Error

If we subtract True quantity from both sides of this equation we get:

Measured quantity − True quantity = True quantity − True quantity + Error

The right side of the preceding equation includes the expression True quantity − True quantity. Whenever a quantity is subtracted from itself we end up with 0 (for example, 5 − 5 = 0). Thus, we're left with:

Measured quantity − True quantity = Error

The idea behind the preceding three equations is that when we measure something like the unemployment rate, inflation rate, GDP, or the like, we end up with a measured quantity. This quantity is made up of the true quantity (the population unemployment rate in the preceding example) along with some error, which we've been calling measurement error. The problem is that we rarely, if ever, know true quantities. Typically, all we have to work with are measured quantities.

Earlier we discussed the validity of a method of measurement. Given that social researchers assume that all measured quantities are estimates or approximations of some true quantity, it should be clear that no method of measurement is absolutely valid in the sense of exactly reflecting the true quantity of interest. You should remember this point the next time you come across two politicians fighting over whether this month's unemployment rate is really 4.3% or 4.5%. Neither of these two quantities are likely to be the true unemployment rate. So, measures of unemployment—and a host of others which enter into policy debates—should be seen for what they are: attempts to get at an underlying reality that will ultimately, to some degree, remain elusive.

INDEX NUMBERS

As I mentioned earlier in the book, there is a US government program called Temporary Assistance for Needy Families (TANF). This program provides cash benefits primarily to women with young children. TANF is more commonly called "welfare," and one of its features is that there is no federal law that requires benefits be adjusted to keep up with the rising "cost of living." Increases in the cost of living are measured with something called the *consumer price index* (CPI). The CPI is an example of an *index number*.

Bennet and Briggs provide a nice discussion of index numbers in their book *Using and Understanding Mathematics: A Quantitative Reasoning Approach* (2008). They regard an index number as a comparison of measurements made in two different areas or at two different times. The quantity at one time or place serves as the *reference value*. Mathematically, an index number takes the following form:

$$\text{Index number} = \frac{Value}{Reference\ Value} * 100$$

The numerator and denominator of this expression will have the same unit of measurement. So, as we learned from Chapter 1, these units will cancel. The result will be multiplied by 100, a pure number, so an index number is a pure number (a number without an associated unit of measurement).

As an example, suppose the average price of a private practice social worker's services in 1980 was $55 per hour. Suppose today the average price of such services is $100 per hour. We could use the index number formula to calculate how today's average price compares to the one in 1980:

$$\frac{\$100 \ per \ hour}{\$50 \ per \ hour} * 100$$

Since the units in both the numerator and denominator cancel, we can ignore the "$ per hour." Once we do, we up with 100 divided by 50. This is 2 because 50 goes into 100 two times. So we're left with 2 * 100 = 200.

In Chapter 1, we saw that whenever a decimal number is multiplied by 100, that number becomes a percent. We usually had in mind decimal numbers like .87, .99, .07, and the like. But 2 can also be written as a decimal number; one version would be 2.00. In general, any whole number X can be written as a decimal number by inserting a decimal point and two zeros to the right of it to get X.00. Thus, 2 * 100 = 2.00 * 100 = 200% (by moving the decimal point two places to the right, as we discussed in Chapter 2). So, the average price of a private practice social worker's services today is 200% of what it was in 1980.

The CPI is very similar to the index of a private social worker's services. It's computed by the US Bureau of Labor Statistics (BLS) and is based on the average price of a sample of goods and services purchased by those residing in urban areas. This average price is what's meant by the phrase "the cost of living" I used earlier. The gory details about how the BLS does this isn't our concern. The main thing we'll care about here is how the CPI is interpreted.

Consider the index number formula again:

$$\text{Index number} = \frac{Value}{Reference \ Value} * 100$$

And here's the CPI version:

$$\text{CPI}_{\text{given year}} = \frac{Average \ price \ in \ given \ year}{Average \ Price \ from \ 1982 - 1984} * 100$$

The little "given year" after CPI is an example of a *subscript*. Subscripts appear frequently in mathematical writing. What it means here is that the formula is used to calculate the CPI for a specific year in question. The CPI is equal to the average price for that same year divided by the average price for the years 1982–1984, all multiplied by 100. Comparing the CPI to the generic formula for an index number, we see that the average price for the years 1982–1984 is the reference value.

If you want to see how prices have changed over time, you take the ratio of the CPIs for the two periods you want to know about. For example, in 1996, the CPI was an estimated 156.9, and in 2014 it was estimated to be 226.7 (rounded to one decimal place).[9] So, to see how prices in 2014 compare to those in 1996, you'd calculate the ratio

$$\text{CPI}_{2014} / \text{CPI}_{1996} = \frac{226.7}{156.9} = 1.4$$

So, the cost of living in 2014 was almost one and half times higher than the cost of living in 1996.

Now suppose you wanted to figure out the effect of inflation on the purchasing power of TANF benefits, where by "purchasing power" I mean how far your TANF benefits would take you when it came to buying stuff in the marketplace. Since TANF benefit levels vary by state, suppose a given state provided its TANF recipients with $4,476 per year.[10] What would that $4,476 per year figure have to be to adjust for higher prices in 2014?

The following formula can be used to answer the previous question:

$$\text{TANF}_{2014} = \text{TANF}_{1996} * \frac{CPI \text{ for } 2014}{CPI \text{ for } 1996}$$

Substituting the appropriate numbers:

$$\$6,266.40 \text{ per year} = \$4,476 \text{ per year} * \frac{226.7}{156.9}$$

So, in order for TANF recipients in this state to have the same purchasing power in 2014 that they had in 1996, they'd need to receive about $6,266.40 per year in benefits.

Anyone who's been exposed to the media, especially about economic topics, has likely heard the term *rate of inflation* or *inflation rate*. Conceptually speaking, the inflation rate is the change in average price, or the cost of living, over a given time period. Typically, the change in price is an increase, so the rate of inflation can be thought of as the rise in the average price over a given time period.[11] Often the time period in question is a year, but change in the cost of living can be tracked over a 6-month period, a 3-month period, a 1-month period, or whatever period suits the analyst. We'll focus here on change over a year. The formula for the inflation rate over a year is:

$$\text{Inflation rate} = \frac{CPI \text{ one year later} - CPI \text{ one year earlier}}{CPI \text{ one year earlier}}$$

This type of calculation comes up in adjusting some federal social benefits for inflation.

Social Security is a federal program that provides cash benefits to people who've worked for at least 10 years in a job covered by the program. Supplemental Security Income (SSI) is a federal program that provides benefits to disabled or low-income elderly persons. Unlike TANF, these two programs adjust for inflation, and the inflation rate is used to do so.

Suppose the government is trying to figure out what Social Security or SSI benefits should be in 2015. Suppose that, in 2014, the CPI was 231.5, whereas in 2015 it was 235.7. Using the preceding formula, the inflation rate over this period was:

$$\frac{235.7 - 231.5}{231.5} = .018, \text{which multiplied by 100 is 1.8\%}$$

That is, our measure of the cost of living would have increased by 1.8% between 2014 and 2015. So, whatever Social Security and SSI benefits were in 2014, by 2015 they'd need to be increased by 1.8% to keep up with the rise in the cost of living.

MEASUREMENT OF POVERTY

I said earlier that measurement is about assigning numbers to represent amounts or qualitative attributes of some object. One of the attributes we're often interested in, where the object in question is an entire nation, is the degree to which residents of the nation are poor. As you might know from your policy course, in the United States, we decide if people are poor by determining whether their income falls below a certain threshold given their family size. The *poverty rate* is the US government's attempt to measure the magnitude of poverty in the United States. It's simply

$$\text{Poverty rate} = \frac{Number \text{ of people below relevant threshold}}{overall \text{ population}}$$

In 2013, the United States had an estimated population of 312,965,000 people. An estimated 45,318,000 of them had incomes below the relevant poverty lines for their family sizes.[12] So, using the preceding formula, the poverty rate in 2013 was an estimated

$$\frac{45,318,000}{312,965,000} = .145 \text{ or } 14.5\%$$

Suppose the table here showed the poverty thresholds on which the preceding calculation is based:

Family Size	Poverty Threshold (in US Dollars)
1	11,888
2	15,142
3	18,552
4	23,834
5	28,265
6	31,925
7	35,384
8	40,890
9	51,594

These thresholds result from the following procedure. The US government estimates how much money families of given sizes need to meet their basic food needs. To create poverty thresholds, the amount needed for food is multiplied by three. This is in keeping with a practice that started in the 1960s, when this way of determining poverty thresholds was first developed. In other words, for families of a given size, the government uses the following formula:

Poverty threshold for a family of a given size =
    3 * Amount needed for food for a family of that size

Now, in the table we see that, in 2013, the poverty threshold for a family of four was $23,834. Thus, anyone in a family of four with an income of less than $23,834 was considered poor. Using this same equation means we have:

$23,834 = 3 *$ Amount needed for food for a family of four

Suppose we divide both sides of this equation by 3. This is "mathematically legal" because, as you may recall from algebra, you can do anything you want to an equation as long as you do the same thing on both sides of the equals sign. So, carrying out this division, we end up with

$$\frac{\$23,834}{3} = \frac{3 * Amount\ needed\ for\ food\ for\ family\ of\ four}{3}$$

The "3s" on the right side of the equals sign cancel, leaving us with

$$\frac{\$23,834}{3} = Amount\ needed\ for\ food\ for\ family\ of\ four$$

You can use a calculator or computer to divide $23,834 by 3, and you'll end up with about $7,944.68. Whenever you divide a number with a unit of measurement by a pure number, as we've done here, the answer will always have the same unit of measurement as the number in the numerator. This is why we ended up with $7,944.68 instead of simply $7,944.68.

So, according to the US government, a family of four in 2013 needed about $7,944.68 to meet its food needs.

You might be wondering why the government multiplies the amount needed for food by three. This is because when the poverty threshold methodology was first developed, it was estimated that families typically spent about a third of their income on food, which meant that about two-thirds was spent meeting other needs. One-third of income plus two-thirds of income equals three-thirds of income or a family's total income. Seen more mathematically, 1/3 + 2/3 = 3/3 = 1, where "1" here refers to the family's whole income.

Now, here's a potential problem. The 1/3 figure comes from the 1960s. The poverty thresholds just given are for 2013. Suppose that, by 2013, the 1/3 figure was terribly outdated by. For example, suppose that, by 2000, the estimated proportion of income spent on food was about 14% as opposed to 1/3, which is about 33%. Now the multiplier of 3 comes from taking the reciprocal of 1/3, which is 3. So, if we assume that the 14% figure for 2000 also held in 2013, to get the proper multiplier we should take the reciprocal of 14/100 (since 14% is the same as 14/100). This reciprocal is 100/14 and comes out to about 7. This would mean that our formula for poverty thresholds should become:

Poverty threshold for family of given size =
    7 * Amount needed for food for a family of a given size

If we multiply $7,944.66 (the amount to meet the food needs of a family of four) by 7 instead of 3, we get a poverty threshold for 2013 of about $55,612.76.

A poverty threshold of $55,612.76 in 2013 versus one of $23,834 means that all the people whose incomes were above $23,834 but under $55,612.76 would have been categorized as poor. So, the number of poor people would've increased, but the overall population would've remained the same. Now recall that the poverty rate is the ratio of the number of people with incomes below the relevant threshold to the number making up the total population. So, the numerator of this fraction would have increased, but the denominator would have stayed the same. Whenever the numerator of a fraction increases but the denominator stays the same, this causes magnitude of ratio to increase. Since the ratio in question is the poverty rate, this means that the poverty rate would have risen. That is, if the multiplier in 2013 should've been 7, yet the government used 3 instead, we would've seriously underestimated the true magnitude of poverty in the United States during that year.

At this writing, we still use the multiplier of 3 in the United States, so we still might be underestimating the degree of poverty in this country. But what politician in office, Democrat or Republican, wants to change how we measure poverty when doing so would mean the number of poor people in the country would increase by millions?

So far, I've been talking about poverty as if it's an "all or nothing proposition." Either a family has an income less than the poverty line for a family of their size, rendering them poor, or they have one at least as large as the poverty line, rendering them not poor. However, poverty thresholds form the basis of two other measures: *the income deficit/balance/surplus* and *the ratio of income to poverty*. Both of these can be regarded as measures of how severe a family's poverty is.

The income deficit/balance/surplus is the difference between a family's income and the poverty threshold for a family of that size:

Income deficit / balance / surplus = $Family income − $Poverty threshold

The "$" is included to indicate that the US dollar is the unit of measurement.

The difference on the right side of the equals sign can be positive, negative, or 0. If a family's income were less than the poverty threshold, that family would be living in poverty. It would also have an income deficit, and the bigger that deficit the more severe its poverty would be.

For example, suppose the Jones family has four members, and its income in 2013 was $20,000. Now $20,000 − $23,834 = $-3,834 (remember when a larger number is subtracted from a smaller one, the result will be a negative number); so the Jones family would have a $3,834 income deficit.

When a family's income is the same as the poverty threshold, they have an income balance. So, any family of four in 2013 with an income of $23,834 would've had such a balance. A family whose income exceeds the poverty threshold would, of course, not be poor.

The ratio of income to poverty is defined mathematically as follows:

$$\text{Ratio of income to poverty} = \frac{\$Family\ income}{\$Poverty\ threshold}$$

Since the numerator and denominator of this ratio have the same unit of measurement, these will cancel. So, the ratio of income to poverty is a pure number.

If the ratio of income to poverty for a given family were greater than or equal to 1, that family wouldn't be poor. If a family's ratio were less than 1, the family would be poor. The further below 1 the ratio of income to poverty is, the higher the severity of poverty. Going back to the Jones family, its ratio of income to poverty would be $20,000/$23,834, which comes out to about .84 or 84%. So this family's income would be about 84% of what it would need to avoid poverty.

This chapter has dealt with measurement, along with its relationship to social issues. Two types of measures which come up frequently in social discussions are demographic and epidemiological ones. For example, mortality rates, life expectancies, and similar measures come up frequently in such discussions, especially those related to health and public health. Yet social workers tend not to be exposed to the technical aspects of these measures. Presumably, the thinking is that social workers don't need to know much about such technicalities since we're neither demographers nor epidemiologists. This point of view is understandable, but it may render us ill-equipped to participate in an informed manner in certain types of policy discussions. The next chapter is a modest attempt to address this problem by providing basic exposure to demographic and epidemiological measures of policy significance.

NOTES

1. As far as I'm concerned in this book, social work is an applied social science.
2. See Hand (2004).
3. See Knoema, *Wealth of the World's Richest People vs. GDP of Countries*.
4. From now on, unless stated otherwise, when I mention dollars I'll mean US dollars.

5. The term "goods" is meant to include material goods, like cars, as well as services, like those provided by teachers, doctors, social workers, and the like.

6. Note that the term "validity" is being used here differently from the way it was in Chapter 1.

7. A *util* is an imaginary unit of measurement for well-being sometimes used in the writings of economists.

8. We'll talk more about populations and samples in a later chapter.

9. See US Inflation Calculator, *Consumer Price Index Data from 1913–2017*.

10. In reality, TANF benefits will differ across recipients in any given state because benefit levels depend on recipient family size. That is, larger recipient families will tend to receive higher benefits, at least up to a point. Also, even though the CPI is meant to apply to prices in the whole country, price levels will vary by state. I'm ignoring these complications in this example because considering them isn't necessary for me to make the my point.

11. Average price can also decrease over time; this situation is usually called *deflation*.

12. See DeNavas-Watt and Proctor, *Income and Poverty in the United States: 2013*.

4

DEMOGRAPHY AND SOCIAL ISSUES

DEMOGRAPHY IS USUALLY defined as the study of the size, distribution, composition, and growth of human populations. In our required policy courses, social workers are usually exposed to demographic issues, but such issues aren't typically the focus of such courses. That is, measures like mortality rates, dependency ratios, and the like are mentioned in these courses, but the mathematics of the measures are downplayed. This chapter will delve a bit more deeply into the mathematical aspects of demographic, as well as a couple of epidemiological measures. Understanding at least the basics of such aspects is helpful for comprehending a number of policy issues in which demographic measures figure prominently.

DEMOGRAPHIC RATES

We'll start with the concept of a *demographic rate* or, more simply, a *rate*. In demography, a rate takes the following form:

$$\text{Rate} = \frac{\textit{Number of events of interest that occur over some period}}{\textit{All those at risk of experiencing the event over the same period}}$$

The period appearing in the numerator and denominator is usually, but doesn't have to be, a period of 1 year. Examples of events are dying in the first year of life, dying at some point after the first year of life, giving birth, and so forth. What goes into the numerator of a demographic rate equation is probably pretty clear to you. What may be more puzzling is what goes into the denominator. That is, you might be wondering what's meant by "All those at risk of experiencing the event?"

Demographers usually focus on two dimensions of risk. One is the *number of people* who could possibly experience the event. If the event is getting pregnant, for example, those without certain body parts and who aren't within a certain age range (about 15–44 years old) aren't at risk of this happening to them. These folks, therefore, wouldn't appear in the denominator of what we'll in a moment call a pregnancy rate.

The other dimension of being at risk of experiencing an event is trickier. It's the period of time during which a given person could possibly experience the event. For example, suppose the event in question is becoming pregnant, and we want to figure out the *pregnancy rate* for a given year. The pregnancy rate would be:

$$\text{Pregnancy rate} = \frac{\textit{Number of pregnancies over some period}}{\textit{All those at risk of experiencing a pregnancy over the same period}}$$

Suppose Jill and Theresa are both of child-bearing age. Jill is in perfect health (whatever that means), frequently has sex with fertile men, and never uses protection when she does so. This, of course, means she may be at risk of other things, like contracting a sexually transmitted disease, but we won't worry about those. A demographer would consider her to be at risk of becoming pregnant for the whole year in question unless she becomes pregnant during some part of the year. If Jill becomes pregnant at any point in the year, she's no longer considered to be at risk of becoming pregnant for the rest of the year, unless she gets pregnant earlier enough in the year for there to be time for her to get pregnant again before the year ends. For example, if Jill gets pregnant in February and we assume she'll give birth in November, then she'll have only been at risk of becoming pregnant for the months of January and December.[1]

Theresa is as healthy and sexually active with fertile men as Jill is for the first half of the year. However, she contracts a serious illness which requires a complete hysterectomy, resulting in her not having a uterus for the second half of the year. Since she no longer has a uterus, Theresa would no longer be at risk of becoming pregnant.

Demographers combine the person and time components of being at risk of experiencing an event into a special unit called *person-time*. The time part of this unit is typically a year, so person-time usually becomes *person-year*. Going back to Jill and Theresa, they'd contribute 1.5 person-years to the denominator of the pregnancy rate (1 year from Jill, assuming she doesn't become pregnant at any point during the year and .5 year from Theresa, since her hysterectomy rendered her at risk of becoming pregnant for only half the year). So, returning to our general rate equation, we can present it like this:

$$Rate = \frac{Number\ of\ events\ of\ interest\ that\ occur\ over\ some\ period}{Number\ of\ person-years\ of\ exposure\ to\ risk\ if\ event}$$

And we can present our pregnancy rate equation like this:

$$Pregnancy\ rate = \frac{Number\ of\ pregnancies\ over\ some\ period}{Number\ of\ person-years\ of\ exposure\ to\ risk\ of\ pregnancy}$$

Now, there is a problem with this way of presenting rate equations—not a problem in principle, but in practice. There are often decent estimates available of the *number* of people at risk of experiencing an event, typically from censuses, government vital statistics, and similar sources. But there isn't as much good data available on the time period over which people are at risk of experiencing various events. To get around this problem, demographers usually estimate the denominators of rate equations using the total population, at mid-year, of people who could possibly experience the event. So, with this method in mind, the general rate equation can also be presented like this:

$$Rate = \frac{Number\ of\ events\ of\ interest\ that\ occur\ over\ some\ period}{Mid-year\ population\ of\ people\ who\ could\ possibly\ experience\ the\ event}$$

From this point on, as a shorthand, I'll leave "Mid-year" out of rate equations. But you should realize that when you see "population . . . " in the denominator of such equations, I'm referring to some population at the mid-point of a given year.

As an example, suppose we assume any woman 15–44 years old in a given year can become pregnant and that the number of such women at the mid-point of that year is 200,000. Among those 200,000 women, suppose there were 200 pregnancies. Then the pregnancy rate for that year would be:

$$Pregnancy\ Rate = \frac{200}{200,000} = .001$$

This is interpreted as a rate of .001 pregnancies per person over the year in question.

Because rates, as is the case here, are often very small and therefore hard to interpret, demographers often multiply them by 1,000. Let's see what that does here:

$$\frac{200}{200,000} = .001 = \frac{001}{1} = \frac{.001*1000}{1*1000} = \frac{1}{1000} = 1 \text{ per } 1000 = 1 \text{ per thousand}$$

What I've done here is applied some basic laws of arithmetic. Any number is the same as that number divided by 1; so $.001 = \frac{.001}{1}$. If the numerator of a fraction and the denominator are multiplied by the same number, the value of the fraction doesn't change. That's why $\frac{.001}{1} = \frac{.001*1000}{1*1000}$. Thus, a rate of .001 pregnancy per person is the same as a rate of 1 pregnancy per thousand people. From now on, when rates are calculated in this chapter, we'll always multiply them by 1,000. The rate equation would now appear like this:

$$\text{Rate} = \frac{\text{Number of events of interest that occur over some period}}{\text{Population of people who could possibly experience the event}} *1000$$

If you've been reading closely, you may have noticed that the poverty rate discussed in the previous chapter is an example of a demographic rate. Here is the poverty rate formula again:

$$\text{Poverty rate} = \frac{\text{Number of people below relevant threshold}}{\text{overall population}} *100$$

The "number of people below the relevant threshold" can be thought of as referring to the number of people, over a given time period, experiencing the event of being poor. That event, of course, is defined as one's income falling below the relevant poverty line. "Overall population" refers to the mid-year population, over the period in question. This can be thought of as estimating the population at risk of falling into poverty. I've multiplied by 100 to show that poverty rates are typically expressed as percentages, or per 100 people, as opposed to multiplying by 1,000 (per 1,000 people) as is typical for most demographic rates.

The unemployment rate, discussed in the preceding chapter, is also an example of a demographic rate:

$$\text{Unemployment rate} = \frac{\text{Number of unemployed persons}}{\text{Total labor force}} *100$$

Here, we can think of being unemployed as the event of interest and those in the labor force as those at risk of being unemployed. Again, I multiplied by 100 to get the unemployment rate in the form of a percentage.

MORTALITY RATES

As you may know from your social policy course, Canada has a system of national health insurance whereby the Canadian government functions much like a public health insurance company for the entire nation. The system is financed by taxes, which function like premiums, so, when Canadians see doctors, they pay little or no "out of pocket costs."

The US healthcare system is different, with the bulk of the population receiving health insurance from private companies. Many of those who obtain such insurance do so through their employers, although employers often require employees to share the cost with them. Others get insurance through government programs like Medicaid or Medicare. Since passage of the Affordable Care Act of 2010, many residents get subsidies from the government to help them purchase private insurance.

In their social policy text mentioned in the previous chapter, Blau and Abramovitz (2007) include a chapter on healthcare. Near the beginning of that chapter, they discuss the US healthcare system and briefly compare it to Canada's. They point out that the United States has a higher infant mortality rate (IMR) than does Canada. They also suggest, but don't come right out and say it, that this difference may be due to the differences, mentioned earlier, in the two nation's healthcare systems. Whether or not this suggestion is true, it should be clear that a nation's healthcare system *could* have something to do with its IMR. And this is why infant as well as other measures of mortality have policy relevance. Before homing in on infant mortality, let's look at how demographers measure mortality more generally. They often do so using the *crude death rate*.

The crude death rate is equal to

$$\frac{\text{Number of deaths in a given year}}{\text{Population}} * 1000$$

According to data from the World Health Organization (WHO), the US crude death rate in 2013 was about 8 deaths per 1,000 persons.[2]

The reason the crude death rate is called "crude" is because those making up the denominator of the rate don't all face the same risk of dying. Recall that mid-year population is an estimate of the number of people at risk, as well as the time over which they're at risk, of experiencing some event. When that event is death, the mid-year population is intended to estimate all those who could die over the year in question. But a 12-year-old doesn't face the same risk of dying in a given year as an 80-year-old does. The crude death rate ignores this reality and treats 12-year-olds and 80-year-olds as though they face the same risk of dying. A measure that addresses this shortcoming is called the *age-specific death rate* (ASDR).

The ASDR is

$$\frac{Number\ of\ deaths\ in\ a\ given\ year\ at\ a\ given\ age}{Population\ at\ that\ age} * 1000$$

Notice the "at a given age" part of the formula. This means we're taking the formula for the crude death rate and modifying it by considering the deaths of those at a specific age. Age-adjusted death rates don't have to be based on only one age. Such rates can cover an age interval. For example, the age-adjusted death rate for 20- to 24-year-olds would be:

$$Age\text{-specific deathrate} = \frac{Number\ of\ deaths\ in\ a\ given\ year\ between\ ages\ 20-24}{Population\ between\ ages\ 20-24} * 1000$$

Here, we're focused only on deaths among those 20–24 years old, and we'd expect this rate to be lower than that among 80- to 84-year-olds.

Generally, the age-specific death rate for those in a given age group is:

$$Age\text{-specific death rate} = \frac{\textbf{Number of deaths in a given year between ages x and y}}{\textbf{Population between ages x and y}} * 1000$$

Here "x" refers to the lower and "y" to the higher limit of the age interval being considered. If we only want to look at those of a specific age, instead of an age interval, we can make the interval in the equation from "between ages x and x."

Not only do demographers adjust crude death rates for age, but they also consider specialized rates based on sex, race, and other kinds of differences as well. For example, here is the death rate for females:

$$Female\ death\ rate = \frac{\textbf{Number of deaths of females in a given year}}{\textbf{Population}} * 1000$$

There are also death rates derived from those suffering certain diseases and other health mishaps. That is, we can calculate death rates from cancer, heart disease, automobile fatalities, gun violence, and the like. Many policy and public health debates are focused on such rates.

For example, the Council on Foreign Relations tells us that, in 2007, an estimated 3.21 per 100,000 US residents were murdered with a firearm. Japan in that same year, had an estimated 0.01 per 100,000 residents killed with a firearm. Other European countries had similarly low numbers compared to the United States.[3]

There has been a great deal of debate regarding why the United States has a higher firearm homicide rate and what, if anything, government should do about it. Such debate is a stark illustration of the relevance of "dry" mathematical calculations to important policy questions.

By the way, you might be wondering why I said "per 100,000" instead of "per 1,000," as I did earlier. Recall that the reason for multiplying rates by 1,000 is because they're sometimes very small; multiplying them by 1,000 makes them easier to interpret. Thankfully, homicide from a firearm, even in the United States, is a relatively rare event. This results in homicide rates being very, very small, and, to make a very, very small rate easier to interpret you have to multiply by a bigger number than 1,000. Demographers typically settle on 100,000.

We're now ready to look at the IMR. Although it has a slightly different appearance, the IMR is a special type of age-adjusted death rate:

$$\text{Infant mortality rate} = \frac{\textit{Number of deaths of those under } 1 \textit{ year of age}}{\textit{total live births in calender year}} * 1000$$

I said earlier that Canada has a lower IMR than the does the United States. At this writing, according to *The World Factbook*, Canada's IMR is estimated at 4.65 deaths per thousand, while infant mortality in the US is 5.87 deaths per thousand.[4] Let's round these to 5 per thousand for Canada and 6 per thousand for the United States. An obvious question could be asked about this difference: what does it really mean? An obvious answer would be that it means a difference of one infant death per thousand, but that's not what the question is really after.

Although I don't want to suggest that a dying infant isn't a big deal, that's exactly what the question is "getting at." Is one more dying infant per thousand really that much? To see what's at issue, consider the IMRs of two other nations.

Japan's IMR is estimated at 2.08 or about 2 deaths per thousand, while Afghanistan's is estimated at 115.08 or around 115 per thousand. I suspect almost anyone would conclude that this is a difference that really "tells us something." We could use our rounded numbers to compare how much bigger the US IMR is than Canada's to how much bigger Afghanistan's is than Japan's. To see how to do so, consider a formula you saw in the previous chapter:

$$\text{Inflation rate} = \frac{CPI \text{ one year later} - CPI \text{ one year earlier}}{CPI \text{ one year earlier}}$$

Although I didn't say so earlier, the inflation rate[5] is actually a special case of a more general formula that Bennett and Briggs (2008) call the *relative change* formula:

$$\text{Relative change} = \frac{Comparison \text{ value} - Reference \text{ value}}{Reference \text{ value}}$$

Notice that in the inflation rate formula "CPI one year later" plays the role of the comparison value, and "CPI one year earlier" serves as the reference value. The relative change formula can be used in any situation where we want to compare the difference between a comparison value and a reference value to the reference value itself. This may sound confusing at first, but some more examples should help.

Suppose we want to compare the US IMR to Canada's. We would do this as

$$\frac{Comparison \text{ value} - Reference \text{ value}}{Reference \text{ value}} = \frac{U.S. \text{ IMR} - Canada \text{ IMR}}{Canada \text{ IMR}} = \frac{\left(\frac{6}{1000}\right) - \left(\frac{5}{1000}\right)}{\left(\frac{5}{1000}\right)} = .2$$

So, the US IMR is .2 = 2/10 = 1/5 larger than Canada's. If we multiply .2 by 100, we get 20%, meaning that the US IMR is 20% higher than Canada's.

Now let's see how much bigger Afghanistan's IMR is than Japan's:

$$\frac{Comparison \text{ value} - Reference \text{ value}}{Reference \text{ value}} = \frac{Afgh. \text{ IMR} - Japan \text{ IMR}}{Japan \text{ IMR}} = \frac{\left(\frac{115}{1000}\right) - \left(\frac{2}{1000}\right)}{\left(\frac{2}{1000}\right)} = 56.5$$

So, rounding to a whole number, Afghanistan's IMR is 57 times bigger than Japan's. IMRs are often thought of as measures of how healthy a nation or group is. If, for the moment, we entertain this idea, the United States appears to be only about 1/5 less healthy than Canada. Assuming, for the sake of discussion, that it's Canada's superior healthcare system which results in Canadians being healthier than US residents, one could argue that these systemic differences in healthcare don't result in that much of a difference—at least not compared to what's going on with Afghanistan versus Japan.

One could also argue that comparing Afghanistan to Japan is ridiculous because Japan is a so-called advanced industrialized nation while Afghanistan is not. I'll concede the point. The only reason for the Afghanistan versus Japan comparison was to give you a sense of what it means to have a big difference in IMRs.

So far, we've been talking about IMRs for a whole nation. But IMRs can also be calculated for specific groups. For example, these rates for whites, blacks, American Indians or Alaska Natives, Asians or Pacific Islanders, and Latinos/Hispanics might be 5, 12, 8, 4, and 5 deaths per thousand, respectively. Using the numbers for blacks and whites and applying the relative difference formula again, we'd get:

$$\frac{\left(\frac{12}{1000}\right)-\left(\frac{5}{1000}\right)}{\left(\frac{5}{1000}\right)}=1.4$$

So the IMR for blacks in the United States in 2010 was about 1.4 times higher than that for whites. This is nothing like the Afghanistan versus Japan difference, but it's clearly bigger than the United States versus Canada one. There has been extensive debate regarding what accounts for the black–white difference in infant mortality, and my intention here isn't to resolve that debate. What I want you to focus on for this book is the role mathematics plays in it. That role is simple—mathematics provides the terms of that debate. That is, it would be very difficult to have this debate if we didn't have relatively valid and reliable measures of infant mortality at our disposal.

PREVALENCE RATES

Mortality rates aren't the only ones relevant to policy issues. Policymakers, especially those dealing with matters of public health, also focus on other measures of how well populations are doing. One measure used in this type of work is called the *prevalence rate*.

The formula for the prevalence rate is:

$$\frac{\textit{Total number persons in a given year with some health condition or illness}}{\textit{population}}*k$$

where "k" is usually 1,000 or 100. According to the 2014 National Survey on Drug Use and Health, among those at least 18 years old, the prevalence of mental illness in the United States was about 18% (or 18 per 100 people).[6]

Prevalence rates, like other demographic rates, can vary by group. For example, for adults aged 18–25 in 2014, the prevalence rate for mental illness was about 20%. That rate was also around 20% for those 26 to 49 years old, and about 15% for those at least 50 years old.

Policymakers can use data such as these to inform social planning. Knowing that older persons had a lower prevalence of mental illness than younger ones could lead to further investigations to determine if this difference persist over time or is merely a 1 year "blip." If it turned out that the difference persisted over time, policymakers could consider interventions with younger persons which might improve their mental health.

LIFE EXPECTANCY, THE DEPENDENCY RATIO, AND SOCIAL SECURITY

Recall that Social Security is a federal program which provides income to people upon retirement as long as they've work for at least 10 years and have met other conditions of eligibility. The benefits received depend on how much one made while working. The higher a person's earnings when they were working, the lower the proportion of those earnings they receive in benefits.

Even though Social Security provides benefits only to those who've retired, people have a certain degree of choice when it comes to when they retire. The age at which someone can retire at full benefits depends on when they were born. Someone born in 1937 or earlier can get full benefits at age 65. Those born between 1943 and 1954 can receive full benefits at age 66. And those born after 1960 can't receive full benefits until age 67. A person can retire at age 62 or at any other time before their "full benefits retirement age." If they do, however, their monthly benefits will be reduced below the amounts they'd receive if they'd waited.

When it comes to financing, Social Security is a "pay as you go" program. This means that current workers and employers are taxed by the federal government, and those tax revenues are transferred to current Social Security recipients.

At this point, you might be wondering why I'm bringing up Social Security in a chapter on demography. The reason is simple: two fundamental demographic concepts are intimately related to this program: *life expectancy* and the *aged dependency ratio*.

Life expectancy, at a given age, is the average number of years someone who's reached that age can expect to live. For example, in the United States, life expectancy at birth (meaning someone between 0 and 1 year old) might be about 79 years. In other words, an infant born in the United States could expect to live to about 79 years. Life expectancy for someone between 50 and 51 years old might be about 31 years, meaning that such a person could expect to live to be about 81 years.[7]

Life expectancy, like infant mortality, varies by race. It also varies by gender. The table here illustrates some of this variation.

Group	Life expectancy starting from age 65–66 (rounded to whole number ages)[8]
Males	18
Females	20
Whites	19
White Males	18
White Females	20
Blacks	18
Black Males	16
Black Females	19
Hispanics/Latinos	21
Hispanic/Latino Males	19
Hispanic/Latino Females	22

It's clear from this table that females aged 65–66 have more years ahead of them than do males, whites have more years ahead of them than do blacks, and black males in this age range have fewer years ahead of them than any other group in the table.

Even though members of some groups have higher life expectancies than those of others, life expectancy in the United States, overall, has been on the rise. Over the course of the twentieth century, life expectancy almost doubled, and increasing life expectancy is predicted to continue during the twenty-first century.

The aged dependency ratio is another measure relevant to Social Security. It takes the following form:

$$\text{Aged dependency ratio} = \frac{\text{Total number of persons in a given year over 65 years old}}{\text{Total number of persons in a given year between 15 and 64 years old}} * 100$$

The numerator of this ratio is meant to capture the magnitude of the elderly population, while the denominator is intended to capture that of the working-age population. Multiplying the ratio by 100 gives us "the number of aged people per hundred people of working age" (Rowland 2003, p. 86).

The importance of life expectancy and the dependency ratio to Social Security has to do with how these interact with an aging "baby boomer" generation. "Baby boomer" is a term demographers use to refer to those born in the United States between the years of about 1946 and 1964. The issues baby boomers raise for Social Security are (1) there are a lot of them; (2) they're entering their retirement years; (3) given what I said about life expectancy, they'll probably live longer than elderly people of previous generations did; and (4) because the number of new entrants into the work force isn't expected to grow enough to keep pace with the retirement of baby boomers, the dependency ratio is expected to increase. This last point my need some elaboration.

Take a look at the aged dependency ratio again:

$$\text{Aged dependency ratio} = \frac{\textit{Total number persons in a given year over 65 years old}}{\textit{Total number of persons in a given year between 15 and 64 years old}} * 100$$

In this formula, more people entering the workforce would increase the denominator. More people entering retirement and living longer would increase the numerator. If demographers are right that growth in the number of retirees will exceed growth in the workforce, this means that the numerator of the aged dependency ratio will grow more than the denominator. If the numerator of a ratio increases by more than its denominator does, this results in a bigger ratio. And a bigger ratio here would mean slower growth in the number of people paying for benefits, while there would be faster growth in the number of people requiring those benefits.

There have been several proposals made to address this problem. Since you're likely to encounter these in your policy course, I won't say much about the details of these proposals here. I'll discuss one, though, that's related to the mathematics we've discussing.

Some have argued that we can address the increasing dependency ratio problem by raising the retirement age, perhaps to as high as 70 years. Doing this would change the age range of the denominator of the dependency ratio from 15–64 years old to 15–70 years old. Since people would be working longer, this would tend to increase the denominator of the ratio and decrease the numerator. A bigger denominator and smaller numerator would mean a smaller ratio. And a smaller ratio would mean a more manageable program from a financial perspective.

Even though raising the retirement age would lead to a more financially manageable program, that, by itself, doesn't mean we ought to do this. Maybe we should let people enjoy their longer, healthier lives by allowing them more "golden years" to play, instead of expecting them to work until they almost drop.

Given what I said earlier about race and life expectancy, the increases in health and longevity mentioned earlier might not be evenly distributed by race. That is, perhaps "persons of color" won't enjoy as much of an increase in life expectancy in relatively good health as whites will. Would it be fair to tell them they have to work until they're 70 years old when they, on average, have fewer years to live after retirement?

MARRIAGE AND DIVORCE

In 1996, a US law called the *Personal Responsibility and Work Opportunity Reconciliation Act* (PROWRA) was enacted. This is the law that gave the United States TANF, a policy more commonly known as welfare, which I've mentioned several times.

Although the title of the law gives the impression that it's related to work (and it is), the actual text of the law opens with the follow "findings" from Congress:

1. Marriage is the foundation of a successful society,
2. Marriage is an essential institution of a successful society which promotes the interests of children,

and

3. Promotion of responsible fatherhood and motherhood is integral to successful child-rearing and the well-being of children.[9]

It's pretty clear from these statements that Congress, at the time, felt marriage between a man and a woman (hence, the reference to "fatherhood and motherhood") was of crucial social significance.

Fast-forward over two decades, and the United States is now a country where marriages between people of the same sex must be legally recognized throughout the nation. But there are still those who believe marriage should only be between a man and a woman and who think that allowing two people of the same sex to marry each other somehow threatens the institution of marriage.

Policy debates about welfare, marriage, and who should be allowed to marry are related to two rates that receive a lot of attention in demography: *marriage* and *divorce rates*. These take the following forms:

$$\text{Marriage rate} = \frac{\textit{Total number of marriages in a given year}}{\textit{Population age 15 and over}} * 1000$$

and

$$\text{Divorce rate} = \frac{\textit{Total number of divorces in a given year}}{\textit{Population age 15 and over}} * 1000$$

As I write these lines, the marriage rate in the United States is about 6.9 marriages per 1,000, while the divorce rate is about 3.2 per 1,000.[10] I don't know if these figures would satisfy the architects of PROWRA, but I suspect marriage and divorce rates will continue to figure prominently in a host of policy discussions.

THE MATHEMATICS OF POPULATION GROWTH
AND CARRYING CAPACITY

On September 13, 2013, the *New York Times* published an op-ed piece by environmental scientist Erle C. Ellis.[11] Ellis's article "stepped into" the debate about whether current world population growth is sustainable or whether such growth is subject to natural constraints. In other words, can we continue growing as we are or will nature eventually stop us from doing so? This harkens back to a question raised by the writings of Thomas Malthus, a British demographer, economist, and clergyman whose life spanned the eighteenth and nineteenth centuries.

Malthus contended that food supply tends to grow *arithmetically* while population tends to growth *geometrically*. Arithmetic growth is when some quantity grows by the same *absolute* amount each time period. For example, suppose we're measuring food supply in pounds per person for a given year, and food supply in the year 2016 was by 1,000,000,000 pounds per person. Suppose the food supplies in 2017, 2018, 2019, and 2020 were 1,000,000,100; 1,000,000,200; 1,000,000,300; and 1,000,000,400 pounds per person, respectively. This would be an example of arithmetic growth because food supply would have grown by the same amount, 100 pounds per person, each year. Arithmetic growth is sometimes called *linear growth*.

Geometric growth is when some quantity grows by the same *relative* amount or percentage each time period. For example, suppose the world population in 2016 was 1,000,000 people. (It was actually about 7 billion people, but working with smaller numbers might make the example easier to understand.) Suppose world population in 2017, 2018, 2019, and 2020, ended up being 1,100,000; 1,210,000; 1,331,000; and 1,464,100, respectively. This would mean that, each year, population grows by 10%. Since the percentage growth for each year is the same 10%, this would be an example of geometric growth. Geometric growth is also called *exponential growth*.

Any quantity that's growing geometrically will grow faster than one that's growing arithmetically. This was what concerned Malthus. Since he thought food supply grows arithmetically while population grows geometrically, he thought food supply would grow more slowly than population would. This means there'd eventually be more people to feed than supply of food available to feed them, leading to mass starvation.

Ellis is a biologist, and, in the article mentioned earlier, he raises questions about views such as Malthus's. Much of the debate turns on something called *carrying capacity*. Any species of organism relies on its environment for survival, and one of the most important things provided by a species' environment is food. The carrying capacity of a species is the largest population that can be supported by the environment of that species. If we think of human beings as a species and the Earth as our environment, then our carrying capacity is the largest population of humans the Earth can support. The debate between Malthusian types and Ellis is whether our carrying capacity is a natural constraint or whether it's something determined by technology and economic institutions. By "economic institutions" I mean all the ways human beings organize the production and allocation of good and services.

Malthus, as well as others who see things similarly, thinks the natural resources of the Earth are in limited supply. This means that the size of the human population must also have a limit. We simply can't grow beyond the resources available to sustain us. Ellis, as well as those on his side, contend that there isn't a natural limit on the size of the human population. Instead, how large a population we can become depends on human technological prowess and whether we can design institutions well enough to feed, house, and provide for more and more people as we continue to grow.

It's not my intention here to resolve this debate. I brought it up, of course, as another illustration of the relevance of mathematics to an important social issue. Does the food supply grow arithmetically? Does human population grow geometrically? Is there a natural carrying capacity which provides a check on human population growth, and, if so, what is it? These are all mathematical questions, and the answers to them are relevant to resolving this dispute.

This chapter has focused on the relationship between demographic and social issues, with the theme being the role of mathematics. The next chapter shifts to *personal finance*. Personal finance refers to decisions people make in an attempt to keep themselves and their loved ones financially secure. It's another area of relevance to a number of social issues in which mathematics plays a fundamental role.

NOTES

1. All this assumes that *superfetation* can't occur during the year in question. Superfetation is when someone already carrying a fetus gets pregnant while carrying that fetus. This is rare, but it can happen.

2. See World Health Organization, *Crude Death and Birth Rate Data by Country*.

3. See Masters, *US Gun Policy*.

4. See Central Intelligence Agency, *The World Fact Book*.

5. Economists sometimes use the term "rate" in a way which differs from how demographers use it. As we've seen, demographers use the term to refer to the number of people meeting some condition divided by the number of people at risk of meeting it. Economists sometimes use it to refer to what I've called a relative change. It's unfortunate that the same term is used in two different ways, but that's the current state of the social sciences.

6. See Hedden et al., *Behavioral Health Trends in the United States*.

7. See Arias, "United States Life Tables."

8. See Ibid., tables 2–12.

9. See the United States Congress, *H.R. 3734*.

10. See National Center for Health Statistics, *Marriage and Divorce*.

11. See Ellis, Erle C. "Overpopulation Is Not the Problem."

5

THE MATHEMATICS OF PERSONAL FINANCE

IN THEIR *ENCYCLOPEDIA of Social Work* article on financial social work, Wolfsohn and Michaeli discuss the importance of financial knowledge in a modern economy.[1,2] More specifically, they make the point that, as people face the perennial problem of trying to assure their economic security throughout the life course, the financial products that may help them do so have become increasingly complex. People are faced with decisions such as whether to embark on higher education themselves or whether their dependents will, whether to obtain insurance of various kinds, how to plan for retirement, and a host of other issues. Yet, as Wolfsohn and Michaeli point out, people aren't very knowledgeable about financial matters.

Another point Wolfsohn and Michaeli make is that social workers, in their work with clients, often have to address financial issues. Yet social workers receive little training in personal finance, resulting in their being no more knowledgeable about such matters than their clients are.

Not only might it benefit direct practitioners to know a little more about personal finance, but social workers interested in policy-related issues would benefit from such knowledge as well. Consider the debate about what should be done regarding Social Security. In the previous chapter, I said this program is predicted to face a good deal of financial stress in the coming years. Many commentators debate what to do about this, and some have argued that Social Security should be privatized. Privatization could take different forms, but what all forms have in common is the idea that people would play a larger role in planning for their own retirement.

Those who support privatization say it would be better than the current system because it would result in a higher average return than we see under the Social Security system. Opponents of privatization counter that this higher average return would come with higher risk, risk that many people wouldn't be able to afford. A social worker without knowledge of how the terms "return" and "risk" are being used in this debate won't really be able to follow it. Having some exposure to the technicalities of personal finance provides a way of acquiring such knowledge.

This chapter attempts to provide enough information about personal finance that social workers who need to know something about these matters will understand some of the basics. Personal finance is an area where mathematics appears a lot, but, as math goes, none of the stuff you'll see will be very difficult. We'll start with household financial statements.

HOUSEHOLD FINANCIAL STATEMENTS

One of the things financial planners often advise people to do is create *balance sheets* as well as *cash flow statements* for their households. These are documents that roughly tell a household how financially healthy it is, but each one does so in a different way. A balance sheet provides an indication of a household's financial well-being at a given point in time by showing how assets compares to liabilities. A cash flow statement provides a record of where a household's income came from, as well as where its spending went.

The main components of a balance sheet are *assets* and *liabilities*. Back in Chapter 3, I defined net worth as the monetary value of what someone owns minus the value of what they owe. Well, a household's assets are the monetary value of what it owns, and its liabilities are the value of what it owes. Thus, another way to define a household's net worth is:

Net worth = assets − liabilities

A household's balance sheet is essentially a record of its net worth. What you want to focus on is whether net worth is 0, greater than 0, or less than 0.

The subcomponents of a household's assets are *monetary assets*, *tangible assets*, and *investment assets*. Monetary assets are the cash in a household's checking and savings accounts, as well as other holdings which can easily be converted into cash. Tangible assets are material goods that people typically use in their daily lives and which have been acquired primarily for this use value. Examples are cars, furniture, homes, and the like. Investment assets are those which have been obtained primarily because the owner of the asset wants to benefit from an increase in the asset's value. Examples are stocks, bonds, and other such objects.

A household's liabilities are what it owes, and a household can owe several kinds of things: credit card debt; money owed for services provided by doctors, social workers, or other professionals; unpaid taxes; past-due rent or utility bills; auto loans; real estate loans; educational loans; and a host of others.

You can use the net worth preceding formula to obtain a measure of a household's financial health. If a household's assets equal its liabilities, the household's net worth is zero. This means that if it were to convert its assets to cash (or *monetize* them), it would have just enough to meet its liabilities. If a household's assets exceeded its liabilities, its net worth would be positive or greater than zero. So, if it were to monetize its assets, it would have more than enough to meet its liabilities. And if a household's assets were less than its liabilities, its net worth would be negative or less than 0. This could mean trouble because, if it were to monetize its assets, it would not have enough to meet its liabilities.

I just said that a negative net worth *could* mean trouble because whether it did would depend on the composition of the household's liabilities. Going into debt isn't necessarily a bad thing. If one goes into debt to buy a house, for example, that might turn out to be a good investment if the value of the house increases to a point where it ends up being worth far more than what's owed on it. Or, to take another example, if someone borrowed money to finance their education and this eventually resulted in them making a very high income in their "high flying" job, this might mean that, over time, their net worth will come into balance or move into positive territory.

Another way of assessing how well a household is doing financially is to focus on how much cash is going into and leaving the household. This brings us to the notion of a *cash flow statement*. A cash flow statement is simply a summary of the amount of money that's flowed into a household and the amount that's been spent over a specific time period. Such a statement has three sections.

One section focuses on income or the total amount of money received by the household over the time period in question. Another section concerns itself with *expenses*, which refers to total spending by the household over this period. And the third section is *net income*, which is the difference between income and expenses. Mathematically, net income is:

Net income = income − expenses

If net income is positive, the household has a cash flow surplus. If net income is negative, it has a cash flow deficit. And if net income is 0, the household has a cash flow balance.

Examples of income sources for a household are wages and salary, scholarships and grants, monetary gifts, social welfare benefits, and a host of others. Expenses can be further divided into two categories: *fixed expenses* and *variable expenses*.

Fixed expenses are those that occur in the same amount over each time period. For example, if you've borrowed money to buy a house, each month you may have to pay the same amount of money to the bank. If you don't own your home but rent it, you'll have to pay your landlord a set amount of money each month; this amount of money is, of course, called *rent*. Some people have different types of insurance. I'll have more to say about private-sector insurance arrangements in a later chapter. For now, all you need to know is that when people have insurance, they typically have to pay the insurance company a set amount of money, called a *premium*, each quarter or other time period.

Variable expenses are those that change over each time period. For example, a household may spend money for entertainment each month. If the amount spent isn't the same each month, we're dealing with a variable expense. Other examples of possibly variable expenses are those for transportation, telephone bills, gas and electricity bills, credit card bills, child care costs, and clothing costs.

Obviously, when it comes to a cash flow statement, a household would at least want a 0 net income and preferably a positive one. It definitely wouldn't want to spend more money than it takes in per time period. The only way it can keep doing this is by borrowing money or dipping into savings. But these two strategies of financing a negative net income tend to increase the probability of a household having a negative worth. And we've already talked about why that is something a household would want to avoid.

RATIOS FOR ASSESSING A HOUSEHOLD'S FINANCIAL HEALTH

In Chapter 2, I introduced ratios. These come up a lot in personal finance. For example, we can calculate a household's *basic liquidity ratio* (BLR). The formula for this is:

$$\text{Basic liquidity ratio} = \frac{\text{mometary (liquid) assets}}{\text{monthly expenses}}$$

There is a new term here, "*liquid*," which I need to define. You already know what an asset is. A liquid asset is either cash or one that can easily be converted to cash.

Examples of assets that can easily be converted to cash are stocks and bonds, both of which I'll discuss in more detail later in this chapter.

The value of a household's BLR is an estimate of how long it could pay its bills if all income flowing into the household stopped. For a given household, the higher this ratio the better, but finance experts recommend a BLR of at least 3.

To consider an example, suppose a household's liquid monetary assets were $5,000 and its monthly expenses were $4,500. This household's BLR is:

$$\frac{\$5000}{\$4,500} = 1.1$$

Since 1.1 is quite a bit less than 3, if this household's income were to drop to 0, we'd predict that it would quickly face financial difficulty.

The *asset to debt ratio* (ADR) is another measure which can help in assessing a household's financial health. It takes the form

$$\text{Asset to debt ratio} = \frac{total\ assets}{total\ debt}$$

Financial health is indicated by an ADR greater than 1; the higher above 1 it is, the better. An ADR of less than 1 would mean the household owes more than it owns. As I said when discussing net worth, owing more than you own, over the long term, isn't a good place to be.

For example, suppose a household has assets of $500,000 but a debt of $100,000. This would result in an ADR of 5:

$$\text{Asset to debt ratio} = \frac{\$500,000}{\$100,000} = 5$$

This household would be in decent financial shape because if it had to convert its assets to cash to pay off its debt, it would have more than enough to do so.

A third ratio for assessing a household's financial well-being is the *debt payments to disposable income ratio* (DDR), which takes the form

$$\text{Debt payments to disposable income ratio} = \frac{monthly\ nonmortgage\ debt\ repayments}{disposable\ income}$$

As you know by now, the number that results from applying this formula can be converted to a percentage by multiplying that number by 100. According to Garman and Forgue (2010), a DDR of 15% or less is preferable. Once a household gets above 15%, they're thought to be in the danger zone; that is, if their income were disrupted in some way, they'd be at risk of not being able to pay off their debt.

Suppose a household had non–mortgage-related monthly debt payments of $1,000 and a monthly income of $3,000. Inserting these numbers into the debt payments to disposable income formula would tell us that this household's DDR would about 33%. Since 33% is well above 15%, this household could face serious financial troubles if it lost its income.

INSURANCE AND PERSONAL FINANCE

It should be clear by now that personal finance is largely about the income and other resources a household possesses. Among the major threats to a household's resources are very costly events that could occur to at least one of its members— car accidents, serious health problems, the death of a loved one, and a host of others. Let's look more closely at the example of serious health problems.

Modern medicine may be a miracle, but if it is, it's a very expensive one. A broken bone may cost hundreds or thousands of dollars to treat. A lot of families may not be in a position to absorb an unexpected layout of, say, $2,000 to get a broken leg fixed. Having to unexpectedly pay someone such an amount of money could mean going with less food or other necessities. There is a type of agreement in the world, however, which allows households to gain protection from such calamities: *insurance*.

Insurance is a kind of contract. Like all contracts, it's an agreement between two parties, each of whom makes promises to the other. One, called the *insurer*, promises to pay the other, called the *policy holder*, financial benefits in the event that the policy holder encounters a certain outcome. There is one type of insurance, *life insurance*, where the policy holder doesn't receive benefits in the event that something happens to them, but those who depend on the policy holder's income do. In return for these contingent financial benefits, the policy holder promises to periodically pay the insurer a certain amount of money called a *premium*.

This type of arrangement relies on people's distaste for uncertainty. As I said earlier, a person may break a bone or experience some other health problem, but the use of the word "may" indicates that we don't know for sure if this will happen. There are a host of other uncertain outcomes that would be quite costly to a household were they to occur. Were it to experience any of them, car accidents, robberies, and fires could also be financially disastrous to a household. And if a breadwinner dies leaving behind a number of dependents, those dependents' financial prospects could quickly take a turn for the worse. People's willingness to pay for protection from such uncertainty is part of what makes insurance possible. Insurance arrangements are also possible because of a mathematical idea called the *law of large numbers*.

The law of large numbers, as it relates to insurance, is essentially about the predictability of events in which there is uncertainty about whether or when they will occur. It's an idea that's really based on two sub-ideas.

The first is that it's very difficult, perhaps impossible, to predict whether a given individual will experience a particular event. The second sub-idea is that it's easier to predict how many times an event will happen among a large number of individuals. You might be wondering at this point, "how large is large?" The law of large numbers doesn't provide an exact answer to this question but simply says that the larger the number, the better our prediction will be.

I said earlier that policy holders usually pay a premium to get protection from adverse events. Now, insurance companies are for-profit businesses and therefore want the gap between their revenue and their spending to be as large as possible. The premiums are what insurance companies take in. The cost of workers, the cost of other resources (e.g., computers, desks, etc.) needed to provide insurance, and the cost of "pay outs" to policy holders make up insurance companies' expenditures. The problem is that, like policy holders, insurance companies don't know whether a given policy holder will experience the event and, therefore, don't know when they will have to pay out benefits. What the law of large numbers does for insurance companies is allow them to use data on what's happened to a large number of policy holders to improve their predictions about what will happen to any given policy holder. And this is what allows insurance companies to set premiums in such a way that they can make profits.

All this can be seen by considering a simplified version of the formula insurance companies use to set premiums:

$$\text{Premium} = \text{pay out to policy holder} * \frac{no.\ of\ people\ who\ have\ experienced\ the\ event}{no.\ of\ people\ who\ could\ have\ experienced\ event}$$

$$* \frac{1}{time}$$

What this formula tells us is that, in order to figure out what premium to charge an individual policy holder, insurance companies multiply the amount of the payout to the policy holder by a fraction containing the number of people who have experienced the event in its numerator and the number of people who could have experienced the event in its denominator.[3] The $\frac{1}{time}$ part of the formula is there because insurance companies typically charge premiums over some agreed upon time period (e.g., per month, per quarter, etc.).

For example, suppose an insurance company is contracted to pay out $10,000 if a policy holder experiences some event of interest. Suppose also that the company has data telling it that each quarter (that is, each 3-month period), about 1 out of 500 of its policy holders encounters this event. Then, a given policy holder should be charged a premium of:

$$\text{Premium} = \$10,000 * \frac{1}{500} * \frac{1}{quarter} = \$20 \text{ per quarter}$$

I referred to the preceding formula as "simplified" because I've left out two complications. As I said earlier, insurance companies are for-profit operations that incur a cost of doing business. In order to profit, they add an amount to the premium to reflect their costs and desire for profit. So, the hypothetical policy holder would not pay $200 per quarter but some amount above that.

The second simplification is that policy holders typically have different characteristics, and at least some of these are related to how likely they are to experience the event. If the event is needing to be hospitalized for heart disease, for example, a 58-year-old man is more likely to encounter this event than a 20-year-old woman. This means that $\dfrac{no.\ of\ people\ who\ have\ experienced\ the\ event}{no.\ of\ people\ who\ could\ have\ experienced\ event}$ varies depending on the traits of the people who make up the numerator and denominator. So there isn't one premium formula which applies to every policy holder but instead several of them, depending on the traits of different types of policy holders.

So far, the cost to policy holders I've focused on are premiums. But policy holders often face other costs, too; these take the form of *deductibles* and *copayments*. A deductible is an amount of money, in addition to a premium, a policy holder must pay "out of pocket" in order to receive any other benefits promised by the insurance company. A copayment is an amount of money, in addition to a premium, a policy holder must pay each time a service covered by an insurance contract is used. Deductibles and copayments are frequently required of health insurance policy holders.

Imagine Mary has health insurance through the ABC insurance company. She might be covered for inpatient surgery, but the contract may require her to pay $200 "out of pocket" before it will pay any other benefits she's entitled to. This $200 would be a deductible.

When she feels ill, Mary may visit her doctor on an outpatient basis. ABC may cover most of the cost of these visits but require her to pay $20 "out of pocket" for each of them. These $20 payments would be examples of copayments.

Deductibles and copayments are ways of addressing a problem endemic to insurance arrangements called *moral hazard*. Moral hazard is the incentive that insurance coverage provides the policy holder to engage in behavior which is more likely to result in the event the policy holder is covered for. This is a concept we get from economists. What they're contending is that the fact someone has health insurance provides them with an incentive to engage in the very behaviors likely to cause the outcomes they're insured against. If policy holders have to pay "out of pocket" through deductibles and copayments some of the cost of receiving treatment for their conditions, this should mitigate the moral hazard problem, or so economists think.

The fact that policy holders typically face different risks of experiencing the event they're covered for is related to another problem endemic to insurance arrangements: *adverse selection*. Adverse selection refers to the tendency for those at higher risk of experiencing the event to be the ones to obtain insurance contracts. Again, health insurance provides a good example.

As I said earlier, a 58-year-old man is more likely to be hospitalized for heart disease than a 20-year-old woman. In fact, older people are more likely to face a number of health problems than are younger folks. If people are aware, at least to some extent, of the health risks they face, younger people might be less likely to purchase health insurance than are older people. And, if this were to happen, health insurance policy holders would tend to be older and sicker than they'd be if younger and healthier persons opted to join the pool. This is adverse selection.

The mathematical issue posed by adverse selection is that it tends to increase premiums. Take a look at the premium formula again:

$$\text{Premium} = \text{pay out to policy holder} * \frac{no.\ of\ people\ who\ have\ experienced\ the\ event}{no.\ of\ people\ who\ could\ have\ experienced\ event}$$

$$* \frac{1}{time}$$

Adverse selection tends to result in $\frac{no.\ of\ people\ who\ have\ experienced\ the\ event}{no.\ of\ people\ who\ could\ have\ experienced\ event}$ being higher than it would be if younger, healthier people were in the pool. To see this, suppose there were two insurance companies, one with all young, healthy people I'll call company A and the other with all older, sicker people I'll call company B. Both A and B have 1,000 people who could experience a health-related event. Both companies also have the same $\frac{1}{time}$ and the same payout to policy holders. Yet company A saw 200 people per time period experience the event while company B only saw 20 people experience it. Since 200 divided by 1,000 equals

20%, and 20 divided by 1,000 equals 2%, company A will be multiplying $\frac{1}{time}$ and the payout by a bigger number than will company B. Therefore, company A will charge a higher premium than company B.

It should be clear by now that insurance companies aren't merely for-profit operations—they're mathematical ones as well. The math gets so complicated, in fact, that such companies usually hire mathematically minded people, called *actuaries*, to help them work it all out. But at the core of all this is the law of large numbers.

SAVINGS AND PERSONAL FINANCE

One of the things financial consultants tell us is that we should save some of our money. In order to do this, of course, you need some money left over after meeting your basic expenses. Math plays a huge rule when it comes to savings; this section will cover some of the basics.

When financial consultants advise us that we should save some of our money, they don't mean that we should put our savings under our mattresses. At the very least, we're advised to open a savings account in a bank. The reason is that banks must pay you in return for leaving your money with them. And the reason they must pay you is because after you've put your money in a bank, that bank is not likely to leave it there. It will typically loan this money to someone else and profit from doing so. That is, the bank will use your money to make money for itself and must, therefore, pay you for this privilege. The money paid to someone for the use of their money is called *interest*.

Not only does the bank pay you interest to use your money. When it loans your money to others, it charges them interest as well. Banks profit from this arrangement by charging others more interest than they pay you for the use of your money. For example, a bank might pay you $50 in interest but charge the person it's loaned your money to $100 in interest, for profit of $50. Much of the math involved in savings is related to interest, and there are two types of interest: *simple* and *compound interest*.

Suppose you put $100 of your savings into a bank. Suppose the bank agrees to pay you 5% yearly interest on your $100. This means that, at the end of a year, the bank would owe you $100 plus 5% of $100. You can figure out what's 5% of $100 by multiplying $100 by the decimal form of 5%, which is .05. That is, you solve the equation $100 * .05 which equals $5. So, at the end of a year, the bank would owe you $100 + $5 = $105.

The initial amount of money placed in a savings account, the \$100 in this example, is called the *principal*. You'll also see this term when we discuss loans; there, it will refer to the initial amount of money that's loaned to someone. You might be wondering why we're using a word reserved for loans when talking about saving money in a bank. The reason is that when you save money in a bank, you're technically loaning money to that bank. So the bank pays you interest just as any other borrower would.

The percent interest, also called the *interest rate*, paid on the principal of a loan, is called the *simple interest rate*, which is where the term simple interest comes from. In our example, .05 or 5% is the simple interest rate.

Notice in this example that interest was paid on the principal after a certain time period. This is always the case. In other words, the unit of measurement of an interest rate is always percent per time period. In the example, it's .05 or 5% per year.

The relationship between the simple interest rate, the principal, the time (in years) over which simple interest is paid, and the total amount of simple interest earned is

$$\text{Simple interest earned} = \text{Principal} * \frac{simple\ interest\ rate}{year} * \left(number * year\right)$$

This formula may look terrifying so let's go through it step by step. "Principal" refers to the amount of money that's loaned or borrowed. It will be in units of dollars. The simple interest rate, since it's the decimal form of a percentage per year, is a pure number divided by year. The "number*year" in the formula stands for the number of years over which simple interest is earned. Since the interest rate per year is multiplied by number*years, the year in the "number*year" cancels with the year in the denominator, meaning we are left with

$$\text{Simple interest earned} = \text{Principal} * simple\ interest\ rate * number$$

Since the Principal is in dollars and the simple interest rate is a pure number, the result of multiplying these should be in dollars. This makes sense because the amount of interest earned should be in dollars (assuming the dollar is the currency in use).

The balance in a savings account after a certain number of years of simple interest has been added to the principal is given by the formula:

$$\text{Account balance}_{simple\ interest} = \text{Principal} + \text{Simple interest earned over certain number } of \text{ years}$$

$$= \text{Principal} + \text{Principal} * \frac{simple\ interest\ rate}{year} * number * year$$

To go back to our example, the principle was $100 and the interest rate was .05 per year. So, after 1 year, the balance is:

$$\text{Account balance}_{\text{simpleinterest}} = \$100 + \$100 * \frac{.05}{year} * 1\text{year} = \$100 + \$5$$
$$= \$105 \text{ (since } \$100 * .05 = \$5)$$

If you were to apply the account balance formula for 2 years of interest, you'd get $100 + $10 = $110. After three years, you'd get $100 + $15 = $115. I think by now you get the idea.

Many accounts, in the real world, including many bank savings accounts, don't pay simple interest but instead pay compound interest. To understand how this works, consider our example again. We said that after the first year of simple interest, the account balance would be $100 + $5 = $105, after year two it would be $110, and after year three it would be $115. But suppose the bank did the following.

After paying a first year of simple interest on the principal of $100, instead of paying simple interest on the principal for the second year, it paid it on the $105 balance accumulated after that first year. Using the same interest rate of 5% per year, after the second year, the account balance would then be $105 + $105 $* \frac{.05}{year}$ * 1 year = $110.25. If, for the third year, the bank paid interest on the $110.25, the account balance after year three would be $110.25 + $110.25 $* \frac{.05}{year}$ * 1 year = $115.76. In theory, the bank could continue paying interest this way indefinitely.

When simple interest isn't paid on the principal but instead is paid on accumulated balances, as just described, this is called *compounding*. Hence, the term "compound interest," a term you may have seen before.

Mathematicians have, of course, come up with a formula to calculate account balances when interest is compounded. That formula is

$$\text{Account balance after t periods}_{\text{compound interest}} = \text{Principal} * \left(1 + \text{Period interest rate}\right)^t$$

It's important to realize that "t" in the exponent is a pure number.[4] It stands for the number of periods over which interest has been compounded. What I mean by this should become clear shortly. The "Principle" in the formula is in units of dollars. The *period interest rate* is a new concept which I'll now explain.

When interest is compounded, it's done a given number of times over the course of a year. Suppose, for example, that interest were compounded monthly. Since there are 12 months in a year, interest would be compounded 12 times in a given year. If interest were compounded quarterly, it would be compounded 4 times a year. This is because a quarter is a 3-month period, and there are four 3-month periods in a given year. If interest were compounded daily, this would amount to interest being compounded 365 times a year. And if interest were compounded annually, it would be compounded once in a given year. The interest rate used for annual compounding has a special name: the *annual percentage rate* (APR). The period interest rate quantity in the previous formula is given as follows:

Period interest rate = APR / Number of times interest is compounded in a year

Since the APR is a pure number and the number of times interest is compounded in a year is as well, the Period interest rate is a pure number.

Now let's go back to the compound interest account balance formula:

Account balance after t periods$_{\text{compound interest}}$ = Principal $*\left(1 + \text{Period interest rate}\right)^{t}$

This formula could also be written as

Account balance after t periods$_{\text{compound interest}}$

$= \text{Principal} *\left(1 + \text{APR} / \text{Number of times interest is compounded in a year}\right)^{t}$

Since, as I said above, "t" in the exponent of this formula is a pure number, the quantity in parenthesis is a pure number, and the principal is in dollars, so the account balance is in dollars multiplied by a pure number. So it, too, must be in dollars.

As an example, suppose you put $100 in the bank (the principal) and the bank agrees to pay you a 5% APR. It's also agreed to compound interest monthly. Let's assume you keep the money in the bank for 5 years. Since 5 years is five 12-month periods, t in the formula would be 60 periods (5 * 12 = 60). That is, interest will be compounded 60 times over a 5-year period. First, let's apply the period interest rate formula:

APR / Number of times interest is compounded in a year = .05 / 12 = .004

The number "12" appears in the denominator because when interest is compounded monthly, it's compounded 12 times in a given year. Now we can apply the compound interest version of the account balance formula.

Account balance after t periods$_{\text{compound interest}}$

$= \text{Principal} *\left(1 + \text{APR} / \text{Number of times interest is compounded in a year}\right)^{t}$

$= \$100 *\left(1 + .004\right)^{60} = \$127.06$

So, after 5 years, the $100 you put into the bank, thanks to monthly compounding of interest, will grow to about $127. Recall that when a simple interest rate of .05

was paid on a principal of $100, after a year you ended up with $105. So, over 5 years, you'd end up with $125. This can be seen by applying the account balance formula for simple interest:

$$Principal + Principal * \frac{simple\ interest\ rate}{year} * number * year$$

$$= 100 + 100 * \frac{.5}{year} * 25years = \$125$$

So, over a relatively short period of 5 years, compounding would only get you about $2 more than simple interest.

What would happen if the bank compounded more frequently, say, daily instead of monthly? The compound interest version of the account balance formula has our answer:

$$\$100 * (1 + .0001)^{1825} = \$128.40$$

So compounding more frequently increased the compound versus simple interest difference to $3.40 ($128.40 − $125 = $3.40). In case you're wondering, the ".0001" in this formula comes from the period interest formula given earlier: namely, APR/Number of times interest is compounded in a year = .05/365 = .0001. The "1825" in the preceding equation refers to the number of days in a 5-year period.

There is a version of the compound interest account balance formula for what's called *continuous compounding*. You can think of continuous compounding as the bank compounding interest at every moment of each day. That formula is

$$Account\ balance_{continuous\ compounding} = Principal * (2.71828)^{(APR*Number\ of\ years\ of\ compounding)}$$

If we insert our APR of .05 and our 5 years of compounding, we get

$$Principal * (2.71828)^{(.05*5)} = \$128.40$$

It appears that daily compounding and continuous compounding resulted in the same answer: $128.40. This resulted from rounding.

The actual value for daily compounding was $128.4003, while the actual value for continuous compounding was $128.4025. But since US currency doesn't come in units of thousandths or 10 thousandths of a cent, I just rounded to $128.40. Let's see what happens if we extend the amount of time the money stays in the bank to 40 years while compounding continuously:

$$\text{Principal}*(2.71828)^{(.05*40)} = \$738.90$$

And if the bank compounded daily, we'd get

$$\$100*(1+.0001)^{14600} = \$738.40$$

The "14600" refers to the number of days in a 40-year period. Using the account balance formula for simple interest, we'd get:

$$100 + 100*\frac{.05}{year}*40 \text{ years} = \$300.$$

So it appears that to really benefit from compound interest, you should put your money in a bank that compounds frequently, and you ought to leave it there for a long time.

I shouldn't leave the topic of saving without talking about *Individual Development Accounts* (IDS). These accounts are directed at low-income persons and are designed to encourage them to save some of their money. Encouragement results from a matching arrangement. If a person (or family) chooses to save some of their money, the government will match whatever they save at a minimum dollar-for-dollar match, up to a maximum of $2,000 for an individual and $4,000 for a family.[5] That is, if a person chooses to put $400 in the bank, the government will match that savings at a minimum of $1 for each $1 saved, meaning the government would match the $400 saved with at least another $400. So the person would end up with at least $800 in the bank instead of just $400, and they'd earn interest on this savings, just as they would with any other. But the matching stops once (at the time of this writing) the match reaches $2,000 or $4,000, as spelled out earlier. This matching rate can be stated in the form of an equation:

$$\text{Amount in IDA} = 2*(\text{Amount saved by account holder})$$

So, in our last example, we would have:

$$\$800 = 2*(\$400)$$

The crucial parameter of an IDA policy is what the multiplier in equations like these should be. If we made it 3, then a $400 savings would amount to $1,200 in total, while a multiplier of 4 would make the total 4 * ($400) = $1,600. Of course, the bigger the total amount in the account for a given interest rate, the more the account holder could earn in interest. Once again, we see the role played by mathematics in a relevant policy issue.

BORROWING AND PERSONAL FINANCE

So far I've focused on people lending money to banks. But banks, of course, lend us money, too. One of the biggest loans a person can take on is a *mortgage*. You can think of a mortgage as a loan to finance the purchase of a house or other real estate. The borrowed money is combined with a person's "out of pocket" money, and this "out of pocket" money is usually called the *down payment* on the house. Typically, a person isn't allowed to obtain a mortgage without a certain amount of money as a down payment.

Even though the person who takes out a mortgage is allowed to live in the house, before the mortgage is paid off the real owner of the dwelling is the bank or lending institution. If it turns out the person doesn't pay the bank back, it has the right to kick the person (or family) out of the house, take possession of it, and sell it to make up for its losses. Failing to pay back a mortgage (or any other type of loan for that matter) is called *defaulting*. When a bank repossess someone's home after default, that's called putting the home in *foreclosure*. Much of the mathematics of mortgages has to do with how repayment of the loan is scheduled.

A mortgage is an example of an *installment loan*. An installment loan is when money is borrowed for a specific period of time, with regular payments plus interest being paid to the lender over this period. The period of an installment loan is called the *term* of the loan.

When a person borrows money to buy a house, the term is often 30 years, and the regular payments often occur monthly. There are actually two types of mortgages: *fixed-rate mortgages* and *adjustable-rate mortgages*.

A fixed-rate mortgage is one in which the interest rate remains the same as the loan is paid back. An adjustable-rate mortgage is one in which the interest rate may change as the loan is paid back. I'll focus primarily in this section on fixed-rate mortgages.

Before discussing the formula for calculating monthly payments for a fixed-rate 30-year mortgage, I should tell you about a short cut I'm going to take. For the most part in this book, when I've discussed formulas of various kinds, I've been careful about attending to units of measurement and showing how such units often cancel out. Since the formula for mortgage payments is more complicated, I think it may be less accessible if I'm so careful about units in this context. What I'll do instead is show the numbers on the right side of the equals sign and show both numbers and units only on the left side. You'll have to take my word for it that if I were to show units on the right side as well, everything would work out as it should. Mathematicians, physicists, and engineers probably wouldn't agree with this, but since I'm writing for social workers, I think this should be okay.

The formula for monthly payments for someone who takes out a 30-year mortgage at a fixed interest rate of 5% (or .05) is:

Monthly mortgage payment

$$= \left[\frac{\text{Amount borrowed} * \text{Monthly rate} *}{(1+\text{Monthly rate})^t} \right] \Big/ \left[(1+\text{Monthly rate})^t - 1) \right]$$

In this formula, "Monthly rate" stands for the interest rate compounded monthly, "t" stands for the number of months over which the loan is paid off, and "Amount borrowed" should be self-explanatory.

Suppose someone borrowed $100,000 to buy their "dream home," and the interest rate the bank charged is .005. Then they would owe:

$$\$599.55 = [100,000 * .005 * (1+.005)^{360}] / [(1+.005)^{360} - 1)]$$

per month or almost $600 per month. Now if they paid this every month for 360 months (30 years), they would end up paying $599.55 * 360 = $215,838.20 to the bank. Since $215,828.20 – $100,000 = $115,828.20, this person would have paid more than $100,000 for the privilege of being able to borrow money from the bank.

Let's call the person we've been talking about Erica and suppose she has a yearly income of $65,000. Let's round Erica's monthly mortgage payment to $600 per month. If we multiply this by 12 months, we see that her mortgage payment comes out to $7,200 per year. If we divide this by her annual income of $65,000, we find that, each year, Erica pays about 11% of her annual income in mortgage payments.

If Erica's mortgage were fixed-rate, she'd pay the same .005 interest rate throughout the life of the mortgage. But suppose it was an adjustable-rate mortgage and the bank raised the interest rate it charges her to .007. Using the monthly mortgage payment formula, an interest rate of .007 would result in a monthly payment of $761.82, which comes out to $9,142.05 per year. This is about 14% of Erica's annual income. This may not seem like a big difference from what she was paying before, but you can see the problem. If Erica's income stays more or less the same, but the interest rate she must pay keeps going up, she could face financial disaster, resulting in her defaulting on the loan and losing her home.

Borrowing money to buy a house isn't something only "well-off" people do. But again, in order to qualify for a mortgage you usually need enough money to make the down payment on the place, and this is something which may not apply to those without much income. There is a type of loan, though, that many low-income people can qualify for: a *payday loan*.

A payday loan is a short-term loan that people, many of them low-income, take out when they need cash quickly. To see how these types of loans work, suppose Mark is in need of cash to fix his car. He gets paid in a couple of weeks but doesn't have the cash on hand now. He could go to a neighborhood "check cashing" place and take out a loan for, say, $200. The check cashing place may charge him a $50 fee and give him 2 weeks, or 14 days, to pay the loan back. So he'd owe $250.

The formula for calculating simple interest rates for payday loans is[6]:

$$\text{Payday loan annual interest rate} = \frac{amount\ of\ interest\ plus\ fees}{Amount\ of\ loan} * \frac{365}{number\ of\ days\ of\ loan} * 100$$

So, in Mark's case, this would be:

$$652\% = \frac{50}{200} * \frac{365}{14} * 100$$

That is, if we state Mark's $50 fee as a yearly simple interest rate, it comes out to one much higher than any other interest we've discussed in this chapter. Such high annualized interest rates is make payday loans controversial.

Some argue that such loans are simply a way for lenders to take advantage of the financially desperate, while others argue that payday lenders provide legitimate financial services to meet an important market demand. You can make up your own mind about this debate. What matters for this book is the following "take-away": the mathematics of interest rates has an important role to play in payday loans.

Another type of loan related to personal finance is *credit card* debt. A credit card is a piece of plastic that a bank or other institution grants someone. It allows the person to buy things on credit, meaning they can buy things without having to pay for them up front. Instead, the issuer of the credit card pays the bill, and the person issued the card pays them back with interest. Credit card payments are usually due each month, at which time the person issued the card is required to make a minimum payment.

Some of the math involved in credit card debt has to do with calculating how much money the person issued the card must pay interest on. The formula for doing so is

Amount subject to finance charges = Previous Balance − Payments + Purchases

Finance charges is the term issuers of credit cards use to refer to interest charges. Suppose it's the beginning of July and you're trying to figure out what amount of money for June you owe interest on. Your previous balance for the month of June (based on purchases made in May) was $250. You made payments of $50 in June and bought $112 worth of goods and services. So the amount subject to finance or interest charges would be:

$312 = $250 − $50 + $112

Suppose the yearly interest rate you owe on the card is 25% or .25. To figure out the monthly interest rate, you divide this by 12, since there are 12 months in a year. In general, to go from the annual interest rate you owe on a credit card to the monthly one, you use this formula:

$$\text{Monthly interest rate on credit care} = \frac{annual\ interest\ rate}{12}$$

Since $\frac{.25}{12}$ = .02, the monthly interest rate on the $312 subject to finance charges would be 2% (.02 * 100 = .02). In order to calculate that amount of interest owed for the month, you would use the formula:

Amount of interest for the month
  owed on credit card = Monthly interest rate * Amount subject to finance charges

In this case, that would be .02 * $312 = $6.24.

I could go into more math about credit cards, but this is enough for you to see how credit card debt could get you into a world of trouble. Take a look at the Amount subject to finance charges formula again:

Amount subject to finance charges = Previous Balance − Payments + Purchases

You can see from this formula that the more you spend on purchases and the less you make in payments, the larger the amount subject to finance charges will be.

For example, suppose instead of having bought $112 worth of goods and services, you bought $400 worth. And suppose that instead of making payments of $50, the credit card issuer only required you to make a minimum payment of $20 and you only paid that minimum. Suppose the previous balance was still $250. The amount in finance changes would then be

Amount subject to finance charges = Previous Balance − Payments + Purchases =
$250 − $25 + $400 = $625

The amount owed in interest would then be

Amount of interest for the month
    owed on credit card = Monthly interest rate * Amount subject to finance charges
$$= .02 * \$625 = \$12.50$$

more than double the amount of interest owed from before. If instead of $400 in purchases you made $1,000, the amount subject to finance charges would be

Amount subject to finance charges = Previous Balance − Payments + Purchases
$$= \$250 − \$25 + \$1000 = \$1225$$

and the amount owed in interest would be

Amount of interest for the month
    owed on credit card = Monthly interest rate * Amount subject to finance charges
$$= .02 * \$1225 = \$24.50$$

If you consider the fact that people can have three or four credit cards, with all the issuers charging interest, as well as the fact that folks could use these cards to go on extravagant monthly shopping sprees, it should be clear that it's easy to get into an extreme amount of credit card debt. This is something we're advised to avoid, but this may be hard to do in a society as consumption-oriented as ours.

INVESTMENTS AND PERSONAL FINANCE

Another aspect of personal finance related to mathematics is *investment*. Investment is the allocation of money with the intention of ending up with more money than you initially invested or at least avoiding a loss. There are many ways to invest money, but I'm going to focus primarily on one of them: buying *stock* in a company. This is because the buying and selling of stock nicely illustrates many of the mathematical issues related to investment.

Stock represents partial ownership of a *corporation*. So, to fully understand what stock is you need to know what a corporation is. A corporation is a type of business which, from a legal perspective, is treated like a person. This means that corporations can do many of the things people can, like borrow money, enter into contractual arrangements with other parties, and own property.

The way a corporation is structured is that it's owned by a set of *shareholders*. These are people who own stock in the company, where stock can be thought of as a piece of paper which gives the holder certain ownership rights. One of these is the right to elect members of what's called the *Board of Directors* (the Board) of the corporation. Members of the Board are the ones who are authorized to run the business, but they usually hire others to do this for them. Those they hire are called *managers*. These managers, in turn, hire people to actually do much of the work of the corporation.

Another right that shareholders have is that, under certain circumstances, they can receive *dividends*. Dividends are part of the profits of corporation. So shareholders have the right to receive some of the corporation's profits, which makes sense, given they're the owners.[7]

A third right shareholders have is that they can sell their stock if they want to. As I said earlier, the buying and selling of stock is what I'm going to focus on as we take a look at the mathematics of investment.

Suppose Erica decides to buy stock in the ABC Corporation. Let's say she buys 10 shares of this company's stock, and it was sold to her for $10 per share. This would mean she paid $10 * 10 = $100 for the stock. Even though this would make Erica a partial owner of the company, this may not be the main reason she bought the stock. The main reason she may have bought it is because she believes the company is going to do very well in the future, and, as a result, its stock price per share is going to increase. If this were to happen, Erica would be able to sell her shares at that time for a profit. The magnitude of profit would depend on how much the per-unit share price of the stock had increased.

Suppose, for example, Erica was right and the share price of the stock increased to $20 per share. This would make the stock she owns worth $20 * 10 = $200. If she sold it for that amount, her profit would be $200 − $100 = $100. In general, the profit from the sale of stock can be found by the formula:

Profit from sale of stock = amount received for stock − amount paid for stock

People don't only profit from owning stock by trying to "buy low and sell high." In our previous example, Erica assumed the price of the stock she bought would increase. Suppose, instead, she thought the stock price would decline. If so, she could implement what's called a *short* strategy. A short strategy for stock, also called *selling a stock short*, is when someone tries to profit from a decline in the price of a stock. Here's how it works.

Erica could borrow shares of stock from someone in order to sell them on the open market. Suppose she borrows 10 shares and is able to sell them for $20 per share, earning her $200. Suppose, after some time has passed, the share price has declined to $10 per share. She could buy back the shares at $100 less than what she paid for them. Once she bought the shares back, she could give them back to the person she borrowed them from, but, in the meantime, she'll have earned a $100 profit.

Stocks aren't just bought and sold directly, but they can also be the basis of other financial instruments called *derivatives*. Derivatives are financial instruments whose market value depends on the value of some other instrument or on some other contingency. The mathematics of how to price or value derivatives is very complex—so complex, in fact, that real rocket scientists are sometimes hired to figure out how to price the things. We won't go into all that here. Instead, what I'll do is explain the basics of how one type of derivative, a *stock option*, works.

A stock option is a contract that allows the buyer of this type of agreement the right to buy (known as a *call option*) or sell (known as a *put option*) stock for an agreed upon price at a later date. Suppose, as before, Erica has bought her 10 units of stock for $10 per share. This time, she bought the stock because she really believes in the company and plans to remain an owner for the long term. But she isn't naïve, and she understands that things could go very badly for the company, causing the price of her stock to plummet. If the per-unit price were to decline to, say, $2 per share; her stock would be worth only $2 * 10 = $20. If she sold at that price, her return would be $20 – $100 = –$80. A negative return is, of course, a loss.

In order to prevent this scenario, Erica could buy a put option which would allow her to sell her stock at a later date for, say, $13 per share. This way, no matter what happened to the stock price, she'd be guaranteed a profit from the sale of shares of $13 * 10 – $10 * 10 = $130 – $100 = $30. Of course, the price of the option wouldn't be $0; capitalism tends not to work that way. But as long as the price of the option was less than $30, Erica would enjoy a positive profit from this arrangement.

One of the things any investor has to contend with is the *risk* of an investment. The risk of an investment is the uncertainty about the magnitude of the return on that investment. And the *return* on an investment can be thought of as any amount of money gained over and above the cost of that investment. Just keep in mind that the return on an investment can be negative, meaning that it's really a loss. The idea of risk versus return might be better understood if we apply these concepts to our earlier examples.

In the first example, Erica bought the stock thinking the share price would later increase. She, of course, could've been wrong because the share price could've decreased instead (resulting in a negative return or a loss). In other words, she faced uncertainty regarding what the share price would be at a later time.

In the second example, Erica assumed the share price would be lower at a later date. But she had no way of knowing for sure if this would turn out to be the case. The price could've remained the same or increased by a later date. Again, Erica faced uncertainty about what the future share price would be.

It should be clear that Erica faced the same type of uncertainty in our third example. In fact, the reason she bought the option was an acknowledgment of this uncertainly as an attempt to protect herself from it.

One of the "laws" of finance is that investments of any kind typically have some risk associated with them. Another "law" is that how much one can expect to gain from an investment tends to be directly associated with the risk of that investment; that is, the higher the expected gain from an investment, the higher the risk associated with it. This is something any investor would do well to keep in mind.

INCOME TAXES AND PERSONAL FINANCE

Benjamin Franklin is supposed to have said that "in this world nothing can be said to be certain, except death and taxes." Whether he really said this or not, taxes are a fact of life, *income taxes* in particular. An income tax is simply a portion of a person's (or family's) income which must be turned over to the government. Income taxation is virtually a marriage of mathematics and public policy. One of the ways to see this is by considering the distinction between *marginal* and *average tax rates*.

The marginal tax rate is the percentage of an extra dollar of taxable income a person must pay in taxes. For example, suppose Enrico earns one more dollar of income and has to pay 35 cents of that dollar to the federal government. Then Enrico would be faced with a marginal tax rate of 35% (or .35 in decimal terms) because 35 cents is 35% of $1. To see how the concept of marginal tax rate applies to the US income tax system, take a look at Table 5.1:

This is a table of income tax brackets faced by single US taxpayers for 2015. The qualifier "single" is used because the tax rate a person faces depends on their marital

TABLE 5.1

2015 US Federal Income Tax Rates/Brackets for Single Person[8]

Annual Taxable Income	Tax Owed
$0 to $9,225	10%
$9,226 to $37,450	$922.50 plus 15% of the amount over $9,225
$37,451 to $90,750	$5,156.25 plus 25% of the amount over $37,450
$90,751 to $189,300	$18,481.25 plus 28% of the amount over $90,750
$189,301 to $411,500	$46,075.25 plus 33% of the amount over $189,300
$411,501 to $413,200	$119,401.25 plus 35% of the amount over $411,500
$413,201 or more	$119,996.25 plus 39.6% of the amount over $413,200

See U.S. Tax Center, 2015 Federal Tax Rates, Personal Exemptions, and Standard Deductions, https://www.irs.com/articles/2015-federal-tax-rates-personal-exemptions-and-standard-deductions.

status. The table ignores deductions, credits, and other "tax breaks" people may be entitled to. To make sure you understand how to read it, take a look at the first row.

It tells us that a single person with an annual income greater than $0 but less than $9,225 would have to pay 10% of their income in taxes. So, if their income were, say, $9,000, they would owe $900 in taxes because .10 * $9,000 = $900. Now suppose the next year this person gets a raise to $9,001. This is a ridiculously low raise, but I chose it to better illustrate the concept of marginal tax rate. This person's income has increased by $1. The amount they would owe in taxes after the increase in income would be .10 * .9001 = $900.10. So their income would have gone up by $1, but the amount owed in taxes would have only gone up by 10 cents. Since 10 cents is 10% of a dollar, the marginal tax rate faced by this person would be 10%. In fact, as long as the person's income stays under $9,225 per year, they will face a marginal tax rate of 10%.

Once someone's income moves into the $9,226 to $37,450 range, the portion of their income in this range would be subject to a marginal tax rate of 15%. This can be seen by turning what appears in the second column of row two into an equation:

$$\text{Amount owned in taxes for income within } \$9,226 - \$37,450 = \$922.5 + .15 * \left(\begin{array}{c} \text{Annual} \\ \text{income} \end{array} \right)$$

You may recall from algebra that this is an example of a *linear equation*. The version found in algebra textbooks often takes the form: y = m + bx. Here "y" is amount owed in taxes, "m" is $922.5, "b" is .15, and "x" is annual income above one threshold, in this case a threshold of $9,225, but below another one, in this case one of $37,450. The key part of this equation for us is "b." It's called the *slope of* the equation and tells us how much y changes when x changes by one unit. If b is positive, then y increases when x changes by one unit; whereas if b is negative, y decreases when x changes by one unit.

In our amount owed in taxes version of a linear equation, .15 is the slope and it's positive. So it tells us how much amount owed in taxes increases when annual income goes up by $1 (assuming we're measuring income in dollar units). That is, the slope in this equation is the marginal tax rate faced by those with incomes in this range.

To see this, suppose Terry has an annual income of $19,225. All we would have to do is insert $10,000 into the preceding equation (because $10,000 is the amount of his $19,225 annual income that's above $9225 but below $37,450):

$$\text{Amount owned in taxes for income within } \$9,226 - \$37,450 = \$922.5 + .15*(\$10,000)$$
$$= \$2,422.5$$

Now suppose Terry's income increases to $10,001. Then the amount he owes in taxes would be:

$$\text{Amount owned in taxes for income within } \$9,226 - \$37,450 = \$922.5 + .15*(\$10,001)$$
$$= \$2,422.65$$

So Terry's income has gone up by $1, and his tax bill has gone up by $2,422.65 - $2422.50 = .15. Since 15 cents is 15% of $1, the marginal tax rate Terry faces is 15%.

You can turn what appears in the second column of each row of the tax table into an equation just like we did for the first row. And it will turn out that each of the percentages found in each of these rows is a marginal tax rate faced by taxpayers in the relevant income ranges. For example, taxpayers with incomes between $90,751 and $189,300 face a marginal tax rate of 28%.

The level at which marginal tax rates should be set is a perennial issue in public debate. You can see from the table that the highest marginal tax rate is set at 39.6% for incomes of $413,201 or more. But whatever the marginal rate ends up being, it seems Republicans usually think it's too high, while Democrats usually think it's not high enough. One of the things at issue in this debate is the effect of tax rates on economic growth.

Republicans tend to think that when marginal tax rates are too high, people work and invest less than they would if rates were lower. This is because with higher rates people take home less of their incomes than they would if marginal rates were lower; that is, with higher rates they have to give over more of their money to the government. This means they have less incentive to work and invest. And with less incentive, people work and invest less than they would if they faced lower marginal tax rates. This supposedly results in the economy growing more slowly than it would otherwise.

Democrats tend to counter this view, contending that there is little evidence to support this Republican story. They deride it as "trickle-down economics" and allege that Republicans are merely trying to rationalize policies which primarily benefit the rich. If you want to take part in this debate, knowing something about the mathematics of marginal tax rates might allow you to do so in a more informed manner.

Let's move now to the *average tax rate*. This is the percentage of a person's taxable income that they pay in taxes. That is:

$$\text{Average tax rate} = \frac{Amount\ paid\ in\ taxes}{Total\ taxable\ income} * 100$$

Suppose Steven's taxable income for 2015 was $45,000. Using Table 5.1, we can figure out how much he owed in taxes. We go to row three of the table because Steven's income of $45,000 is between $37,451 and $90,750. That row tells us to start with $5,156.25 and add to that amount the difference between $45,000 and $37,450 multiplied by .25 (the decimal form of 25%). So Steven's tax bill is:

$$\$5,156.25 + \left(\$45,000 - \$37,450\right) * .25 = \$7,043.75$$

Since $7,043.75 divided by $45,000 is about .16, once we multiply by 100 we get an average tax rate of about 16%.

The average tax rate is used to define three types of taxes: *regressive, progressive*, and *proportional taxes* (also called *flat taxes*). A regressive tax is one where the average tax rate a person pays declines as their income rises. That is, under a regressive tax, the higher a person's income, the lower the percentage of their income they pay in taxes.

A progressive tax is where the average tax rate increases as income rises. So, under a progressive tax, the higher a person's income, the higher the percentage of their income they pay in taxes.

A proportional tax is where taxpayers pay the same percentage of their income in taxes regardless of their income level. So a "filthy rich" person and a "working-class" person could both be subject to an average tax rate of, say, 25% under a proportional or flat tax.

An example of a regressive tax in the real world is a sales tax. Another is the payroll tax used to finance Social Security. Let's first take a look at how sales taxes work. A sales tax is typically a set percentage of the amount paid to buy certain goods and services. For example, someone buys a tube of toothpaste and is subject to a sales tax of 8%. If this toothpaste cost them $2.50, they would owe $2.50

+ $2.50*.08 = $2.70 in total. What I've done is start with the amount paid for the item and added .08 (or 8%) of the amount paid for it, since the sales tax is 8% of the price of the good or service in question. Since $2.50 * .08 = $.20, the sales tax amounts to 20 cents.

The formula for the total amount owed on an item (or on several items), including sales tax, is written more generally as:

$$\text{Total amount owed including sales tax} = \text{total cost of item(s)} + \text{total cost of item(s)} * \text{sales tax rate}$$

In our example, the total cost of the item was $2.50 and the sales tax rate was 8% or .08.

To see why a sales tax is regressive, consider Jack and Jill. Jill's annual income is $60,000 and Jack's is $40,000. Suppose Jack and Jill make the same purchases throughout the year, and each has paid $1,000 in sales taxes. Jack's average tax rate will be $1,000/$40,000 = .025 or 2.5%, and Jill's will be $1,000/$60,000 = .017 or 1.7%. Since Jill's 1.7% average tax rate is less than Jack's 2.5% and her income exceeds Jack's, the sales tax is regressive. If a tax is regressive, it's considered to be harder on lower income persons since it takes a larger share of their lower incomes.

The payroll tax is used to collect revenue to finance Social Security, a program we discussed earlier in the book. To see why this tax is regressive takes a fair amount of work.

A payroll tax, for our purposes, can be thought of as an income tax which is only imposed on incomes up to (at this writing) $118,500. That is, all income below $118,500 is subject to a tax rate of .062 or 6.2%. So, anyone with an income of $118,500 or less would pay $7,347 in payroll tax.

Now suppose someone has an annual income greater than $118,500—say, $200,000. Because the tax is capped at $118,500, this person would still only owe $7,347 in payroll tax. Now we already know that $7,347 divided by $118,500 is 6.2%, since this is the legislated tax rate. It's also the payroll's taxes' average rate for someone at this income level. But $7,347/$200,000 = .037 or 3.7%, a lower average tax rate than 6.2%. This means that, for incomes of greater than $118,000 per year, the payroll tax becomes regressive.

The personal income tax is an example of a progressive tax. To see this, suppose Buffy has an annual income of $295,000 and Spike has one of $35,000. Using the tax brackets from Table 5.1, Buffy's total tax bill would be:

$$\$46,075.25 + (\$295,000 - \$189,300)*.28 = \$80,956.25$$

TABLE 5.2

Hypothetical 2015 US Federal Income Tax Rates/Brackets for Single Person

Annual Taxable Income	Tax Rate
$0 to $9,225	10%
$9,226 to $37,450	$922.50 plus 15% of the amount over $9,225
$37,451 to $90,750	$5,156.25 plus 25% of the amount over $37,450
$90,751 to $189,300	$18,481.25 plus 28% of the amount over $90,750
$189,301 to $411,500	$46,075.25 plus 50% of the amount over $189,300
$411,501 to $413,200	$157,175.20 plus 60% of the amount over $411,500
$413,201 or more	$158,195.20 plus 70% of the amount over $413,200

And Spike's would be:

$$\$922.50*.10 + (\$35,000 - \$9,225)*.15 = \$4,788.75$$

This means that Buffy's average tax rate would be $80,956/$295,000 = about .27 or 27% and Spike's would be $4,788/$35,000 = about .14 or 14%. We see that Buffy has both a higher income and a higher average tax rate, indicating that the income tax is progressive.

The federal income tax could be more progressive if we increased marginal tax rates at higher income levels. Take a look at the marginal tax rates in Table 5.2:

These are hypothetical 2015 marginal tax rates. Notice that the rates are higher for the top three brackets in this table than is the case for the previous one.

If Spike, possessing the same income, faced the rates in Table 5.2, nothing would change for him since those in his income bracket would face the same rates as before. That is, his average tax rate would still be 14%. But here's what would happen to Buffy:

$$\$46,075.25 + (\$295,000 - \$189,300)*.50 = \$98,925.25$$

With a tax bill of $98,925.25, her average tax rate would be $98,925.25/$295,000 = .34 or 34%, which is clearly higher than the previous 27% average tax rate she faced. And, if she faced a higher average tax rate than before while Spike faced the same one as before, we can say that the federal income tax is more progressive under the system with higher marginal rates. And this is precisely where the math meets the policy/political debate.

Those located "left of center" on the political spectrum tend to argue for higher marginal tax rates for those in higher income brackets. They believe those who have more are obligated to pay more; they see this is a simple matter of social justice. Those closer to the political right typically argue that marginal tax rates should be decreased, instead of increased, and this should be done across the board. The reasons they offer appeal to social justice concerns, as well as those about economic growth.

I've already discussed the economic growth argument in an earlier section of this chapter. The social justice concerns of the political right are usually couched in terms of people being able to decide what to do with their own money instead of having the government decide this for them. The social justice, as well as economic growth effects of marginal tax rates are debated endlessly. Once again, my purpose in this book isn't to resolve this debate. Instead, I'm hoping to equip you with some basic mathematical tools that will help you become a more informed participant in it.

Earlier I mentioned certain types of tax breaks. Let's now go over some of the details of how these work, focusing mainly on three kinds: *exemptions*, *deductions*, and *credits*. An exemption is a tax benefit that lowers your taxable income. That is, exemptions reduce the amount of your income that is subject to taxation. There are actually two types of exemptions, the *personal exemption* and the *dependent exemption*. A personal exemption can be taken for yourself and your spouse if you're married. Dependent exemptions can be taken for your children or other relatives.

As an example, suppose Buffy and Angel are married, have two children, and are filing their taxes as a married couple. In 2015, the exemption amount was $4,000 per person. If their gross annual income were $100,000, assuming they only qualified for the four exemptions (two personal ones for the two adults and two dependent ones for the two children), their gross income would've been reduced by 4 * 4,000 = $16,000. Since $100,000 − $16,000 = $84,000, the amount of income subject to taxation would be $84,000 instead of the $100,000 gross income. And this would put them in the third row of the tax table ($37,451 to $90,750) instead of the fourth one ($90,751 to $189,300).

The personal exemption phases out at certain income levels. For a married couple filing jointly, the phase out begins at incomes greater than $309,900. If a couple's gross income exceeds the phase-out level ($309,900) by more than $122,000, that couple would no longer be eligible for exemptions. If a couple's gross income exceeds the phase-out level by $122,000 or less, the dollar amount of the couple's exemption is decreased by 2% for each $2,500 by which their income exceeds $309,900. The Internal Revenue Service (IRS) provides a method for figuring out how much a couple's exemptions are reduced when their gross income exceeds the phase-out level by $122,000 or less. To see this method in action, assume that, in 2015, Buffy and Angel's gross income was $350,000. To figure out how much their exemption is reduced, you would follow these steps:

1. Divide amount above phase-out by $2,500 (if the answer isn't a whole number, round it up to the nearest whole number).
2. Multiply the amount from line 1 by .02 (retain at least three decimal places in the answer).
3. Multiply line 2 by $4,000 * Number of personal and dependent exemptions.
4. Subtract line 3 from $4,000 * Number of personal and dependent exemptions.

Let's apply this method to Buffy and Angel's income of $350,000, keeping in mind that they're entitled to four personal and dependent exemptions:

1. $350,000/$309,900 = 16.04 = 17 (rounded up to the nearest whole number)
2. 17 * .02 = .34
3. .34 * $4,000 * 4 = $5,440
4. ($4,000 * 4) − $5,440 = $10,560

So, if their gross income had been $100,000, Buffy and Angel would've been entitled to a total exemption of $16,000 for a taxable income of $84,000 ($100,000 − $16,000 = $84,000). But had their income instead been $350,000, they would've been entitled to a total exemption of only $10,560 for a taxable income of $339,440 ($350,000 − $10,560 = $339,440).

Tax deductions are similar to exemptions in that they also lower your taxable income. But they differ from exemptions in that they're typically associated with people's spending. In other words, deductions usually become available to you if you buy certain things. A good example is the *mortgage interest deduction*.

The mortgage interest deduction allows you to deduct interest paid on your mortgage. Recall that a mortgage is a loan you take out to buy a home or other real estate. If you've taken out a mortgage to buy a home, you'll be required to pay interest on that mortgage, meaning that, each year, you'll have paid a certain amount in interest. Without going into all the "gory details," you're able to subtract from your gross income a percentage of the interest you've paid on your mortgage. This would then allow you to figure out the portion of your income subject to taxation. Assuming, for the sake of simplicity, that the only tax break you qualify for is the mortgage interest deduction, your taxable income (income subject to taxation) for a given year would be:

Taxable income = Gross income – Amount paid in interest * Percent for tax bracket

So, if your gross income for a given year were $75,000, the amount you paid in interest that year was $5,000, you were in the 25% tax bracket, and you qualified for no other tax breaks; your taxable income would be $75,000 – $5,000 * .25 = $75,000 – $1,250 = $73,750.

Another type of deduction you may have heard of is the one for *charitable contributions*. Under certain conditions, if someone gives money to a charity— including, you might be happy to know, one that hires social workers—they can deduct this expense from their gross income.

Tax credits are different from deductions and exemptions in that credits reduce your tax bill, not your taxable income. That is, unlike deductions and exemptions, a tax credit allows you to subtract the value of the credit from the amount you owe in taxes. An example should make this clear.

Suppose Spike is in the 25% tax bracket and he's entitled to a $5,000 deduction. The value of this to him would be $5,000 * .25 = $1,250 because that's the amount by which he would be able to reduce his gross income to figure out his taxable income. If the $5,000 was a credit instead of a deduction, this would be worth $5,000 to him because he'd be able to reduce the amount he owed to the government by the full $5,000, instead of just 25% of it. This example highlights a general point. Tax credits are more valuable than tax deductions and exemptions.

There are two types of tax credits: *nonrefundable* and *refundable*. These can best be defined with help from the following equation:

Difference between tax bill and tax credit = Tax bill – Tax credit

If Tax bill – Tax credit is greater than 0, you owe more in taxes than the value of the credit you're entitled to, and you simply pay this difference to the government. If Tax bill – Tax credit = 0, you pay nothing to the government and the government owes you nothing. If Tax bill – Tax credit is less than 0, and you neither pay money to the government nor receive money from it, the tax credit is nonrefundable. If Tax bill – Tax credit is less than 0 and you receive this difference from the government, the tax credit is refundable.

An example of a refundable tax credit you may have studied in social policy is the *earned income tax credit* (EITC). The EITC is a refundable tax credit that low- to moderate-income workers are entitled to. If a working family has no obligation to pay income taxes, they get a check from the government for the EITC amount they're entitled to. You might be wondering how a working family can owe nothing in income taxes, given that the tax table shows a positive marginal tax rate (10%) even for those in the lowest income tax bracket. The answer is that tax exemptions, deductions, and/or credits can reduce such persons' tax liabilities to 0.

So far, we've considered tax credits, deductions, and exemptions separately. In the real world someone could qualify for any or all of these types of tax breaks. The math gets a little more complicated, but there aren't really any new principles involved; it all comes down to arithmetic.

Ending this chapter with a discussion of taxes is a great place to stop. This is because it's a nice segue into a major topic of the next one: the US federal budget. It shouldn't surprise you that a whole lot of math comes up in this area.

NOTES

1. This chapter draws from Garman and Forgue (2008).

2. See Wolfsohn and Michaeli, "Financial Social Work."

3. This fraction is an example of what in a later chapter I'll call a *probability*. Although I'll use terms like "chance," "likely," and the like at several points in this chapter, I'll be relying on your intuitive notions of probability. I'll define the concept more carefully in Chapter 7.

4. It actually results from cancelling of units in the appropriate numerator and denominator; we've seen such cancelling at several places in this book. But the way this happens in the exponent of the compound interest version of the account balance formula is fairly complicated; I'll leave such complications for texts in finance.

5. See Falk, *Individual Development Accounts (IDAs)*.

6. See Drake, *Calculating Interest Rates*.

7. Actually, not all shareholders have this right, but I'll leave such details to business courses.

8. See US Tax Center, 2015 *Federal Tax Rates, Personal Exemptions, and Standard Deductions*.

6

THE MATHEMATICS OF BUDGETS

THE PREVIOUS CHAPTER focused on household budgeting. This one scales up to the budgets of larger organizations, the main one being the US federal government. However, we'll spend a little time as well on budgetary matters regarding nonprofit organizations (NPOs).

Anyone who follows the news has, no doubt, heard a lot about the US federal budget. They've heard that the federal government's debt and deficits are too high, that we spend too much on social programs, that we spend too little on social programs, that we spend too much on defense, that we spend too little on defense, that taxes should be raised, that taxes should be lowered—the list goes on. Although social workers are exposed to budgetary issues in our policy courses, the mathematics of budgets is often downplayed. That is, the emphasis tends to be on the provisions of various social programs, with the quantitative aspects of budgets being more in the background. This chapter will have the opposite emphasis. I'll focus on the mathematics of budgets, while my references to social programs will be primarily to certain mathematical ideas. Before we get going, let me say a word about why I chose to include in this chapter a focus on the budgets of NPOs.

Many of those who currently do or will work as social workers are employed in an NPO. An NPO can be thought of as a type of business, but one where any profits must be put back into providing those services which have been authorized by the organization's mission. That is, these profits can't be allocated to shareholders.

In fact, NPOs don't have shareholders, the way many for-profit businesses do. For-profit businesses provide goods and services of various kinds and may even intend to do so at high quality. But their main goal—or one of them at least—appears to be making profits for their owners who, in the case of corporations, are shareholders.

Since many social workers will find themselves employed by NPOs, and some will eventually serve as middle managers or executives of such organizations, it may be prudent for social workers to know something about how these organizations work, especially at it relates to budgetary matters. Before getting to this topic, though, we'll start with a look at the federal budget.

FEDERAL INCOME

Many of the ideas discussed in the previous chapter carry over to this one. For example, just like a household, the US federal government has an income. It obtains this income from taxes and other fees it charges for its services. An example of one of these fees is the money you pay the post office for stamps. If you've renewed a passport lately, you've paid for that service, too.

In the previous chapter, we talked a lot about taxes, but the focus was on the individual income tax. There are other types of federal taxes, though, and discussing some of them will help me illustrate more connections between mathematics and social issues.

One tax that comes up in a lot of economic debates is the *capital gains tax*. To understand what a capital gains tax is, you first need to understand what a capital gain is. A *capital gain* is the difference between the price someone paid for an asset and the amount they sold it for. Suppose Angel bought a painting for $1,000 and sold it for $3,000. Since $3,000 − $1,000 = $2,000, Angel's capital gain would be $2,000. Capital gains can be negative, and, when they are, we call them *capital losses*. If Angel had bought the painting for $3,000 but sold it for $1,000, he would have lost $2,000 because $1,000 − $3,000 = −$2,000.

An important distinction in the capital gains world is between an *unrealized capital gain* (or loss) and a *realized* one. An unrealized capital gain is when someone *could* sell an asset for more than they paid for it but haven't yet done so. A realized one is when the person sells that asset and actually enjoys the gain. If Angel bought the painting for $1,000, and, over time, its market value increases to $3,000 but he doesn't sell the painting and get the $2,000 gain, this would be an unrealized gain. But if he actually sells the painting and collects the two grand, he would experience a realized gain.

Another important distinction is between *long-* and *short-term capital gains* (or losses). If you held onto an asset for 1 year or less before selling it at a profit, your capital gain would be a short-term gain. If you held onto it for longer than a year before selling it at a profit, your gain would be a long-term gain.

Net long-term capital gain is the difference between your long-term gains and your long-term losses. *Net short-term capital gain* is the difference between your short-term gains and your short-term loses.[1] If Willow made a long-term capital gain of $3,000 on the sale of some asset and a long-term capital loss of $1,500 on the sale of another one, her net long-term capital gain would be $1,500 ($3,000 – $1,500 = $1,500). If Tara made a short-term gain of $4,000 and a short-term loss of $3,000, her short-term capital gain would be $1,000.

Another concept we need is *net capital gain*. This is the difference between net long-term gain and net short-term loss. If Xander's net long-term gain is $5,000 and his net short-term loss is $2,000, his net capital gain would be $3,000. By now, you've probably figured out that a capital gains tax is a tax on capital gains.

Net short-term capital gains are treated, for tax purposes, like ordinary income. This means that, for single people, the tax rates in Table 5.1.

In other words, your net short-term capital gain gets added to your other income, and this puts you in a given tax bracket. The tax rates that apply to someone in that bracket would then apply to you.

Net capital gain is treated differently. Table 6.1 tells the story.

Notice that the highest tax rate for net capital gain is considerably lower than the highest tax rate for ordinary income. One of the assets a person may own is stock in a company. When you buy a company's stock, you're providing it with money it can use to expand its business. Thus, it can hire more people, which is usually thought of as a good thing. It can also buy new plant and equipment. Since someone—until the robots take all our jobs—needs to build and/or maintain this new plant and equipment, this also leads to more hiring. Such purchase of plant

TABLE 6.1

2015 US Capital Gains Tax Rates/Brackets
for Single Person

Tax Brackets	Capital Gains Tax Rate
0$–$9,225	0%
$9,226–$413,200	15%
More than $413,200	20%

and equipment is called *investment*. So, when you buy stock in a company, you're helping provide it with resources that can be used to increase its investment. Now consider the following.

When you work outside the home, to an economist, you're selling your labor. That is, you're offering your ability to work for someone in return for a salary or wage. People selling their labor (if they can) is also regarded as a good thing. The salary or wage you get for doing so is part of your income and may be subject to the highest tax rate in Table 5.1, 39.6%. If you could claim net capital gain, that would also be part of your income and would be subject to the *lower* highest tax rate in Table 6.1, 20%. So it looks as if US politicians believe selling stock (as long as you've held it for more than a year) is better than selling labor. This could explain why income from the sale of stock is taxed at a lower rate than income from the sale of labor.

Now maybe, in some sense, it is better for someone to sell stock they've owned for more than a year than to sell their labor. But it isn't really *the sale of stock* that might warrant special treatment but the fact that *it was bought* that does. The more-than-a-year qualification is there to discourage you from buying stock in the hopes of a short-term rise in the stock price so you can quickly sell it for a profit. When you sell your labor, you provide one worker to the economy. When you've bought stock, you've been partly responsible for providing, perhaps, many more than one worker—or the so argument might go.

I suspect there are some who aren't convinced by this argument. They would contend that the reason capital gains get taxed at a lower rate is because higher income people enjoy more capital gains, and they've simply bought off politicians to get preferred tax treatment.

As you've been reading about how capital gains are taxed at a lower rate, a question may have occurred to you—doesn't the lower tax rate mean less tax revenue for the government? And doesn't that make it harder for the government to meet its obligations, at least those that cost money? It does seem reasonable to expect this outcome. However, there is a school of thought in economics called *supply-side economics* which contends that this may not necessarily be the case.

According to this school, it's possible for a lower tax rate on capital gains, or any type of income, to generate more revenue for the government than a higher rate would. This is because the higher rate on capital gains might discourage the purchase of stocks and other assets since people will have to turn over more of those gains to the government in the form of higher taxes. And this would mean that the jobs that would have resulted from those purchases don't get created, and, therefore, the incomes that workers in those jobs would have had don't get taxed to generate revenue for the government. A lower capital gains tax means more buying of stocks and other assets, more jobs created, and, therefore, more incomes to tax to obtain government revenue.

Opponents of supply-side economics pejoratively call it *trickle-down economics*. The idea seems to be that if we make the rich better off, the rest of us will be better off as well as the gains at the top trickle down to the rest of us. These opponents contend that there isn't much evidence to support this way of seeing things, and they regard supply-side economics as just a veiled attempt to justify preferred tax treatment for the rich. The general public wouldn't stand for rich people telling us that "we deserve preferred tax treatment because most capital gains come to us and we can afford to buy off politicians so they'll lower our taxes." So supply-side economics had to be invented to convince the rest of us that helping the rich would help us as well.

I'll leave it to you to decide whether you think the preferred tax treatment of capital gains is justified. For now, just notice all the math involved. Capital gains tax rates, the amount of job creation associated with different such rates, and the impact of all this on government revenue are inherently mathematical topics. Once again, we see the relevance of mathematics to an important policy debate.

Another tax that gets a lot of attention in policy debates is the *corporate income tax* (or *corporate tax* for short). As I'm sure you've guessed, a corporate tax is paid by *corporations*. But what's a corporation? A corporation is a legal form of business in the United States. It differs from two other forms you may have heard of, the *sole proprietorship* and the *general partnership*.

A sole proprietorship is a business with just one owner. For this type of business, the owner and the business are the same. So any profit the owner makes is subject to personal income taxes and, therefore, the tax rates in Table 5.1. Any debts of the business are also debts of the owner. This means that the owner, under some circumstances, may be legally obligated to use their personal assets (car, house, etc.) to pay off the business' debt. This is called *unlimited liability*.

A general partnership is essentially a proprietorship with at least two owners. So, as with sole proprietorships, the *partners'* (what the owners of a general partnership are called) incomes and debts are also the business's income and debt.

Corporations are structured quite differently from sole proprietorships and partnerships. First, the owners of corporations are called *shareholders*. This is because, to be one of the owners of a corporation, you must own at least one share of its stock. Second, there is a legal distinction between the corporation and its owners. That is, the corporation is considered a separate entity from those who own it. So the incomes and debts of its shareholders are distinct from the incomes and debts of a corporation. This means that the personal assets of shareholders aren't legally at risk when it comes to paying off a corporation's debts. This is called *limited liability*.

From a legal point of view, corporations are treated like people. For example, corporations can have incomes, just as people can. This is where the corporate tax comes in; it's simply a tax on corporate incomes. Table 6.2 contains US federal tax rates on corporations for the year 2016.

Although Table 6.2 looks a little different from Table 5.1 (the one for personal income tax rates), it's interpreted similarly. So, a corporation with an income of $70,000 would pay a tax of $7,500 + .25(20,000) = $12,500 (since the decimal form of 25% is .25 and $20,000 is the difference between ($70,000 and $50,000).

There are some who vehemently oppose the corporate income tax. They do so because, in their view, it taxes the same income twice. And, in so doing, it prevents the economy from growing as fast as it would otherwise. Let's consider an example to see what they mean by "taxing the same income twice."

Suppose Klaus has bought shares in a corporation and is entitled to receive dividends. Now, when the business first earns income, that income is taxed at the rates in Table 6.2, the corporate tax rates. This is the first time that income is taxed. If Klaus receives part of the corporation's income as dividends, this now becomes part of his income and is taxed at the rates in Table 5.1, the personal income tax rates. This is the second time that income is taxed.

Why is this double taxation thought to impede growth of the economy? As I said earlier, according to a number of economists, people work harder when they can

TABLE 6.2

2016 US Corporate Tax Rates[8]

Annual Corporate Income	Tax Owed
$0 < Income ≤ $50,000	15% of amount over $0
$50,000 < Income ≤ $75,000	$7,500 plus 25% of the amount over $50,000
$75,000 < Income ≤ $100,000	$13,750 plus 34% of the amount over $75,000
$100,000 < Income ≤ $335,000	$22,250 plus 39% of the amount over $100,000
$335,000 < Income ≤ $10,000,000	$113,000 plus 34% of the amount over $335,000
$10,000,000 < Income ≤ $15,000,000	$3,400,000 plus 34% of the amount over $10,000,000
$15,000,000 < Income ≤ $18,333,333	$5,150,000 plus 38% of the amount over $15,000,000
Over $18,333,333	35% of the amount over $0

See World Wide Tax Summaries, United States Corporate-Taxes on Corporate Income, http://taxsummaries.pwc.com/uk/taxsummaries/wwts.nsf/ID/United States Corporate Taxes on corporate income keep more of their income. This is no less true of the "people" we call corporations. That is, when they can keep more of their income, they also work harder. The "work" corporations do is invest in new plant and new equipment, as well as in new workers (by hiring them). This investment leads to more production of goods and services, resulting in faster economic growth. Again, whether you buy this or not is up to you. Just notice the mathematics surrounding the entire discussion.

Another type of tax which sometimes receives attention in policy debates is the *estate tax*. The Internal Revenue Service (IRS) of the US government defines an estate tax as "a tax on your right to transfer property at your death."[2] So, if a deceased person leaves property to their heirs, the recipients of that property is subject to the estate tax. Those who don't like this tax call it "the death tax." I think it's obvious why they grace it with that term.

The way the estate tax works is that there is an assessment made of the market value of the deceased person's property. This property can be money, stocks and bonds, real estate, and a host of other things. The market value of all such property is called the deceased's *gross estate*. There are a number of deductions and other adjustments, the details of which we'll leave for the tax lawyers, which reduce the gross estate to that which is subject to taxation.

Table 6.3 contains the 2016 estate tax brackets, tax rates, and taxes owed for those falling within given brackets. However, there is something of a catch.

TABLE 6.3

US 2016 Federal Estate Tax Rates[9]

For Taxable Estates Between	You'll Pay This Amount of Tax
0 < Estate ≤ $10,000	18% of amount over $0
$10,000 < Estate ≤ $20,000	$1,800 plus 20% of amount over $10,000
$20,000 < Estate ≤ $40,000	$3,800 plus 22% of amount over $20,000
$40,000 < Estate ≤	$8,200 plus 24% of amount over $40,000
$60,000 < Estate ≤ $80,000	$13,000 plus 26% of amount over $60,000
$80,000 < Estate ≤ $100,000	$18,200 plus 28% of amount over $80,000
$100,000 < Estate ≤	$23,800 plus 30% of amount over $100,000
$150,000 < Estate ≤ $250,000	$38,800 plus 32% of amount over $150,000
$250,000 < Estate ≤ $500,000	$70,800 plus 34% of amount over $250,000
$500,000 < Estate ≤ $750,000	$155,800 plus 37% of amount over $500,000
$750,000 < Estate ≤ $1,000,000	$248,300 plus 39% of amount over $750,000
Over $1,000,000	$345,800 plus 40% of amount over $750,000

See Frankel, Max. 2016 Estate Tax Rates, https://www.fool.com/retirement/general/2015/12/18/2016-estate-tax-rates.aspx

According to federal law, only the value of an estate that exceeds $5,450,000 is subject to taxation.

So, if Hayley were to die leaving a $6,000,000 estate, her heirs would only pay taxes on $550,000 of it. Looking over Table 6.3, we see that this would put them in the $500,000 < Estate ≤ $750,000 bracket. So they would owe $155,800 + .37 * $50,000 = $174,300 in taxes (since $50,000 is the difference between their taxable estate of $550,000 and $500,000). Since this tax is only imposed on the amount of an estate exceeding $5,450,000, it looks like one paid only by the extremely wealthy, assuming we can think of those with estates of more than $5,000,000 as extremely wealthy.

FEDERAL SPENDING

The fiscal year of the US federal government runs from October 1 of a given year to September 30 of the following year. So, the fiscal year for 2015 runs from October 1, 2014, to September 30, 2015. During that fiscal year, the federal government spent about $3.7 trillion. Just to see how big that number is, let's write it out in full: $3,700,000,000,000.00.

Table 6.4 contains the programs and services that most of this $3.7 trillion paid for.

This table is probably self-explanatory for the most part, but there may be a couple of categories that require a bit of elaboration.

TABLE 6.4

Major Federal Spending in Fiscal Year 2015[10]

Program/Service	Program/Service Spending	Program/Service as Percentage of Total Spending (rounded to two decimal places)
Social Security	$888 billion	24%
Medicare, Medicaid, CHIP, Marketplace Subsidies	$938 billion	25%
Defense and International Security	$602 billion	16%
Safety Net Programs and Interest on the National Debt	$362 billion	10%

CHIP is an acronym for *Children's Health Insurance Program*, a federal program that provides health insurance to children and families with moderate incomes. *Market Subsidies* refer to a part of the *Affordable Care Act* (also known as *Obama Care*), a controversial piece of legislation signed into law during President Barach Obama's first term. It contains a number of provisions you probably covered (or will cover) in your policy course. One of them was the provision of subsidies to help low- to moderate-income persons purchase health insurance in the private marketplace. *Safety Net Programs* refer to a host of programs for low- to moderate-income people, such as Supplemental Security Income (SSI), child care and afterschool programs, and housing assistance programs.

Interest on the national debt refers, as you might have guessed, to interest payments the US federal government has to make to those it's borrowed money from. This topic segues nicely into our next one: how federal spending relates to federal revenue.

You already know that federal spending in fiscal year 2015 was about $3.7 trillion. Federal revenue that year was about $3.2 trillion.[3] This means that the difference between revenue and spending was about $3.2 trillion − $3.7 trillion = −$.5 trillion. And $.5 trillion is the same as $500 billion. It might be easier to see what's going on if we write these numbers out in full: $3,200,000,000 − $3,700,000,000 = −$500,000,000. Notice that the difference between revenue and spending is negative; this always happens when the government takes in less revenue than it spends. When this happens, we say that the government has run a *deficit*. When the government takes in more revenue than it spends, we say it's run a *surplus*. And when it takes in the same amount in revenue as it spends, we say it has a *balanced budget*.

You may be wondering how the government could have spent more money in 2015 than it received in revenue. The answer is borrowing. The federal government borrows money by selling bonds. So, when people buy government bonds, they're really lending money to "Uncle Sam." And, like any lenders, they expect to eventually be paid back with interest. This is the same interest we were talking about a few paragraphs ago.

So we've now seen that when the government runs a deficit, it does so by borrowing money. And it typically doesn't pay off all the money it owes by the start of the next year. That is, by the beginning of the next fiscal year, it typically still owes money from the previous year. As this happens each year, the government's borrowed money keeps adding up, and this accumulation of borrowed money is called *debt*. Let's take a slightly more mathematical, but hypothetical, look at this:

Table 6.5 assumes that (1) the US federal government has only been around from 2014–2019, and (2) it borrowed nothing in fiscal year 2014 and therefore owed no debt from the previous year by the time fiscal year 2015 rolled around. These are, of course, ridiculous assumptions; I only make them because simplifying things to this extent will help me better explain debt accumulation.

We've already discussed the first column of Table 6.5. In 2015, the federal government spend $3.7 trillion but received only $3.2 billion in revenues. This resulted in a budget deficit of $500 billion. In fiscal year 2016, the government, once again, spent more than it had in revenue, $600 billion more. This $600 billion just gets added to the previous year's debt, which again was $500 billion. Now $500 billion plus $600 billion is $1.1 trillion. However, column 2 of Table 6.5 tells us that $100 billion was paid on the 2015 accumulated debt of $500 billion. So, for 2016, the accumulated debt is $600 billion + $500 billion − $100 billion = $1 trillion. That's where the number at the bottom of column 2 comes from. The other numbers at the bottom of the other columns are calculated the same way:

Accumulated debt

for a given year = Gross debt for a given year + Accumulated debt from previous year
− Amount paid on accumulated debt from previous year

Back in Chapter 3, we discussed the distinction between a stock and a flow (something different from stock you can own in a company). Recall that a *stock* is something which occurs at a *given point* in time. It's typically measured as a pure number or a number with some unit of measurement attached, but time isn't a part of that unit of measurement. A *flow* is something which occurs *over some period of time*. That is, a flow is measured in a given unit per unit of time or as number of units/time or number of units per unit time. A deficit is a flow variable because it tells us how much spending exceeds revenue *per fiscal year*. A debt is a stock variable because it tells us the total amount of money the government owes *at a given point in time*.

So far, we've only considered debt the government must repay as a consequence of borrowing money from those other than itself. This includes citizens and residents of the United States, as well as those of foreign countries. However, the federal government does also borrow from itself. An example of this is related to the Social Security program.

As mentioned earlier, Social Security is financed by a payroll tax. Revenue from this tax is used to pay benefits to current recipients. The rest goes into a *trust fund*. Ideally, the money in this fund would be invested in order to grow it to pay benefits to future recipients. This isn't what happens, though. Instead, the federal

TABLE 6.5

Hypothetical Federal Revenue, Spending, Deficits, and Debt Over the Period of 2015–2019

	2015	2016	2017	2018	2019
	Spending = $3.7 trillion	Spending = $3.6 trillion	Spending = $3.5 trillion	Spending = $3.7 trillion	Spending = $3.7 trillion
	Revenue = $3.2 trillion	Revenue = $3.0 trillion	Revenue = $3.2 trillion	Revenue = $3.2 trillion	Revenue = $3.2 trillion
	Deficit = $500 billion	Deficit = $600 billion	Deficit = $300 billion	Deficit = $500 billion	Deficit = $500 billion
	Addition to debt = $500 billion	Gross addition to debt = $600 billion	Gross addition to debt = $300 billion	Gross addition to debt = $500 billion	Gross addition to debt = $500 billion
	Amount of debt paid off in previous fiscal year = $0	Amount of debt paid off in previous fiscal year = $100 billion	Amount of debt paid off in previous fiscal year = $100 billion	Amount of debt paid off in previous fiscal year = $100 billion	Amount of debt paid off in previous fiscal year = $100 billion
	Accumulated debt = $500 billion	Accumulated debt = $1 trillion	Accumulated debt = $1.2 trillion	Accumulated debt = $1.6 trillion	Accumulated debt = $2 trillion dollars

government uses money from the trust fund to finance other federal programs and services, effectively borrowing money from itself. This is thought of as borrowing because, legally, the federal government is required to pay the trust fund back. As long as Social Security remains in place, presumably people will keep getting older, retiring, and having a right to benefits. The money that's been borrowed from the Social Security trust fund will be necessary to meet these future obligations.

As of this writing, the federal debt is around $20 trillion.[4] This is a huge sum of money, so huge in fact that its magnitude may be hard to wrap your mind around. So let's compare it to something that might be easier to picture: the circumference of the Earth.

You may recall from geometry that the circumference of a sphere (a three-dimensional circle, like a basketball) is the distance around the sphere. The Earth can be thought of as a giant sphere. Its circumference is about 24,900 miles. Now imagine that each mile is a dollar. Then the US federal debt is so large that, tied end to end, it could wrap around the earth about 803,212,851 times (20,000,000,000,000/24,900 = 803,212,851). An obvious question is whether a debt this large is a bad thing.

A common sense way to approach this question is to view the federal government as similar to a household. Both have incomes and both spend money. And both may have savings they can borrow from. In the case of a household, savings might be in the form of a bank account. As we saw earlier, in the case of the federal government, savings may be in the form of a government account, such as the Social Security trust fund. So here's the question: what might happen when a household runs deficits year after year, going deeply into debt?

One thing that might happen is lenders notice the amount the household owes, get nervous about its ability to pay off its debt, and decide not to loan it any more money. Or, a common practice when dealing with borrowers thought to be at high risk of defaulting, they might agree to lend the household more money but only at a very high interest rate. If a household isn't able to borrow money at all or only at a very high interest rate, and it can't dip into savings, it'll be under tremendous pressure to increase its income, decrease its spending, or both. And this could cause a drastic change in its standard of living.

According to many commentators, the federal government faces a similar situation. They argue that if our federal debt keeps growing, lenders will either stop loaning money to the United States or will only agree to loan it at much higher interest rates. Neither of these would be good outcomes.

If the federal government could only borrow at very high interest rates, paying interest on the federal debt would become much more expensive. So the United States would have to spend even more money paying down the debt, money that couldn't be used to provide other valuable public services. If lenders decided not to loan the US government any money *at all*, and it couldn't dip into government trust funds to make up for this loss, it would have to increase taxes, cut federal spending, or both. This could result in a sharp decline in economic activity, a huge increase in unemployment, and a substantial amount of pain and anguish associated with job loss.

Even though the federal government–household analogy is instructive up to a point, there are key differences that should be taken into account. If a household prints money to pay off its debt, the money so printed would be called *counterfeit*, and the household (well, the person in this household) that engaged in this behavior could spend some time in a federal prison. But the federal government is allowed to print money to pay off all or some of its debt. So why doesn't it just do so?

The reason the federal government doesn't print money to pay off its debt is because doing so would increase the amount of money circulating in the economy, which, according to many economists, would cause a substantial increase in inflation. We discussed inflation in an earlier chapter, but we didn't say much about why it should be avoided. High inflation is bad for two groups in particular: those on a fixed income and lenders.

Inflation is bad for those on fixed incomes—those, that is, whose incomes don't rise fast enough to keep up with inflation—because inflation results in lower real incomes. And lower real incomes mean higher food, housing, and other costs. High inflation is bad for lenders because, as prices rise, the value of money declines. This means that lenders are paid back in money which is less valuable than it was when it was loaned out. To see what I mean, consider the following example.

Suppose in January of 2016, the bank loans Luke $500 and he must pay this back a year later. To keep things simple, we'll ignore the fact that Luke would also owe interest. Suppose the consumer price index (CPI; see Chapter 3) in 2016 is 231.5, and, by 2017, it's risen to 235.7. Entering the appropriate numbers into the inflation rate formula from Chapter 3, we see that the inflation rate for the period of 2016–2017 is

$$\frac{235.7 - 231.5}{231.5} = .018, \text{ which multiplied by 100 is } 1.8\%$$

This would mean that the general price level over this period increased by 1.8%, and, therefore, $500 in 2017 is 1.8% less valuable than it was in 2016. So, again, the bank would be getting paid back in money worth less than it was before.

The government may not have to worry much if inflation is bad for those on fixed incomes. But if something is bad for bankers, this might not so easily be ignored. So, even though the federal government could print money to pay off some or all of its debt, this is not something it'll do lightly. But the fact remains that it could do so and avoid jail, while a household couldn't.

Another problem with the United States having such a large debt has to do with where some of it is owed: China. About 8% of the amount the federal government owes is to China.[5] A figure of 8% might not sound like much, but it's apparently big enough for some to worry. The concern is that China may try to exert undue influence on US policy in return for keeping the money coming—that is, if United States doesn't play, China might not pay. And if China stopped paying, the United States would face that problem of having to drastically cut spending, raise taxes, or both, sending the economy into a tailspin. A question one could raise about this line of argument has to do with the fact that China sells a lot of goods to the United States.

For 2016, the United States bought about $423 billion worth of goods from China.[6] If China were to significantly decrease the amount it loans the US federal government and the US economy were to tank as a result, this wouldn't just hurt the United States. It would also hurt China because a major market for its goods and services would be in the midst of an economic calamity instead of buying Chinese goods. Since China probably doesn't want this to happen, it may not decide to severely cut back on loaning money to the US government.

NPO BUDGETING

Just as households and the federal government do, NPOs have sources of income. The type of NPOs that social workers have the most contact with, because many of us are employed by them, is the *direct service provider*. These NPOs do exactly what their name suggests—provide services of various kinds directly to members of the community. Examples of this type of NPO are hospitals, clinics, agencies that provide child welfare services, substance abuse treatment, family counseling, and a host of others. These types of NPOs typically have three main funding sources.

One is individual donors. Executive directors of NPOs, at least the more successful ones, typically spend a lot of time cultivating relationships with people who have "deep pockets." Large NPOs can have overall budgets of millions of dollars, and some of those millions tend to come from rich donors. Donors may contribute money for various reasons: to receive a tax deduction for a charitable contribution, out of a genuine desire to "do good," for "naming rights," or a host of other reasons. (For readers who may not be familiar with the practice, "naming rights" are given when an NPO names a building or other publicly accessible structure after a large donor or someone else of that donor's choosing.)

Another funding source for NPOs is *foundations*. A foundation is itself a kind of NPO, but, unlike direct service providers, they don't provide services directly to clients. Instead, they often focus on getting direct service NPOs the money they need to do their jobs. The way the process typically works is that foundations ask direct service providers for proposals describing what problems the agencies intend to address, as well as the programmatic approaches which will be used to address them. Increasingly, foundations are also requiring NPOs to include, as parts of their proposals, plans for how they intend to evaluate the impacts of their interventions. Foundations review proposals they receive, awarding grants to NPOs they deem worthy of receiving such support.

The third funding source for NPOs is government. An NPO's funding can come from any level of government (federal, state, or local), depending on what it intends to do and which level has jurisdiction over that area. The process of receiving a grant from the government is similar to that regarding foundations but a bit more exacting since taxpayer money is involved.

When it comes to the spending of NPOs, this depends, of course, on what services a given NPO specializes in providing. But there are some spending categories which apply to most, if not all, NPOs. One such category is salary/wage spending.

Until computer scientists and engineers find some way to fully automate family therapy, substance abuse counseling, community organizing, and similar services that NPOs provide, the work of such agencies will always be pretty labor intensive. And since many people won't sell their labor free of charge, one expense that NPOs typically face is having to pay people to work for them.

Connected to the salary/wage expense is the payroll tax. This tax came up when we discussed Social Security. At that point, we focused on how this is a tax on workers. What we didn't mention is that the payroll tax is actually a "shared tax" in the sense that workers and their employers both pay it. If a person is self-employed, they pay both the employer's and employee's shares. Since NPOs employ people, they have to pay the same payroll tax their employees do. To see how this works, consider the following example.

In 2016, Luke Cage worked for a Harlem NPO providing outreach services to "at risk" youths. Luke made $50,000 a year, and, based on a payroll tax rate of .062, the payroll tax amount he owed was $50,000 * .062 = $3,100. The NPO Luke worked for would've also owed a payroll tax amount of $3,100.

Another expense related to workers is *fringe benefits*. When an NPO hires someone, they often don't stop at paying a salary and payroll tax on that salary.

They may have to cough up money to provide for that employee's healthcare, fees to provide training for professional development, paid vacation, and possibly other expenses.

The number of workers an NPO hires will typically depend on how much it is doing. That is, the more services it provides, the more workers it needs; and the more workers it needs, the higher its labor costs. Costs whose level depends on the level of goods produced or services provided are called *variable costs*.

Other costs that NPOs typically face are rental cost, cost of vehicles, office supplies, and the like. Rental cost will often not depend on the magnitude of service provision. That is, an NPO might have to pay $5,000 per month for a space whether 100 kids are served within it or 500. Costs which don't depend on the level of goods produced or services provided are called *fixed cost*.

Given the different types of costs and revenue sources we've discussed, it should come as no surprise that NPOs tend to write up budget plans, just as the federal government does, although on a much smaller scale. And, just like the federal government, an NPO's actual revenue and spending patterns could result in the organization facing a balanced budget, a surplus, or a deficit.

When an NPO faces a deficit, it will either have to dip into its savings (often called its *reserves*) or borrow money. Unlike the federal government, however, NPOs typically aren't able to incur deficits and accumulate debts indefinitely.

The type of NPO we're discussing in this chapter typically isn't legally allowed to allocate any part of a surplus to shareholders. In fact, these NPOs don't have shareholders because they're not owned in the way that private for-profit firms are owned. So, when it comes to what to do with a surplus, an NPO basically has two choices, assuming a funding source doesn't simply require surpluses to be given back.

One option is to use surplus funds to continue or expand the NPO's services. Its second option is to put some or all of that surplus into a reserve fund, assuming it doesn't face certain restrictions, one of which I've already mentioned: when the government provides funding for a specific program, and that program enjoys a surplus, the NPO must typically give that money back to the government.[7] But foundations and individual donors may also impose restrictions on the use of funds they provide. A common one is that funds can only be used for specific programs or types of programs. This may mean that an NPO can't simply put surplus funds into a reserve if doing so would run counter to restrictions imposed by a funding source.

In Chapter 5, I said that households typically possess both assets and liabilities; assets are the monetary value of what a given household owns, and liabilities are the value of what it owes. NPOs also have assets and liabilities, and one measure of the financial health of an NPO is called the *current ratio*. This quantity is

$$\text{Current ratio} = \frac{Current\ assets}{Current\ liabilities}$$

Both current assets and liabilities are measured in the same currency units (for example, US dollars). So, during division of the numerator by the denominator, these units cancel, leaving us with a pure number.

According to McLaughlin (2009, p. 75), the current ratio tells us how an NPO's "resources that can be converted to cash compare with the liabilities we know to be coming during the same period." "Current," in this context, typically refers to a period of 1 year. For the most part, the higher an NPO's current ratio is, the better, although it should be at least 1.0. That is, for each dollar it expects to owe, an NPO should have at least a dollar on hand to pay it off.

As an example, suppose an NPO's assets were worth $100,000 and its liabilities $90,000. Since $100,000 divided by $90,000 is about 1.1, the minimum of a current ratio of 1.0 would be met for this organization, although it probably wouldn't hurt for it to try to get it a bit higher.

Another important measure of an NPO's financial health is its *total margin*, which is

$$\text{Total margin} = \frac{Revenue - Expenses}{Revenue}$$

An NPO's total margin is its "bottom line." That is, you can think of it as an NPO's profit margin over a specific period of time. For the most part, the higher an NPO's total margin, the better.

Suppose an NPOs revenue over a given period was $100,000 and its expenses were $60,000. After dividing $100,000 by $60,000 we'd get a total margin for this firm of about 1.67.

The revenue and expenses referred to in the total margin formula are an NPO's total revenue and expenses. This may not be the most informative measure of an organization's profit margin because total revenue and expenses may not represent revenue or expenses involved in running the organization on a day-to-day basis. For example, a donor might provide money to an organization but restrict its usage to a special one-time payment on a specific program. Or an organization might have to make a large one-time expense to have the leaks in a roof fixed or something else along those lines. In order to obtain a more accurate measure of an organization's day-to-day operations profit margin, sometimes the following ratio, called an *operating margin*, is used:

$$\text{Operating margin} = \frac{\text{Operating Revenue} - \text{Operating Expenses}}{\text{Operating Revenue}}$$

I could go on discussing the financial aspects of NPOs, but that isn't really my main purpose; after all, this isn't a book on nonprofit finance. Instead, I've been interested in alerting you to some of the mathematical issues that arise in the management of NPOs. It just so happens that one of the most fertile areas for such issues is nonprofit budgeting and finance.

And, of course, what I've just said about nonprofits applies even more perhaps to the US federal government. That is, the budgetary/financial issues it faces also provide a number of mathematical problems to be solved. None of the problems we've discussed in this chapter is mathematically very difficult, so understanding their solution should be within the grasp of most, if not all, readers of this book. Understanding them should also help you see the relevance of mathematical issues to pressing social questions.

NOTES

1. See Internal Revenue Service, *Topic 409-Capital Gains and Losses*.
2. See Internal Revenue Service, *Estate Tax*.
3. See The United States Congress, *The Federal Budget in 2015*.
4. See Treasury Direct, *The Debt to the Penny and Who Holds It*.
5. See Jackson, *Who Holds Our Debt*.
6. See United States Census Bureau, *Trade in Goods with China*, https://www.census.gov/foreign-trade/balance/c5700.html.
7. Personal communication from Eri Noguchi, who's been an NPO administrator for more than 20 years.
8. See World Wide Tax Summaries, *United States Corporate-Taxes on Corporate Income*.
9. See Frankel, *2016 Estate Tax Rates*.
10. See Center on Budget and Policy Priorities, *Where Do Our Federal Dollars Go?*.

7

PROBABILITY AND SOCIAL ISSUES

IMAGINE YOU'RE EMPLOYED by a state child welfare agency and have been asked to visit a certain family's home. The reason you've been asked to do this is that your agency suspects the children in the home are being abused. Suppose you enter the home and don't witness any abuse occurring while you're there. You'd then be faced with trying to figure out how likely it is that the children in the home are being abused based on observing certain things: how the parents interact with their children, whether the children have visible scars or wounds that appear to have been deliberately inflicted, whether the children seem extremely fearful of their parents, and so forth. The thing about all these cues is that none of them would allow you to determine with certainty whether the parents are abusing their kids. That is, even if you were to observe visible scars, fearful gestures on the part of the children, or other things, you still couldn't know for sure whether the parents are abusing their kids. The branch of mathematics typically used to analyze uncertain situations such is this one is called *probability theory*. That branch is what this chapter is all about.

MATHEMATICAL MODELS

In order to understand probability theory, it helps to know a little about *mathematical models*. And since mathematical models are a type of model, it helps to know something about models in general.

A *model* is any idealized representation of some real object or situation. By "idealized" I mean that some features of the real object or situation aren't represented in the model. The purpose of a model is to help its user understand something about the real object being represented. In most cases, not every feature of the real object needs to be represented in order for a model to serve this purpose. Only those features relevant to an understanding of the real object need to be represented in the model. To make this more concrete, consider a model I suspect readers of this book are quite familiar with.

In your human behavior theory course, you no doubt came across Freud's model of the human mind. This model has three components: the *id, ego,* and *superego*. The id represents that part of our minds which cause us to act on impulse, without our giving too much thought to the consequences of our actions, other than whether they might result in us obtaining pleasure.

The superego represents that part of our minds which cause us to engage in actions we regard as socially right, again without too much regard for the consequences, whether good or bad. That is, the superego pushes us toward acting in accordance with social norms, "no matter what."

The ego represents that part of us which mediates between strictly pleasure-seeking, impulsive behavior and strictly social norm–abiding behavior. It tries to help us choose courses of action that might allow us to attain pleasure but which also won't violate any social rules.

Notice that there are things about our minds that Freud's model doesn't capture. Some of us process information slowly, others more quickly. Some of us have good memories, while others of us don't. Some of us can do complicated mathematical calculations in our heads, while others of us find such feats harder to accomplish. None of these differences is captured in Freud's model. This is the sense in which it's an idealized representation of the human mind. But if the purpose of Freud's model is to help us understand how people end up engaging in behaviors intended to attain pleasure but which don't violate any social norms, arguably it's okay for it to leave out these other features—they simply aren't relevant to the purpose of the model.

Readers of this book are no doubt familiar with other types of models. For example, model airplanes and cars, as well as the models of buildings used by engineers and architects, are examples of what are called *physical models*. These may help us understand how real planes or cars move or how winds and movements of the Earth during earthquakes affect buildings. The type of model most relevant to this chapter (really, this whole book) is a mathematical model.

A mathematical model is an idealized representation of some real object or situation through the use of mathematical techniques. We've been using such models throughout this book without calling them such. For example, the difference between the total revenue of the federal government and its total spending can be regarded as a model of its fiscal status. The consumer price index (CPI) formula we covered in an earlier chapter is really a model representing what happens to prices over time. You may be wondering why the need to be so explicit about the use of mathematical models at this point. The reason is that probability theory can be very abstract and, therefore, hard for someone to get a handle on. The task may be easier if the theory is taught through the explicit use of *probability models*, which, as you might guess from the name, are examples of mathematical models.

PROBABILITY MODELS

A probability model is a mathematical representation of a real-world situation involving uncertainty. The language used to talk about such models is set theory, a topic we discussed in Chapter 2. Any probability model contains three parts: a *sample space*, a *set of events*, and a rule for assigning *probabilities* to any member of the set of events. In order to elaborate on these ideas, let's go back to the situation that opened this chapter: a worker trying to figure out whether at least one of a couple of parents are abusing at least one of their children.

This is a situation involving uncertainty because, on the assumption that the worker doesn't witness abuse at it occurs, no matter what else they might observe during a home visit, they can't be absolutely sure whether abuse has occurred. Let's make this example a bit more precise.

Suppose the worker's name is Jennifer, and, during her visit, she sees a kid named Rick. Jennifer observes a large mark on Rick's arm that looks like it might have resulted from a burn of some kind. From the point of view of whether child abuse has occurred, there are two possibilities: either Rick's mark is the result of child abuse or it's not. We can model these two possibilities using the following set: {Rick's mark resulted from child abuse, Rick's mark didn't result from child abuse}. Notice that this set exhaust all the possibilities in this case. It's an example of what probability theory calls a "sample space." More generally, a sample space is the set of all possibilities, or possible outcomes, in a situation involving uncertainty.

Before discussing the second component of a probability model—the set of events—we need to go a bit into the part of set theory dealing with subsets. Recall from Chapter 2 that X is a subset of set Y if every member of X is also a member of Y. Another way to state this, which will become relevant shortly, is that X is a subset of Y if there is no element of X which isn't also an element of Y. So no subset of {Rick's mark resulted from child abuse, Rick's mark didn't result from child abuse} can possess elements which aren't also elements of this set itself.

Keeping the second version of the definition of subset in mind, here are the subsets of {Rick's mark resulted from child abuse, Rick's mark didn't result from child abuse}: {Rick's mark resulted from child abuse, Rick's mark didn't result from child abuse}, {Rick's mark resulted from child abuse}, {Rick's mark didn't result from child abuse}, {}. Let's see how the definition applies.

The first subset of {Rick's mark resulted from child abuse, Rick's mark didn't result from child abuse} is the set itself. Obviously, this subset can't have any elements which aren't possessed by {Rick's mark resulted from child abuse, Rick's mark didn't result from child abuse} since it is {Rick's mark resulted from child abuse, Rick's mark didn't result from child abuse}. This is an example of a general principle in set theory: every set has itself as one of its subsets.

The second two subsets of {Rick's mark resulted from child abuse, Rick's mark didn't result from child abuse} also meet the definition. That is, neither {Rick's mark resulted from child abuse} nor {Rick's mark didn't result from child abuse} possess elements which aren't also possessed by {Rick's mark resulted from child abuse, Rick's mark didn't result from child abuse}.

The last subset of {Rick's mark resulted from child abuse, Rick's mark didn't result from child abuse} is the empty set, one we first met in Chapter 2. This set also meets the definition of a subset, but it may be a little harder to see why, at least initially. Take a look at the second version of that definition again: X is a subset of Y if there is no element of X which isn't also an element of Y. Now the empty set has no elements at all. So it would be impossible for it to contain elements which aren't also elements of {Rick's mark resulted from child abuse, Rick's mark didn't result from child abuse}. And since it can have no element which isn't also an element of {Rick's mark resulted from child abuse, Rick's mark didn't result from child abuse}, it meets the definition of a subset of {Rick's mark resulted from child abuse, Rick's mark didn't result from child abuse}. In fact, the empty set is a subset of every set since it can never contain an element which isn't also an element of any set at all.

Now consider again the sample space for our child abuse example: {Rick's mark resulted from child abuse, Rick's mark didn't result from child abuse}. If we took all the subsets of {Rick's mark resulted from child abuse, Rick's mark didn't result from child abuse} and collected them into a set, we'd get: {{Rick's mark resulted from child abuse}, {Rick's mark didn't result from child abuse}, {Rick's mark resulted from child abuse, Rick's mark didn't result from child abuse}, {}}. This would be the set of events for our child abuse example. More generally, a set of events in a probability model is a set of subsets of the sample space in that model.

The third component of any probability model is a rule for assigning real numbers between 0 and 1 inclusive (or 0% and 100% inclusive, if we're thinking in percentage terms) to elements of the set of events. These numbers are called, as you might've guessed, *probabilities*. Table 7.1 shows a rule that would apply in our case:

The first entry in the events column represents the assumption that, in the real world, either Rick's mark resulted from child abuse or it didn't—at least one of these things is *guaranteed* to have happened. Our probability model represents this idea of guaranteed to have happened as a probability of 1. You read this as saying it's a certainty that either Rick's mark resulted from child abuse or it didn't. The entries in the second and third rows are .5 because we're assuming that each of the corresponding events has a 50% probability of occurring. The 0 in the second column of the last row is meant to represent the assumption that the mark Jennifer observes must have resulted from child abuse or it must not have. In other words, it's impossible for the mark to have resulted both from child abuse *and simultaneously* for it not to have so resulted. In probability theory, impossible occurrences are typically represented by the empty set and are assigned probabilities of 0.[1] Much of the action in probability theory has to do with allowable rules for assigning probabilities to events.

Two of these rules I've already stated: probabilities must be real numbers between 0 and 1 (or 0% and 100%) inclusive, and the probability of the event which corresponds to the sample space must equal 1. The other rule which applies for probabilities is called *additivity*.[2]

To understand additivity you need to go back to a couple of concepts we met in Chapter 2: disjoint sets and the union of two or more sets. Two or more sets are disjoint if they have no elements in common. Since events are just sets, two or

TABLE 7.1

Events and Associated Probabilities

Events	Probabilities
{Rick's mark resulted from child abuse, Rick's mark didn't result from child abuse},	1
{Rick's mark resulted from child abuse},	.5
{Rick's mark didn't result from child abuse}	.5
{}	0

more of them can be disjoint. For example, {Rick's mark resulted from child abuse} and {Rick's mark didn't result from child abuse} are disjoint events.

Recall that the union of two or more sets is the set made up of all those elements which are members of at least one of the sets being "unioned." That is, the union of sets T, W, and Z is the set made up of all those elements which are members of at least one of T, W, or Z. So the union of {Rick's mark resulted from child abuse} and {Rick's mark didn't result from child abuse} is {{Rick's mark resulted from child abuse}, {Rick's mark didn't result from child abuse}}. What additivity says is that if two or more events are disjoint, then the probability of the union of those events is the sum of the probabilities of the events that go into creating the union in question.

So, the probability of {{Rick's mark resulted from child abuse}, {Rick's mark didn't result from child abuse}} is equal to the probability of {Rick's mark resulted from child abuse}, which is .5, plus the probability of {Rick's mark didn't result from child abuse}, which is also .5. Since .5 + .5 equals 1, the probability of the event {{Rick's mark resulted from child abuse}, {Rick's mark didn't result from child abuse}} is just 1.

We now have all the parts we need for probability models: sample spaces, sets of events, and rules for assigning probabilities to events. Other than being real numbers between 0 and 1, inclusive, that follow certain rules, a question may have occurred to you: what exactly is a probability? I'll turn to that question next.

INTERPRETATIONS OF PROBABILITY

In the previous section, I assumed that the probability of the event {Rick's mark resulted from child abuse} and the event {Rick's mark didn't result from child abuse} are both .5. But what exactly am I claiming in saying this; what does such a claim really *mean*? There are two interpretations we'll consider: the *frequentist interpretation* and the *Bayesian interpretation*.

To understand the frequentist interpretation, let's change our child abuse example a bit. Suppose Jennifer has made 1,000 home visits during her career where conditions in those homes were virtually identical to what she sees now in Rick's, including the same type of mark located in the same place on the child's body. It later turned out that in only 50 of those homes were the kids abused by their parents. So we have 50/1,000 or .05. If we multiply .05 times 100, we get 5%. According to the frequentist interpretation, this would be an estimate of the probability that Rick has been abused by his parents.

In general, as frequentists see it, we estimate the probability of a given event by taking the number of times that event has occurred and dividing it by the number of times that event could have occurred. In other words, we estimate a probability by the fraction[3]

$$\text{Probability}_{\text{frequentist}} = \frac{\textit{Number of times event happened}}{\textit{Number of times event could've happened}}$$

And, if we multiply the result by 100, we get an estimated probability in percentage terms. Now let's turn to the Bayesian interpretation of probability.[4]

According to Bayesians, probability is a number representing the degree of belief someone has about the occurrence of an event. So, if Jennifer says the probably that Rick has been abused is .5 instead of .3, the first number represents a stronger degree of belief in the occurrence of this event than does the second number.

According to this degree of belief view of probability, people may legitimately arrive at different numbers to represent the probability of the same event. This is the case because people arrive at degrees of belief based on the information available to them. And since people often have different information, it would stand to reason that they might arrive at different degrees of belief in the occurrence of an event.

As Bayesians see it, if Jennifer has seen a 1,000 kids with marks like Rick's, and she now knows that 50 of them had been abused, it would be reasonable for her to assume that the probability of Rick has been abused is 5%. In other words, if someone decides to base their degrees of belief on frequencies such as this one, a Bayesian assessment of probability can end up at the same answer as a frequentist one. But even if Jennifer has never seen a kid with a mark like Rick's, she could still come up with an assessment of the probability that Rick has been abused. She could base it on conversations she's had with Rick's parents, conversations with neighbors, whether Rick appears atypically afraid of his parents, and other factors.

One of the criticisms Bayesians make of frequentists is that they claim frequentists face difficulty assigning probabilities to novel situations. Suppose Jennifer were a rookie child welfare worker encountering a situation like the one she's in with Rick for the first time. In that case, she wouldn't have a set of similar situations to draw on that would allow her to count the number of times kids in those situations had been abused by at least one of their parents, or so Bayesians claim.

Which of these interpretations of probability is correct? Although there is a long history of thinkers arguing about the answer to this question, this debate seems to have died down a bit. There are still those who emphasize one of these interpretations, almost to the exclusion of the other. But there are also those who see the contributions which can be made by both perspectives (Westfall and Henning, 2013). I suspect most social workers will probably encounter the frequentist view more often than the Bayesian one. So, unless stated otherwise, that's the one I'll focus on in this book.

CONDITIONAL PROBABILITY AND INDEPENDENT AND DEPENDENT EVENTS

Let's change our child abuse example a bit. Suppose Sookie Stackhouse is a social work researcher interested in whether being from a poor family increases the probability that a child will be abused. This would mean Sookie is interested in what's called a *conditional probability*.

In general, a conditional probability is the probability that some event occurs, given (or assuming) that some other event has occurred. To keep me from having to write so much, let's agree on the following notation:

Prob() = the probability that some event (entered inside the parentheses) occurs
| = "given (or assuming) that"

So, in our new version of the problem, what Sookie is concerned with is Prob(child will be abused | child is from poor family). More generally, where A and B are two events, Prob(A | B) stands for the probability that A occurs, given that B has occurred. Let's take a look at how a conditional probability can be estimated.

The basic idea is to start with the assumed event. In our example, Sookie would start by considering all kids from poor families. Suppose she has access to data indicating that there are 2.5 billion kids in the world and that 1 billion of them are from poor families. So Sookie would start by considering only this group of 1 billion poor kids.

Next she'd consider how many of these 1 billion poor kids have been abused by their parents. Suppose she has access to data telling her that 100 million of the 1 billion kids from poor families have been abused. If we divide 100 million by 1 billion we get .1, which, multiplied by 100, is 10%. So Sookie would estimate Rick's chance of having been abused at 10%.

From a conceptual point of view, a conditional probability isn't much different from an unconditional one. Both are about how many times something occurred divided by the number of times it could've occurred. The main difference is that,

TABLE 7.2

Screening Test Results and Conditional Probabilities

True positive	Prob(Screen positive | Child abused)	$\dfrac{\textit{Number of kids screen positive}}{\textit{Number of kids abused}}$
True negative	Prob(Screen negative | Child not abused)	$\dfrac{\textit{Number of kids screen negative}}{\textit{Number of kids not abused}}$
False positive	Prob(Screen positive | Child not abused)	$\dfrac{\textit{Number of kids screen positive}}{\textit{Number of kids not abused}}$
False negative	Prob(Screen negative | Child abused)	$\dfrac{\textit{Number of kids screen negative}}{\textit{Number of kids abused}}$

for a conditional probability, you have to be careful about including only those cases in the calculation which meet the condition of interest.

Conditional probability comes up at lot when screening to see if someone has contracted an illness or is suffering from some social/emotional ailment. Suppose a social worker with expertise in child welfare has developed a tool to screen for whether a child has suffered abuse at the hands of their parents. There are four possible outcomes from using such a tool: *true positive, true negative, false positive*, and *false negative*. These are all conditional probabilities, displayed in Table 7.2.

From this table, we see that a true positive is the probability that a child will screen positive for abuse given that they've actually been abused. Numerically, this is estimated as the number of kids who've screened positive for abuse divided by the number of kids who've actually been abused. So, if 10,000 kids have been abused and 9,000 of them screened positive for abuse, the true-positive probability would be 9,000/10,000 = .9 or 90%.

Anyone designing a tool to screen for child abuse will obviously want the true-positive and true-negative probabilities to be relatively high and the false-positive and false-negative ones low. So it would be helpful for the designer of such an instrument to be familiar with the concept of conditional probability.

True positives, true negatives, and the like don't just apply to screening for child abuse. Social workers, psychologists, medical doctors, and other helping professions screen for all kinds of conditions. Table 7.3, a generalization of Table 7.2, applies to any disease or condition.

The concept of conditional probability is related to another one referred to as *independence*. Two events A and B are independent with respect to one another if Prob(A | B) = Prob(A). Let's take a look at what this means intuitively.

TABLE 7.3

More General Version of Screening Test Results and Conditional Probabilities

True positive	Prob(Screen positive | Condition)	*Number screen positive* / *Number with condition*
True negative	Prob(Screen negative | Free of Condition)	*Number screen negative* / *Number free of condition*
False positive	Prob(Screen positive | Free of Condition)	*Number screen positive* / *Number free of condition*
False negative	Prob(Screen negative | Condition)	*Number screen negative* / *Number with condition*

Suppose A is the event that someone is poor and B the event that this person is also a Virgo. I'm no astrologer, but let's assume that whether someone is poor is independent of whether they're a Virgo. That is, Prob(Person is poor | Person is a Virgo) = Prob(Person is poor). What this means is that, if we know the probability that someone is poor, learning that they're also a Virgo doesn't provide us with any new information about the chance that they are poor. That is, the fact that someone is a Virgo has no effect whatsoever on the probability that they're poor. This is why Prob(Person is poor | Person is a Virgo) and Prob(Person is poor) are the same.

Knowing whether two events are independent is important because this affects how to calculate the probability of both of them occurring at once. If A and B are two events, we write the probability of both occurring as Prob(A and B). When A and B are independent, the probability of both of them happening at once is equal to the probability of A happening multiplied by the probability of B happening or

$$\text{Prob}(A \text{ and } B) = \text{Prob}(A) * \text{Prob}(B).$$

This idea can be extended to any number of independent events. So, if A, B, and C are independent, then

$$\text{Prob}(A \text{ and } B \text{ and } C) = \text{Prob}(A) * \text{Prob}(B) * \text{Prob}(C)$$

Suppose the probability that someone is poor is .15, the probability they're a Virgo is .09, and we assume that these two events are independent. Then the probability that someone is a poor Virgo is (.15)*(.09) = .01. Multiplying this probability by 100, we get a probability that someone is poor and a Virgo of 1%.

Having discussed independent events, it's easy to move to *dependent* ones. If events A and B are dependent, then Prob(A|B) ≠ Prob(A). That is, if we're trying to determine the probability of A, knowing something about whether B also occurs provides important information about the probability of A.

Suppose A is the event that someone is poor and B the event that the person is unemployed. If being poor and being unemployed are dependent events, then Prob(Poor|Unemployed) ≠ Prob(Poor). If the probability that someone is poor is .15 and the probability that someone is poor, given that they're unemployed, is .35, being poor and being unemployed would be dependent events.

Conditional probabilities, where the events in question might be dependent, are extremely important in many discussion regarding social issues. We spend a lot of time thinking about questions such as the following:

1. Does the chance that someone is poor depend on their race?
2. Does the chance that someone is poor depend on their gender?
3. Does the chance that someone is unemployed depend on their race?
4. Does the chance that someone suffering from a mental illness will receive treatment for their condition depend on their income?
5. Does the chance that a kid will end up in the foster care system depend on their income?
6. Does the chance that someone's clinical depression will subside depend on whether they receive treatment from a social worker?
7. Does the probability that someone will work outside the home depend on whether they receive TANF benefits?
8. Does the probability that a political candidate will win an election depend on how much money they received in campaign contribution?

This list of questions could easily be made much longer.

As I write these lines, a US federal court is trying to determine whether to allow certain provisions contained in one of President Trump's Executive Orders to stand. Those provisions ban persons from certain countries from entering the United States. As currently written, some are banned temporarily and others indefinitely.

For some, the debate around these provisions has raised the following question: are the events that someone commits a terrorist act in the United States and that someone is a migrant from Syria dependent events? That is, do we have Prob(Person commits terrorist act in US|Person is a migrant from Syria) ≠ Prob(Person commits terrorist act in US)? Trump, along with many of his supporters, appears to believe this inequality holds. In fact, he seems to believe that Prob(Person commits terrorist act in US | Person is migrant from Syria) > Prob(Person commits terrorist act in United States). Those opposed to Trump's travel ban disagree. Of course, many of them are less focused on this empirical question about the relationship between chance of engaging in an act of terrorism and country of origin but are more focused on constitutional as well as moral issues about the legitimacy of discrimination and the proper scope of executive power. But it is still true that conditional probabilities play a role in this debate.

Now I should be clear here about what I am, as well as what I'm not saying. I'm not suggesting that Trump or his supporters walk around with conditional probability inequalities like the ones in the previous paragraph in their heads. What I'm saying is that such inequalities can be used to represent or model what appears to be Trump's, along with many of his supporters', beliefs. Sometimes mathematically modeling your own as well as others' beliefs can make those beliefs more precise and thereby easier to assess. This is one of the most powerful uses of mathematics.

RANDOM VARIABLES

Earlier in this chapter, I defined a sample space as the set of all possibilities, or possible outcomes, in a situation involving uncertainty. In probability theory, we sometimes find it convenient to work not with a sample space directly but with the numbers assigned to the possible outcomes which make up the sample space. Going back to our example about whether the mark on Rick's arm indicates abuse, there are two possibilities making up the sample space: either Rick's parents have abused him, or they haven't done so.

Suppose we decided to assign numbers to these two outcomes. We might agree that the outcome Rick's parents abused him = 1, while the outcome Rick's parents didn't abuse him = 0. One important thing to remember here is that we don't have to assign 0 and 1 to these two outcomes—any two *real numbers* would do. When we assign real numbers to the possible outcomes of a sample space in this way, we create what probability theorists call a *random variable*. There is also another more intuitive definition of random variable that you sometimes see: a numerical quantity whose value depends on chance (Hasset and Stewart, 1999). Since you may be wondering how these two definitions are related, I'll say a bit about this.

I suspect the numerical quantity part is clear—we create a random variable by assigning *numbers* to possible outcomes. But what about the "whose value depends on chance" part? To see the connection here, go back to the idea of a sample space. There is some situation involving uncertainty. This means that we face a situation where something will occur, but, before observing an actual outcome, we don't know what will occur. We do know what *could* occur: these are the possible outcomes of the sample space in question. And there are probabilities associated with these outcomes—the more probable an outcome (or set of outcomes), the more likely we are to observe it. And since a random variable involves assigning numbers to outcomes, the more probable an outcome, the more likely we are to "see" the number that has been assigned to that outcome. This is the sense in which the value of a random variable depends on chance.

You might be wondering why anyone would care about the numbers representing the possible outcomes of some uncertain situation instead of focusing directly on the outcomes themselves. The main reason is that once we assign numbers to possible outcomes, a host of mathematical tools can be brought to bear. One such tool is probability distributions.

PROBABILITY DISTRIBUTIONS

We started this chapter discussing sample spaces. We next said that random variables are rules for assigning real numbers to the possible values making up sample spaces. This section turns to *probability distributions*.

Probability distributions are rules for assigning probabilities to the possible values of random variables or to intervals of possible values of random variables. When we can assign probabilities to the possible *values* of a random variable, that random variable is *discrete*. When we can only assign probabilities to *intervals of* possible values—say, the values in the interval [0, 1]—that variable is *continuous*. A number of discrete and continuous probability distributions frequently come up in probability theory. In an effort to illustrate how this area of probability theory is related to social work, we'll discuss two such distributions: the *Bernoulli* and *binomial distributions*.

The Bernoulli distribution is one we've already been discussing, although implicitly. This is a distribution where the random variable has two possible values, typically coded 0 or 1. One of the values, often 1, has a given probability of occurring, while the other has 1 minus that given probability of occurring. In other words, if the value 1 has probability p of occurring, the other value has a probability $1- p$ of occurring. Although I referred earlier to *the* Bernoulli distribution, this is a misnomer. There isn't just one such distribution, but an infinite number of them, one for each combination of p and $1 - p$. This actually applies to both of the distributions we'll discuss in this section.

Bernoulli distributions are often used to represent real-world situations of uncertainty where there are just two possible outcomes. Those outcomes, as I said in the previous paragraph, are typically assigned a 0 or a 1, and specific values of p and $1 - p$ are applied to them. Our example involving Rick and whether he's been abused by his parents is such a situation. We assigned a 1 to the outcome that he's been abused and a 0 to the outcome that he hasn't been abused. We also assumed that there is a .10 chance that he has been abused and so a $1 - .10 = .9$ chance that he hasn't been abused.

Another example of a discrete probability distribution relevant to social work and public policy is called the *binomial distribution*. Any given binomial distribution is determined by two numbers. One is the number of observations of some uncertain situation. The other is p, the probability of success in any given one of these uncertain situations. By "success" I don't necessarily mean something good happening. Instead, think of "success" as the value of the random variable which is the focus of interest. The probability of failure in any given uncertain situation is $1 - p$.

Binomial distributions are used to model real-world situations where the following conditions apply, at least approximately so:

1. The observed uncertain situations are independent; that is, what happens in one of them doesn't affect what happens in another one.
2. One random variable value is defined to be a success: again, this is just the value that is the focus of interest.
3. p is the probability of success and remains the same for each observed uncertain situation.
4. $1 - p$ is the probability of failure and remains the same for each observed uncertain situation.
5. Interest is in the probability of a given number of successes over the course of the observed uncertain situations.

Let's consider an example where the binomial distribution would apply.

Suppose Jennifer is considering Rick's case again. But now he has four siblings (five kids in all). She's trying to figure out the probability that all five kids are being abused by their parents. Here, success is the outcome that a kid is being abused (random variable value of 1) and failure is a kid not being abused (random variable value of 0). Suppose the probability that any one of the kids is being abused is .10. That is, this probability is the same for all five of them. This means the probability that any one of them isn't being abused is .90 (since $p = .10$, $1 - p = 1 - .10 = .90$). Also, assume that kids being abused in this family are independent events. That is, whether any one kid in the family is being abused is unrelated to whether any other kid is being abused as well. This is a case where the binomial probability distribution could be used to model the situation.

There is actually a formula that can be used to calculate the probability that all five kids are being abused. But instead of putting you through all that, I had a computer calculate that quantity for us. It turns out that it's about .001%.[5] So it seems that Jennifer can safely assume that it's very unlikely that all five kids are being abused.

Whenever we use mathematics to model a situation, we should ask ourselves whether the assumptions on which the model is based seem realistic. Our model here is based on two crucial assumptions: (1) that each kid has the same probability of being abused, and (2) whether one kid is being abused has no impact on whether another one is being abused.

There are reasons to believe that our first assumption may not true. According to the Centers for Disease Control (CDC), children under age 4 are more likely to be abused than are older ones. Children with special needs (cognitive impairments, etc.) are more likely to be abused than those without such needs. The CDC website also tells us about parental risk factors that render them more likely to abuse or neglect their children:

1. Parents have history of child maltreatment in their family of origin
2. Parents have history of substance abuse or mental health issues
3. Parents have low incomes[6]

Any one of these risk factors might apply "globally" in the home. To see what I mean, suppose a father were suffering from clinical depression and that this condition is associated with a higher chance of neglecting or abusing his children. Assuming he has at least two children, that higher risk may apply to all (or at least more than one) of them. In such a case, whether any one of his children is abused by him may not be independent of whether another one is; that is, the second of our model assumptions also might not hold.

Mathematical models are typically unrealistic in the sense that their assumptions don't exactly apply to the real word. The fundamental question is how closely such assumptions approximate that world. When approximations are close, models can be used to understand more about the world we live in. When approximations aren't close, they're less useful for that purpose. In these instances, a model may need to be refined or discarded. Refinement usually involves reassessing the model's assumptions in an attempt to bring them closer to the real world. However, even as refinement is attempted, the goal typically isn't to make the model's assumptions correspond exactly to the real world. The goal of exact correspondence could make the model too complex, thus rendering it intractable.

An *intractable model* is one which is so complicated that it's difficult to do the calculations required to solve it. This tradeoff between trying to construct a mathematical model which is realistic but yet still simple enough to solve is endemic to mathematical modeling.

Probability theory is important in the sciences, including the social sciences, and I've tried to illustrate this by using it to model a situation known all too well in social work—child abuse. However, the main role probability theory plays in social work, particularly in more policy- and research-oriented social work, is in its connection to the discipline of statistics. The next chapter takes a look at that connection.

NOTES

1. Even though impossible events are assigned a probability of 0, this doesn't mean that if an event has a probability of 0 it can't possibly occur. Understanding why this is the case requires knowledge of calculus and measure theory. See Taboga (2010).

2. Actually, there is distinction between *countable-additivity* and *finite-additivity*. I'm combining these in a way that is unorthodox but not inaccurate.

3. I keep saying "estimate" because, according to frequentists, the true probability is the number such a fraction gets closer and closer to as its denominator gets bigger and bigger. In other words, it's the value of such a fraction as the number of times something could've happened tends to infinity. This may seem like a strange definition, but such notions are routine in certain areas of advanced mathematics.

4. Thomas Bayes was a clergyman who also worked in the area of probability theory. This interpretation of the concept is named after him.

5. The computer program I used is called *R*, a free package used by statisticians, quantitative researchers, and data scientists throughout the world.

6. See Centers for Disease Control and Prevention, *Child Abuse and Neglect*.

8

STATISTICS AND SOCIAL ISSUES

YEARS AGO, I WAS talking to an engineering student while the two of us were waiting on a subway platform. Engineering is well known for being a pretty mathematical discipline. When I told her I sometimes teach statistics, she confessed that she hadn't taken a course in statistics yet but was required to for her major. She also said she was terrified at the prospect of having to do so, so terrified in fact that she'd chosen to take an advanced calculus elective in order to postpone statistics.

In my experience, this attitude toward statistics isn't unusual. To be blunt, most students I've met hate statistics. It strikes them as extremely difficult, as well as extremely boring—a deadly combination if ever there was one. This is unfortunate because statistics, as difficult and boring as many find it, is also very useful, especially in fields like social work and the social sciences. Statistics, as far as social work is concerned, is all about data and what we can find out about social life by focusing on data.

STATISTICS AND DATA

Statistics is usually defined as the science of the collection and analysis of numerical data. So, first and foremost, statistics is a discipline which focuses on *data*.

In social work, as well as the social sciences more generally, numerical data are usually bits of information collected on individual persons, groups of persons, or social institutions.

Examples of numerical data that might interest social workers are the number of times each member of some group of clients has been hospitalized for mental illness, the number of times each member of a set of residents in a given nation has been arrested for illegal drug use, the poverty rate of each member of a given set of nations, and a host of others.

The preceding definition of statistics also tells us that it's a discipline concerned with methods for *collecting* numerical data. You're no doubt aware that large-scale social surveys, smaller questionnaires, and experiments are used to collect data on people. These are just a few examples of the "data collection" part of statistics.

We're also told that statistics deals with *analysis* of numerical data. Here, we're talking about a variety of techniques for examining patterns and relationships in data. Some of the more basic ones will be covered in this chapter, while somewhat less basic ones will be covered in the next chapter. Related to the analysis of numerical data is the interpretation of such data. After using particular methods to analyze data sets, researchers arrive at conclusions regarding what they've found. Such conclusions constitute interpretations of data.

As an example, suppose a researcher is interested in the question of whether people's incomes (defined as poor or not poor) and their emotional states (defined as depressed or not depressed) are related to one another. Using terminology from the previous chapter, this is a question about conditional probability. The researcher is really interested in whether the chance that someone is depressed depends on whether they're poor or not.

Suppose this researcher has a data set containing the following information. For each of 400 people, they have whether the person is poor as well as whether they're depressed. Using a technique from statistics called the *chi-square test*, the researcher could assess whether the probability of depression depends on whether someone is poor. In most cases, one data set may lead to a number of different conclusions/interpretations depending on the type of analysis that was conducted and the interest of the researcher.

I said earlier that statistics deals with numerical data. In order to represent data numerically, researchers have to measure things. Thus, they must concern themselves with the theory of measurement, a topic we introduced in Chapter 3.

WHAT IS MEASUREMENT (AGAIN)?

In Chapter 3, we said measurement[1] has to do with the assignment of numbers to represent different amounts or the qualitative aspects of an object's attributes. A helpful way to think about measurement is to use set theory, a topic we covered in Chapter 2. There are two sets involved.

One is a collection of numbers, which I'll call B. The other is a set of objects I'll refer to as A. Examples of objects are people, countries, towns, cities, social service agencies, cells, married couples, and a host of others. The elements of set A are considered to have attributes of some kind. Using these two sets, measurement can be thought of as a rule that states how a given number from set B is assigned to each member of set A so that (1) each element of A is assigned one, and only one, number from B; and (2) the numbers are assigned in such a way that patterns in the attributes of elements of A are reflected in patterns in the assigned numbers. So, if the members of set A are equal on the trait of interest, the assignment of numbers should reflect this. If set A's members differ on the trait, the assigned numbers should reflect this as well. This might be hard to understand initially so an example should help.

One of the major concerns of clinical social workers is self-esteem. This is because we believe self-esteem may be associated with other outcomes of interests, such as the probability of suicide or other types of self-harm. Let's assume there is a scale which allows us to measure someone's level of self-esteem. Suppose B is a set which contains the numbers 0 to 30, inclusive. That is, set B = {0, 1, 2, 3, 4, 5, 6, 7 . . . , 30}. Suppose A is a set of adolescents. The attribute of interest is a given adolescent's level of self-esteem. Our self-esteem scale would be a collection of procedures telling us how to assign one, and only one, number from set B to a given adolescent from set A, where each adolescent receives just one number to represent their level of self-esteem. Note that a member of set B be can be assigned to more than one member of set A; but, again, each element of set A must be assigned *only one* member from B.

Many statistics books studied by social workers, as well as social scientists more generally, open with discussions about the level of measurement. Even though this isn't exactly a statistics book, we'll spend a bit of time on this topic here because it's another illustration of the role of mathematics regarding issues of concern to social workers.

The *level of measurement* has to do with the types of rules used to assign numbers to traits of interest. Another term you'll sometimes see as a synonym for "level of measurement' is "measurement scale." The typical distinction you'll see is among nominal, ordinal, interval, and ratio levels of measurement.

NOMINAL LEVEL OF MEASUREMENT

If numbers from set B are assigned to objects from set A so that differences in numbers represent *qualitative* differences in the attribute in question, then this is the *nominal* level of measurement. For example, let set B be {1, 2, 3} and A be a set of clients of a social service agency. Suppose the trait of interest is gender, and the clients aren't all the same gender. When traits differ between or among the members of some set of objects, we have what statisticians call a *variable*. So, in this example, gender is a variable.

Suppose gender can take on the following categories: female, male, and transgender. Let the rule which assigns numbers to these categories be the following: female is assigned 1, male 2, and transgender 3. Notice that female, male, and transgender differ qualitatively. For example, females do not have one less level of "maleness" than males. Gender differences are differences in kind not quantity. Thus, the assignment of 1, 2, and 3 reflects the differences in kind among female, male, and transgender. In other words, the numbers are "acting" like labels instead of like quantities of something.

ORDINAL LEVEL OF MEASUREMENT

If numbers from set B are assigned to objects from set A so that differences in numbers represent differences in rankings among the attributes of these objects, then this is the *ordinal* level of measurement. For example, suppose set B is {1, 2, 3, 4} and set A is, again, a set of clients. Suppose a social worker is interested in the highest degree obtained by clients because she's thinking about writing a grant to help fund the agency's job training program.

The clients who make up set A differ in terms of highest degree obtained, with the following categories as possibilities: high school diploma, associate's degree, bachelor's degree, and graduate degree. Suppose 1 is assigned to high school degree, 2 to associate's degree, 3 to bachelor's degree, and 4 to graduate degree. Notice here that trait differences are quantitative, but these quantitative differences are not very precise. They are differences in rankings, with high school degree being the lowest and graduate degree the highest, of formal educational attainment. A person with a graduate degree does not have "3 degree units" more than someone with an associate's degree. in fact, we cannot even assume that a person with a graduate degree spent more time in school than someone with an associate's degree. The degrees can only be ranked, and the assignment of numbers represents these rankings. Furthermore, the assignment of 1–4 is arbitrary. The numbers 1,

1.5, 200, and 3,000,000 could have been assigned, as could any other four numbers that differ in magnitude. As long as the four numbers are assigned to educational attainment levels such that the order of assigned numbers reflects the order of educational attainment rankings, we have an ordinal level of measurement.

INTERVAL LEVEL OF MEASUREMENT

If numbers from set B are assigned to traits of objects from set A, such that (1) patterns in intervals between numbers represent patterns in intervals between amounts of the trait, and (2) assignment of the number 0 does not indicate the absence of the trait, then this is the *interval* level of measurement. Let's start with an example from outside of social work.

Physical scientists and engineers study temperature. You may recall from a long-ago science course that if one increases the temperature of matter, it will expand in size. This trait of matter is the basis of certain types of thermometers. As an example, consider the mercury thermometer. These work because there is a bit of mercury enclosed inside a glass tube. When the glass is heated, the mercury expands, and this expansion is measured by a set of numbers that constitute a temperature scale. In the United States, probably the best-known such scale is the Fahrenheit scale. The units of measurement on this scale are degrees Fahrenheit (°F). This scale is considered to be at the interval level of measurement.

To see why, let B be the set of real numbers in the interval [0, 212], where these numbers represent °F. Let set A be a set of thermometers that vary in terms of the sizes of the columns of mercury inside of them. The Fahrenheit scale assigns numbers in [0, 212], such that the intervals between two numbers represent the intervals between two sizes of mercury columns.

Suppose four thermometers from set A are considered. Thermometer 1 (T_1) is assigned 46 degrees, T_2 is assigned 44 degrees, T_3 is assigned 29 degrees, and T_4 is assigned 27 degrees. 46 − 44 is 2 degrees and so is 29 − 27. The Fahrenheit scale has been created so that the difference between the mercury column of T_1 and T_2 is the same as that between T_3 and T_4. In other words, equal numerical intervals imply equal differences in the trait of interest (here, mercury column size). This is condition (1) in the definition of interval level of measurement. Condition (2) can be seen by considering that, under the Fahrenheit scale, assignment of 0 to a thermometer does not mean that the mercury column completely disappears. The column may be very small, but it still exists.

Now let's leave physical science and return to social work. Earlier, I referred to a hypothetical self-esteem scale. Social workers interested in self-esteem might be inclined to treat the scores from such a scale as interval level values. Consider what would have to be the case for these scores to be at the interval of measurement.

Suppose there are four adolescents named Maria, Leroy, Tomas, and Yvette. Maria scores a 20 and Tomas an 18 on the Rosenberg Scale. Yvette scores a 24 and Leroy a 26 on the scale. If this scale really is at the interval level of measurement, this pattern of scores would mean that the difference between Maria's and Tomas' self-esteem levels would be equal to the difference between Leroy's and Yvette's. Now consider Enrico, another adolescent. Suppose he scores a 0 on the Rosenberg scale. If this is truly an interval scale, this score of 0 would not mean that Enrico has no self-esteem whatsoever.

We said "if this is truly an interval scale" because one could raise a question about whether it makes sense to think of differences in self-esteem in the same way we think of differences in the sizes of mercury columns. The size of a mercury column is a physical quantity which can be directly observed with our eyes, at least among those of us with the sense of vision. This makes it relatively easy to put a temperature scale on a thermometer representing the differences in the sizes of mercury columns. But, arguably, self-esteem is not a physical quantity in the same sense as the size of a column of mercury. So how do we ever know if numbers assigned to differences in self-esteem levels truly represent differences in those levels? In fact, how do we ever know if there are such levels, if self-esteem isn't a physical quantity? What I've just said about measurement of self-esteem also applies to measurement scales used to measure depression, happiness, and other phenomena that interest social workers.

This discussion of interval levels of measurement has taken us into the philosophy of science. Since this isn't a book about the philosophy of science, we won't say much more about the feasibility of interval-level scales in social work. Let it suffice to say that if you come across someone treating a self-esteem, depression, or similar scale as an interval-level one, you should be aware of some of the philosophical baggage this raises.

RATIO LEVEL OF MEASUREMENT

If numbers from set B are assigned to traits of objects from set A so that (1) patterns in intervals between numbers represent patterns in intervals between amounts of the trait of interest, and (2) assignment of the number 0 *does* indicate the absence of the trait, then this is the *ratio* level of measurement. Notice that this definition is almost identical to the definition of interval level of measurement. The difference is in condition (2).

Here's a social work example of the ratio level of measurement. Again, suppose B is a set of numbers and A a set of people. The trait of interest is the number of times a person has been hospitalized for mental illness. The measurement rule is this: assign a number from set B equal to the number of times a person has been hospitalized. That is, if a person has been hospitalized one time, then assign the number 1. If someone has been hospitalized two times, then assign the number 2; if three times, then assign the number 3, and so on. This may seem strange, but it is consistent with the theory of measurement.

There is a set of numbers, a set of objects possessing some trait of interest, and a rule which allows us to assign numbers to traits of objects. It should be clear that condition (1) of the ratio level of measurement is met. To see that condition (2) is met, consider the following. If a person has never been hospitalized for mental illness, then they would be assigned the number 0. Here, 0 does mean absence of the trait of interest; it means that there is been no (that is, 0) hospitalizations for mental illness.

DISCRETE VERSUS CONTINUOUS VARIABLES

We said earlier that measurement has to do with the assignment of numbers to objects and that, when those objects differ on some trait or attribute of interest, we have a variable. Statisticians sometimes make a distinction between *discrete* and *continuous* variables.

A *discrete variable* is one that can only assume a finite or *countable infinite* number of values. I suspect you already know what "finite" means. A countable infinite number of values means that the values the variable can assume can be any number from the set of natural numbers; that is, any number from {0, 1, 2, 3, 4, 5 . . . }.

For example, gender would be a discrete variable taking on male, female, or transgender as possible values. There are only three possible values that this variable can assume—which is, of course, a finite number of them. The number of times one has been hospitalized for mental illness is also a discrete variable because this number must be a natural number. However, in principle, one could argue that the number of times one has been hospitalized could "range" across the natural numbers from 0 to infinity. That is, from a mathematical point of view, the number of times someone has been hospitalized could be 0, 10, 100, 1,000, 100,000, 1,000,000, 1,000,000,000, 1,000,000,000,000, and so on, although no researcher is likely to ever come across someone who's been hospitalized for mental illness a trillion times.

A *continuous variable* is one that can assume an *uncountable infinite* number of values. An uncountable infinite number means that the values the variable can assume can be any number from any subset of the set of real numbers.

For example, the *proportion* of US residents who've been hospitalized for mental illness can take on any value within [0, 1]. This proportion no doubt varies over time, so it's an example of a variable. Also, since [0, 1] is a subset of the set of real numbers, it's an example of a continuous variable.

Earlier we made a distinction between interval- and ratio-level variables, but both of these types of variables, as well as ordinal ones, are often treated as continuous in social work- and policy-related research. This often happens when the variables in question can assume many values, even when, strictly speaking, that variable isn't continuous. For example, income is a commonly studied variable which is often treated as continuous. But, clearly, income isn't a continuous variable since it's measured in some currency unit. A person in the United States, for example, can't really have an annual income of $60,000.555 because the smallest currency unit in the United States is the penny (1 cent).

The thinking behind treating interval-, ratio-, or even ordinal-level variables, especially ones that can assume many values, as continuous is that such a variable is thought to be closely approximated by a continuous variable. This sort of thing came up when we discussed mathematical models. We said that use of approximations in mathematical modeling is common in science. So, in this respect, social work researchers who model noncontinuous variables as continuous ones are behaving similarly to scientists. The advantage of doing so allows more powerful statistical methods to be used.

DESCRIPTIVE VERSUS INFERENTIAL STATISTICS

Statisticians make a distinction between descriptive and inferential methods. *Descriptive methods* refer to techniques used to summarize various aspects of a data set. One of the most commonly used descriptive methods is the *arithmetic mean* or, more simply, the *mean* of a data set.

The mean is more commonly known as the *average*. For a given set of numbers, as you probably know, the mean or average of those numbers is calculated as follows:

1. Add up all the numbers in question to get the total of those numbers.
2. Divide this total by the number of values.

The mean of a set of numbers is considered to be a measure of the typical number in that set. "Typical" in this context means the one number which most represents the set of numbers as a whole.

As an example, suppose the following numbers are the ages of the clients served by a social service agency: 10, 15, 12, 11, 8, 9, 10, 14, 13, and 16 (all measured in years). If we take the sum of these numbers, we end up with a total of 118. Since 118 divided by 10 (since there are 10 values) is 11.8, the mean age is 11.8. So, the typical client served by this agency is about 12 years old.

Even though the mean is a commonly used descriptive method, if we want to measure the typical value in a data set, it's not always the best one to use. To see this, suppose the clients of a social service agency are the following ages: 10, 15, 12, 11, 8, 9, 10, 14, 13, and 106 (again, all measured in years). The total of these ages is 208. Once we divide this figure by 10, we get 20.8. Thus, the typical client at this second agency is about 21 years old.

Notice that the only difference between the ages of clients of the first agency and those of the second is that the age of the tenth person listed for the second agency is much higher that the age of the tenth person listed for the first one (106 vs. 12). Also, notice that the mean age for the second agency is so high that most of the ages in that group are less than the group's mean age. This is what's wrong with using the mean as a measure of what's typical—it's vulnerable to what statisticians call *outliers*. An outlier is a value in a data set which is much larger or much smaller than the other values in that data set. Because of the way the mean is calculated, outliers pull the mean in their direction in such a way that the mean is no longer a measure of what's typical.

An understanding of *inferential methods* in statistics requires you to know something about the difference between a *population* and a *sample*. A population, call it P, is a finite set of objects that some researcher is interested in. A sample, which we'll call S, is a proper subset of P. That is, every member of S is also a member of P, but there are some members of P that aren't members of S.

For example, our population of interest might be the set of all kids in the US foster care system on June 21, 2017. The set of white kids in the US foster care on June 21, 2017, would be a proper subset of this population, assuming not all kids in foster care on this date are white.

Another important distinction is between a *statistic* and a *parameter*. The word "statistics" is often used to refer to an entire academic discipline. But "statistic" is also used to refer to any measurement obtained from sample data. For example, the mean age of the sample of white kids specified in the previous paragraph would be a statistic. A parameter is any measurement obtained from a population. So, the mean age of all kids making up the population of foster care children specified in the previous paragraph would be a parameter.

Inferential methods are those concerned with drawing conclusions about a population on the basis of some measurement obtained from a sample. For example, we might be interested in the mean age of children making up our foster care population. Yet obtaining data on each member of that population may be infeasible. So, we could select a sample from this population, calculate the mean age for that sample, and use it to say something about the population mean age. Inferential methods are fraught with challenges because the ways samples are obtained greatly affect the degree of confidence we can have in our conclusions about populations.

PROBABILITY SAMPLES

Statisticians prefer a type of sample known as a *probability sample*. A probability sample in one in which each member of the population has a known probability of being selected for the sample. Let's consider our population of foster children again. If we know the probability of each kid being selected for our sample before selecting him or her, we'd end up with a probability sample.

A basic type of probability sample is a *random sample*. A random sample is one in which each member of the population has the same probability of being selected for the sample. Suppose there are 400,000 kids in foster care in the United States on June 21, 2017. If we selected 1,000 kids for our sample in such a way that each of the 400,000 kids had a 1/400,000 chance of ending up in the sample, our sample would be a random sample. Courses in statistics focus on how this sort of thing can be done. A fair amount of math, as well as computers are involved. But the basic concept is pretty simple. Notice that if we just selected all the white kids who are in foster care on this date, that wouldn't be a random sample. This is because the probability of any white kid being selected for the sample would be 1 or 100%, while the probabilities for others would not be 1 or 100%.

The reason statisticians are so interested in random samples is because they've developed a number of techniques that allow them to draw conclusions about populations on the basis of such samples; however, these techniques are based on the assumption that the samples in question are random samples. Whether these techniques apply when the samples being used aren't random is an open question.[2]

DATA-GENERATING PROCESSES AND INFERENTIAL METHODS

So far, our discussion of inferential methods is typical of those found in books written for a social science or social work audience. I'll call it the *population approach* to statistical inference because it focuses on drawing conclusions about populations on the basis of samples from such populations. Statisticians often discuss another approach to statistical inference, one that I'll call the *process approach* to statistical inference. The process approach isn't focused on drawing conclusions about populations on the basis of samples but, instead, on drawing conclusions about *data-generating processes* (DGPs) on the basis of samples.[3]

"Data-generating process" is a term that refers to those forces which account for the data we see before us. Any DGP has two components:

1. The natural and social forces operating "out there" in the world
2. The way we've chosen to design our study as well as measure the variables we're interested in

This DGP view of inference is a bit more abstract than the population view, so examples are likely to be very helpful. Let's go back to our kids in foster care example.

Earlier, we assumed that, on June 21, 2017, there were 400,000 kids in foster care residing in the United States, and we called this our population. But if you think about it for a moment, you're likely to conclude that it's kind of strange to only care about foster kids residing in the United States on June 21, 2017. Instead, we're likely to care about the natural and social forces (perhaps poverty, racism, etc.) which result in there being foster kids residing in the United States *at any point in time*. And, if we ended up with 400,000 (or any number of) foster kids residing in the United States at a particular point in time, this could be regarded as a sample. This sample will have resulted from the natural and social forces just referred to, as well as how we designed the study to collect these data, including how we chose to determine (that is, measure) whether a kid is in foster care. From the DGP point of view, inference would be about using these sample data to draw conclusions about the natural and social processes which helped to produce them.

HYPOTHESIS TESTING: THE POPULATION-RANDOM SAMPLE APPROACH

We said earlier that inference has to do with drawing conclusions about populations (or DGPs) on the basis of sample data. In social work, this is usually discussed in terms of *hypothesis testing*. In this section, we'll focus on hypothesis testing as it relates to drawing conclusions about populations on the basis of random samples. The next section will do the same for conclusions drawn about DGPs.

The following steps are involved in hypothesis testing:

1. Determine the critical p value.
2. State the *null hypothesis*.
3. State the *alternative hypothesis*.
4. Collect some data and calculate a *sample statistic*.
5. Transform the sample statistic into a *test statistic*.
6. Determine the *test statistic's p value*.
7. Compare the p value associated with the test statistic to the critical p value.
8. If the p value associated with the test statistic is less than the critical p value, reject the null hypothesis; otherwise, do not reject the null hypothesis.

As shorthand, we'll refer to these steps as the hypothesis-testing algorithm (HTA).

It's easier to explain step 1 within the context of discussing step 6, so we'll come back to it later. Step 2 means that a researcher must start with an assumption about the value of some quantity in some population of interest. They can assume pretty much whatever value they want, as long as the assumption makes mathematical sense. For example, if a researcher is interested in the average number of kids in a family, they shouldn't assume that this average is –2 children, since an average of –2 kids doesn't make sense. Also, it's considered best practice if a researcher's assumption, whenever possible, is based on some combination of theory and what's already known about the issue being investigated.

To make this discussion more concrete, suppose a social work researcher or policy analyst is interested in the average parenting skill level, at a given point in time, of the population of US foster parents (of course, this also assumes we've come up with some way of measuring parenting skill level). So, step 2 amounts to saying that this researcher would start with an assumption about this average level.

Step 3 means the researcher must make another assumption about the average parenting skill level. However, the value assumed in the alternative hypothesis must be mutually exclusive in relation to the value assumed in the null hypothesis. That is, it must be impossible for the average parenting skill level assumed in step 2 to be true, and, simultaneously, the average assumed in step 1 to be true as well. For example, suppose the social worker assumed in step 1 an average parenting skill level of 15 units. Then, in step 2, the assumed value can be any value other than 15 units.

Step 4 means that a sample must be collected, data must be obtained from that sample, and a sample value for the quantity in question must be calculated. How this is done will depend on the quantity of interest, a subject you'll learn more about in your research courses. For this example, an average parenting skill level must be calculated from sample data.

Step 5 is telling us that a given sample value must be transformed into a test statistic. There are a number of ways such transformations can occur. In a situation like the one facing our social worker, the average level of parenting skill calculated from the sample would be transformed into a test statistic. You can think of a test statistic as just a different way of presenting a sample statistic that makes that sample statistic more amenable to hypothesis testing. It's like translating a sentence written in English to one written in Spanish so someone who only reads Spanish could understand it.

For step 6, the critical p value must be chosen. Understanding what the critical p value is requires you to understand what a p value is, in general. A p value is a type of conditional probability. It's the probability that a test statistic value at least as large as the one we've observed would be observed if the null hypothesis were true. That is, if we assume the null hypothesis is true, the p value tells us how likely it is we'd observe a test statistic at least as large as the one we actually observed in our sample.

As an example, suppose our researcher's null hypothesis is that the average level of parenting skill is 15 units, but the average they obtained from their sample—their sample statistic, that is—is 22 units. When this sample value of 22 units is transformed into a test statistic, it becomes 2.00. The p value of .04 means that the probability of obtaining a test statistic value of at least 2.00 (and, therefore, a sample value of at least 22 skill units), assuming the null hypothesis is true, is 4% (.04 * 100 = 4%).[4]

Now that we know what a p value is, we can define "critical p value." A critical p value (referred to in step 1) is simply a "cutoff" p value chosen by a researcher. It's essential that a researcher chooses the critical p value they want to use in the study *before* beginning steps 2–8 of the HTA. Another name for a critical p value is *alpha level*. The alpha level in a given study is a cutoff p value in the sense that the p value associated with a test statistic must be less than the critical p value before the null hypothesis can be rejected. When a null hypothesis is rejected, a researcher decides that the probability of obtaining a test statistic as extreme as the one they did obtain is so low—assuming the null hypothesis is true—that they conclude the null hypothesis actually isn't true.

A common critical p value used in social work as well as in the social sciences more generally is .05 or 5% (.05 * 100 = 5%). That is, if the test statistic p value is less than a critical p value of .05, the researcher will reject the null hypothesis. If the test statistic p value is at least .05, the null hypothesis will not be rejected.

Going back to our parenting skill example, we're assuming that our researcher found a test statistic p value of .04. If the chosen critical p value is .05, they'd reject the null hypothesis that the average level of parenting skill in the US foster parent population is 15 skill units, since .04 is less than .05. That is, they'd conclude that the average level of parenting skill in this population isn't 15 skill units.

Steps 7 and 8 of the HTA should be clear. If a given null hypothesis can be rejected, this is sometimes referred to as a *statistically significant* finding, in the sense that the value of the sample statistic/test statistic is statistically significantly different from the value assumed in the null hypothesis. Rejection of the null hypothesis is also typically taken as evidence in support of the alternative hypothesis. So, our parenting skill researcher, having rejected the null hypothesis of 15 skill units, would conclude that they've obtained evidence in support of the alternative claim that the average parenting skill level is around 22 units.

Before moving to the next section, I should make a crucial point about the difference between statistical and *substantive significance*. I just said that statistical significance has to do with whether, assuming the null hypothesis is true, the probability of obtaining a test statistic value as extreme as the one actually obtained is low. Substantive significance has to do with whether a sample or test statistic is considered sizable enough to guide clinical, policy, or some other kind of intervention. To see what I mean, let's go back to our parenting skills example.

Our null hypothesis was a skills level of 15 units, but we found a sample value of 22 units (which is the same as our test statistic value of 2.00). We rejected the null hypothesis, concluding that a sample value of 22 units (or a test statistic value of 2.00) is unlikely, assuming that the actual value is 15 units. A substantive significance question might be this one: assuming the average parenting skills level is closer to 22 units than it is to 15 units, should we change anything we're doing clinically, in terms of public policy, in regard to how we train social workers to intervene with parents? Substantive significance is about the implications of a finding for what we should do. Given that social work is about intervening in the hopes of bettering people's lives, substantive significance is at least as important—and, arguably more so—as statistical significance.

HYPOTHESIS TESTING: THE DATA-GENERATING
PROCESS-SAMPLE APPROACH

Take a look at the HTA again:

1. Determine the critical p value.
2. State the *null hypothesis*.
3. State the *alternative hypothesis*.
4. Collect some data and calculate a *sample statistic*.
5. Transform the sample statistic into a *test statistic*.
6. Determine the *test statistic's p value*.
7. Compare the p value associated with the test statistic to the critical p value.
8. If the p value associated with the test statistic is less than the critical p value, reject the null hypothesis; otherwise, do not reject the null hypothesis.

One of the key differences between the population-sample and the DGP-sample view of hypothesis testing has to do with steps 2 and 3. The null hypothesis isn't something assumed about a population, but about a DGP. DGPs are represented by probability distributions.

Recall from the previous chapter, that a probability distribution is simply a set of values of some random variable, or intervals of such a variable, along with the probabilities associated with those values or intervals. Also, recall that a random variable is a numerical quantity whose value depends on chance. In other words, before we actually observe them, we can't predict with certainty the values of random variables. But if we know, or assume, that these values are governed by particular probability distributions, we can determine the probabilities of certain values occurring. Let's see how this is related to DGPs.

I said earlier that a DGP has to do with the forces we assume generated the data we actually get to observe. Considering our ongoing example of parenting skills of US-based foster care parents, let's say we end up with a data set of parenting skill levels. These data, in part, will have resulted from how we chose to design the study, including how we chose to measure parenting skill. But there are also social forces that helped to generate these data. The social forces in question would include how foster parents are socialized, what the laws are regarding corporal punishment, the behavior of children in foster care, and a host of others.

To conduct a hypothesis test from the DGP perspective, a researcher would have to "translate" an assumed DGP into a probability distribution. Within the context of our current example, they'd have to go from assumptions about forces which generate data on parenting skill to assuming that parenting skill is a random variable which takes on specific values with associated probabilities.[5] When it comes to step 2 of the HTA, a given probability distribution replaces a given population. That is, instead of an assumption about a population made up of a finite number of cases *at a specific time*, a researcher makes an assumption about a probability distribution made up of an infinite number of values, which is viewed as generating data *at any time*. Just as populations can have averages as well as other relevant quantities, so, too, can probability distributions. Thus, just as we can assume that the average parenting skill level of the population of US foster parents at a given time is 15, we can assume, from the DGP perspective, that the average (also called expected value) of the probability distribution of foster parents' skill levels is 15.

Another key difference between the population-sample and DGP-sample perspectives has to do with the nature of the samples we have in mind. Where the population approach talks about random samples, the DGP approach refers to *independent* and *identically distributed* (IID) samples. To see what an IID sample is, assume that we have, at a given point in time, a data set of 1,000 US foster parents, along with each of their parenting skill levels. This would be an IID sample if two things were true:

1. Whether a given parent ended up in the sample didn't depend on whether another one ended up in it. This is what's meant by "independent" in "IID."
2. Each case in the sample—that is, each parent's skill level—came from *the same* probability distribution; in fact, each case came from the distribution assumed in step 1. This is what's meant by "identical distribution" in IID.

More generally, a given sample is IID if (1) whether a case ends up in the sample doesn't depend on whether another case does and if (2) each case came from the same probability distribution.

With these two differences taken care of, hypothesis testing under the DGP approach is pretty much the same as it is under the population one. That is, once our null hypothesis is stated in terms of a probability distribution assumed to have generated our data and we have our IID sample, we formulate an alternative hypothesis, calculate sample and test statistics, decide on the critical p value, and so forth. Rejecting the null does, however, have a slightly different interpretation under the DGP approach. If a researcher found that the test statistic p value is less than the critical p value and therefore rejected the null, that would mean something like the following: the probability of obtaining a test statistic as extreme as the one obtained is very low, assuming the probability distribution specified in the null hypothesis (which represents the assumed DGP) is true.

ERRORS AND HYPOTHESIS TESTING

We said earlier that the HTA involves a null hypothesis and that the outcome of such a test is either rejecting it or not.[6] When it comes to the question of rejecting the null hypothesis, two types of errors are possible. This is because we're basing our conclusion about a null hypothesis (with respect to either a population or DGP) on something from a sample. Null hypotheses are *assumptions* about populations or DGPs. But what's assumed about such matters and what's actually going on may be very different. And when it comes to the typical statistical study, we have no way of knowing what's actually going on in populations or regarding DGPs. In fact, statistics as a discipline arose in large part to deal with exactly these types of situations of uncertainty. To make matters worse, a given sample may not be a good indication of what's really going on in a population or with regard to a given DGP. One error we might make is to reject the null hypothesis when, in fact, it is true. This is called a *type I error*. We could also decide not to reject the null hypothesis when, in fact, is it false. This is called a *type II error*. The importance of considering the possibility of type I and II errors will be easier to see in the next chapter when we're discussing causal inference. So we'll come back to these types of errors then.

CONFIDENCE INTERVALS

I said in Chapter 3 that social researchers tend to assume that all measurements have some degree of error associated with them. For example, we used the case of a measured unemployment rate of 4.3%. Instead of the actual unemployment rate being 4.3%, it's actually 4.3% ± error. The "±" symbol means our estimate could either be too large (the plus sign) or too small (the minus sign).[7] The problem is that we typically don't know the level of error associated with our measurements. This section is about how statisticians address this problem using *confidence intervals*.

A confidence interval is just what it says—an *interval* of values. To create such an interval, a researcher starts with a measured value of some quantity of interest.

Next, they must decide whether they want a 90%, 95%, 98%, or some other percentage confidence interval. Since one of the most frequently used percentages is 95%, that's what I'll focus on in this section.

Once a researcher has a measured value and has decided they want a 95% interval, they could calculate what's called a *margin of error*.[8] You can think of a margin of error as a quantity that helps a researcher estimate how much their measurement might be "off by." That is, they assume the measured value isn't the true one, but also that they don't know the true value. The marginal of error is added to and subtracted from the measured quantity to create an interval—namely, the confidence interval—in order to account for this uncertainty in the measured value:

Confidence Interval(95%) = measured value ± margin of error

The interpretation of confidence intervals is a bit tricky. A 95% confidence interval tells us the following: if we were to repeatedly select samples of a given size from a given population or DGP and calculate confidence intervals for each one, 95% of those intervals would contain the true value of the quantity of interest. So, if a researcher were to select 10,000 samples from a given population or DGP and calculate a 95% confidence interval for each of them, about 9,500 (.95 * 10,000 = 9,500) of these intervals would contain the true population or DGP value. Of course, researchers tend not to collect 10,000 samples and often only collect one of them. But statistical theory still tells them what would happen if they were to select more. Even if the concept of confidence intervals is new to you, you're probably more familiar with them than you think.

About every four years, around presidential election time, a number of organizations start polling citizens in an effort to forecast who'll win the election. We might hear that a given candidate is forecasted to win 45% of the vote with a margin of error of 3 points. Applying the confidence interval equation to these numbers, we get

Confidence Interval (95%) = 45 ± 3
or
[42%, 48%]

The "[42%, 48%]" is a closed interval and stands for any percentage from 42% to 48%, inclusive. Since 95% of the confidence intervals constructed this way would contain the true percentage, a statistician would say that we can be 95% confident that the true percentage of support for this candidate is between 42% and 48%, inclusive.

CAUSAL INFERENCE

Social workers are in the business of intervening in people's lives or advocating for public policies which do so; the intent of such interventions is to improve things. So we have an interest—at least we should have—in whether or our interventions result in improvements. Put differently, we're interested in whether our interventions cause people's lives to become better. Statisticians are interested in causality, too, and what they have to say about it is something social workers ought to be familiar with, whether or not they intend to be researchers. This is because, for better or worse, our interventions are under increasing scrutiny as many call for "evidence-based" practice. Knowing something about how statisticians, as well as quantitative researchers more broadly, view causality will help us better understand what's at stake in evidence-based practice debates. Such an understanding may also help us become more informed participants in these debates. Currently, the most influential view in statistics regarding causality is the *counterfactual* view. In order to say more about this, a bit of notation is required.

Let "i" stand for an individual who might be exposed to some intervention of interest. Let "Int" stand for the intervention in question, and, for the sake of simplicity, assume that, for a given individual i, Int can only take the value of either 1 or 0 but not both. The value 1 is assigned to i if they receive the intervention; if i doesn't receive it, they're assigned the value 0. $Outcome_i(Int = 1)$ stands for the value of some outcome when i has received the intervention and $Outcome_i(Int = 0)$ stands for the value of the outcome variable when i hasn't received it. According to the counterfactual view of causality, the intervention has a causal effect on the outcome in question for i if $Outcome_i(Int = 1) - Outcome_i(Int = 0)$ isn't equal to 0. That is, if the difference between the value of the outcome variable when i receives the intervention and the value of this variable when i doesn't receive it isn't 0.

In any given study, i couldn't simultaneously receive the intervention and not receive it. So, either we'd end up with $Outcome_i(Int = 1)$ or $Outcome_i(Int = 0)$, but not both. That is, for each case i, only the outcome under the intervention or the outcome under no intervention would be observed, but not both. So, we'd never be able to obtain $Outcome_i(Int = 1) - Outcome_i(Int = 0)$, the causal outcome of interest, for a given case. This is the central problem faced by those who want to estimate causal effects. The outcome for case i that we end up not being able to observe is called the *counterfactual outcome*; hence, the name counterfactual view of causality.[9] A concrete example may help clarify this understanding of causality.

Suppose there is a parenting skill training class and a set of 20 foster parents. The purpose of this class is to increase the quality of each person's parenting, and we assume that there is some interval-level measure of foster parenting quality where the higher the score, the higher the quality of parenting. We want to know whether this class actually improves the quality of care provided by the foster parents. For each foster parent, we can imagine their parenting quality score under two conditions. One is what that score would be if they were to receive the parenting skill class; this is $Outcome_i(Int = 1)$. The other is what the parenting quality score would be if they weren't to receive the class; this is $Outcome_i(Int = 0)$. The causal effect of the class for a given foster parent would be their parenting quality score if they received the class minus their score if they didn't receive it; this is $Outcome_i(Int = 1) - Outcome_i(Int = 0)$. If this difference ended up not being 0, then, by definition, we'd have a causal effect of the parenting skill class on parenting quality. If $Outcome_i(Int = 1)$ were greater than $Outcome_i(Int = 0)$, this would mean that i's parenting improves as a result of the parenting skills class.

As should be obvious from this example, in a real study to assess the impact of a parenting skill class, each person would be assigned to only one of the two groups, either receiving the skills training or not. That is, they won't be exposed to the class and *simultaneously* not exposed to it. Thus, for each person, the parenting quality score difference couldn't be observed. This raises the question of how researchers go about estimating causal effects when the ones we want to estimate can't be observed.

In statistics, there is one highly regarded strategy to estimate causal effects when these are conceived of in counterfactual terms—the *randomized controlled experiment* (RCE). Using this strategy, a set of cases is randomly assigned to either a treatment or control group. In some studies, cases are randomly assigned to any number of treatment or control groups. But, to keep things simple, I'll focus on just one treatment and one control group. The treatment group is the one which receives the intervention of interest, while the control group receives some comparison intervention, which could be no intervention at all.[10]

Random assignment means that a given case has an equal chance of ending up in the treatment or control group. This, according to statistical theory, means there will be no systematic differences between the treatment and control groups on any other variable which might affect the outcome of interest. So, any difference between the outcome variable for a given member of the treatment group and a member of the control group closely approximates $Outcome_i(Int = 1) - Outcome_i(Int = 0)$. Let's relate this to our parenting skill example.

Suppose we randomly assign 10 of the 20 parents to get the parenting skill training (our treatment group) and the other 10 not to receive the training (our control group). Random assignment means that the two groups do not differ systematically on any other variables (perhaps age, number of kids in the home, motivation to be a "good" parent, education level, etc.) that might affect parenting skill. The only difference is that some have been assigned to receive the training and others have not been so assigned. Let's choose a person from the treatment group and one from the control group. If we subtract the control group person's parenting quality score from the treatment group person's score, this approximates subtracting the *treatment group person's score had they not received treatment* from their score under the condition of *having received it*. That is, this difference approximates $Outcome_i(Int = 1) - Outcome_i(Int = 0)$. $Outcome_i(Int = 1) - Outcome_i(Int = 0)$. This approximation works because random assignment has made it likely that the control group member is similar to the treatment group member in every respect except the difference in treatment. In other words, we can think of pairs of treatment and control group members as "statistical clones" of one another.

The problem encountered by social work researchers, as well as social scientists more generally, is that they're often not in a position to conduct RCEs. This could be due to costs or to ethical or other kinds of constraints. For example, if a social worker is interested in the effect of poverty on childhood mental health, they're unlikely to be able to conduct a RCE to study this effect. Not many people would stand for the social worker randomly assigning some kids to live in abject poverty, while others are assigned to live under better conditions. Instead, this social worker would have to work with children who've already been "assigned," by DGPs beyond their control, to be impoverished or not. Data that were not obtained by way of an RCE are called *observational data*. The problem a researcher is faced with when trying to estimate causes on the basis of observational data is called *confounding*.

Confounding occurs when there are variables, called *confounding variables*, which have a causal effect on both the treatment and outcome of interest. In fact, when we're dealing with observational data, some would argue that we really shouldn't be using the word "treatment" anymore but should be using "exposure" or something along those lines. We'll stick with "treatment," though, to highlight the fact that we're still interested in the causal effect of some treatment even if we can't randomly assign participants to its categories.

Suppose we're interested in studying the effect of depression on suicide; that is, depression is our treatment variable. Suppose our two treatment groups are "person is depressed" (which we assign the number 1) and "person is not depressed" (which we assign the number 0). It isn't feasible for us to randomly assign some people to be depressed and others not to be depressed. But nature and social forces will conduct that assignment for us. That is, genetic factors as well as various social conditions will result in some people being depressed and others not. This is precisely what I meant earlier by the term "DGP."

Suppose we find that the proportion of depressed people who commit suicide is higher than the proportion of nondepressed people who do. Have we shown that depression causes a higher probability of suicide? Not necessarily. Suppose there is a gene which causes both a higher probability of depression and of suicide. So, even though we've found that the proportion of depressed people who commit suicide exceeds the proportion of nondepressed people who do, is that because depression causes an increased chance of suicide, this gene does so, or both? Our data on depression and suicide simply don't allow us to answer this question—that's confounding.

There are a number of policy-related issues which come down to the question of confounding. Take the issue of whether poverty causes child maltreatment (child abuse or neglect). There are data which show that poor parents are more likely to neglect or abuse their children than are non-poor parents (Cancian and Slack, 2010).[11] But is this because poverty causes neglect or abuse, or is something else causing them both? As Cancian and Slack discuss in their paper, it may be that mental health status causes both poverty and child maltreatment, and that this is what accounts for the association between these two variables.

This isn't just an academic debate. If poverty is the cause of child maltreatment, and if the magnitude of this effect is large, then we may be able to substantially reduce maltreatment by reducing poverty. But if both poverty and child maltreatment are caused by poor mental health (depression, bipolar disorder, or something along those lines), then addressing poverty may not do much to address maltreatment. Instead, we'd need to address parents' mental health.

Consider another example. There is an association between receipt of prenatal care and the birthweight of a newborn; women who received such care are less likely to have low-birthweight babies. We're told by medical folks that low birthweight in newborns is something we should try to prevent. Could we do so by assuring that all pregnant women has access to prenatal care? The extent to which we could do this depends on whether receipt of prenatal care is a cause of birthweight. That is, if receipt of prenatal care and birthweight are both caused by a mother's income, then we may not be able to do much about low birthweight by targeting receipt of prenatal care.[12] In this case, the association between prenatal care and birthweight wouldn't be because prenatal care causes birthweight but because mother's income causes both.

For yet another example, consider the controversial issue of welfare. As I said earlier, what most people refer to as welfare is actually a program called Temporary

Assistance for Needy Families (TANF). At one time, it was called Aid to Families with Dependent Children (AFDC) and, even earlier, Aid to Dependent Children (ADC). For much of its existence, the program has been despised. This is because many people think it generates "welfare dependency" by causing people to work less than they would if they weren't receiving benefits. So, some have argued that we should reduce such benefits.

But to what degree does welfare cause a reduction in labor supply? If welfare recipients work less because of welfare, we may be able to get them to work more by reducing the level of welfare benefits. But what if lack of motivation causes people to both go on welfare and work less? Then, to get them to work more, we'd need to address motivation instead of their welfare receipt. But actually things can get more complicated than this. It may be that lack of motivation causes one to go on welfare but also that going on welfare causes a lack of motivation. This is sometimes called *reverse causality,* and it can make teasing out causal effects using observational data quite difficult.

Consider another complicating factor when it comes to trying to anticipate the causal effects of a policy intervention. Sometimes an intervention will operate in such a way that it has offsetting effects which makes it very difficult to predict what will happen if the policy is implemented. Economists are very aware of this sort of thing. Take income tax policy.

Suppose a jurisdiction is considering raising marginal tax rates.[13] Economists would assume that such a change would impact labor supply. The problem, however, is that there are two causal effects to consider. One they call the *substitution effect* and the other the *income effect*.

The substitution effect of a marginal tax rate increase concerns the fact that, as the tax rate increases, the amount you take home decreases (because more of your income must be forked over to the government). This means that the "cost" of not working decreases since you give up less income by choosing not to work than you did before the tax hike. And, as economists see it, when the cost of something goes down, we tend to consume more of it. So, in this case, they'd expect you to "consume" more "non-work time." That is, they'd expect you to substitute non-work time for work time.

The income effect of a marginal tax rate hike has to do with the fact that the higher tax rate decreases your income. So, if you want to maintain your standard of living, you'll tend to work more, not less. So, an increase in marginal tax rates would have two causal effects—at least this is what economists think—but these effects pull in different directions. And economic theory offers no guidance regarding which effect will dominate.

In an earlier section of this chapter, I mentioned type I and type II errors and said I'd come back to them during our discussion of causality. A type I error occurs when the null hypothesis is rejected even though that hypothesis is true. A type II error occurs when the null hypothesis isn't rejected when that hypothesis is false. A table may help to see this more clearly:

	Null Is True	Null Isn't True
Reject null	*Type I Error*	Correct Decision
Don't reject null	Correct Decision	*Type II Error*

The thing about type I and II errors is that we typically don't know if we've made one of them. This is because we usually don't know if the null hypothesis is true. And, to make matters worse, you're in a kind of "damned if you do and damned if you don't" situation. That's because it can be shown that the probability of these two types of errors is negatively related one to the other. If you lower the chance of a type I error, then you raise the chance of a type II error and vice versa.

Suppose we're interested in whether poverty increases the chance that a parent will abuse or neglect at least one of their children. That is, we're interested in whether poverty causes a parent to be more likely to abuse or neglect at least one of their children. The null hypothesis here would be that there is no causal effect of poverty on the probability of abuse or neglect. The alternative hypothesis would be that there is a causal effect of poverty on the probability of abuse or neglect. A type I error would occur if we ended up rejecting the idea that there is no causal effect on poverty when, in fact, there isn't such an effect. A type II error would occur if we didn't reject the idea that there is no causal effect on poverty when, in fact, there is such an effect.

You may one day come across the term *statistical power*. Statistical power refers to the probability of rejecting the null hypothesis when, in fact, it's false. If the probability of committing a type II error is referred to as *ProbII*, then statistical power would be (1 − *ProbII*). Suppose, for example, that the probability of a type II error is .20 or 20% (multiplying .20 by 100). Then, in this case, statistical power would be (1 − .20) which is .80 or 80%. Thus, there would be an 80% chance of rejecting the null hypothesis if, in fact, the hypothesis is false. Statistics courses cover how to calculate type I and II probabilities, as well as statistical power. They also cover how we can increase (or decrease) the chance of a type I or type II error.

You may be wondering why we should care about type I and II errors, as well as statistical power. Here's an example which should help you see the significance of such things. Suppose a new drug to treat depression has been created. You're interested in whether this drug, taken in conjunction with cognitive therapy, is more effective at treating depression than cognitive behavior therapy alone is. The null hypothesis here would be that there is no difference in the mean depression level of those exposed to both the drug and therapy combination versus those exposed to therapy alone. The alternative hypothesis would be that there is a difference between these two means.[14] A type I error would occur if we reject the assumption that there is no difference when, in fact, there really isn't one between the two means. A type II error would occur if we failed to reject the assumption of no difference when, in fact, there really is a difference between the two averages. Now recall the damned-if-you-do-damned-if-you-don't dilemma.

If we lower the chance of a type I error here, then we raise the chance of a type II error; and, if we lower the chance of a type II error, then we raise the chance of a type I error. This takes us into why consideration of type I and II errors is important. Ask yourself what's worse: concluding that a drug–therapy combination isn't effective when it really is (type II error) or assuming that it's effective when it really isn't (type I error). I've been told that all drugs have side effects, and some can be quite dangerous. This is something we should consider as we think about which type of error, I or II, would be worse in this context. If we assume that a type II error would be worse, we should lower that error which, because of the (1 −*ProbII*) difference, would automatically increase statistical power. And statisticians have shown that one of the ways to lower the probability of type II error—and thereby increase statistical power—is by selecting large samples.

In general, the importance of type I and II errors is that, if we take them seriously, we're forced to think about what's at stake in what we're studying, as well as how to make adjustments in the types of errors we might make given what's at stake. Those not conducting the studies but instead reading or hearing about those conducted by others would still do well to think about all this. That is, the next time you read or hear about a study someone has conducted, you might want to ask yourself the following questions:

1. What was the null hypothesis?
2. What was the alternative hypothesis?
3. What would a type I error mean in this context?
4. What would a type II error mean in this context?
5. Which would be worse in this context, a type I or II error?
6. Was the sample size big enough to detect an effect of interest (that is, was the chance of type II error low enough)?

I'm not suggesting that you think about these questions because you'll be able to answer all of them. The exercise of considering these questions serves another purpose—helping you review studies you've read or hear about with a "critical ear and eye." There are a lot of studies out there making all kinds of claims. Critically thinking about questions such as these may help inoculate you against a great deal of nonsense "dressed up" as science.

The question of what's involved in trying to estimate causal effects on the basis of observational data is receiving a great deal of attention these days. Two highly regarded books that address this topic are *Counterfactuals and Causal Inference: Methods and Principles for Social Research* by Stephen L. Morgan and Christopher Winship and *Causality* by Judea Pearl. Both of these books are probably tough going for someone unfamiliar with statistics beyond the level of this chapter. But if you have the appropriate background and want to learn more about statistics and causality, these would be excellent places to start.

ESTIMATES OF CAUSAL EFFECTS

I said earlier that you can take the difference between the outcome of a person who received the intervention of interest and one who didn't receive it to estimate the difference between the outcome of a person under the condition that they received the intervention and the outcome *for that same person* under the condition that they didn't receive it. But this isn't typically how researchers estimate causal effects. If the outcome variable is ratio or interval, and confounding is believed to have been addressed, they usually estimate the causal effect of interest by calculating the difference between the averages of the two groups. That is, they calculate the difference $\text{Average}_{\text{group which received intervention}} - \text{Average}_{\text{group which didn't receive intervention}}$.

For example, let's go back to that parenting skills training class. We could compute the average for the groups of parents who received the training, obtaining $\text{Average}_{\text{group which received training}}$. Suppose this equals 20 units. Assume that $\text{Average}_{\text{group which didn't received training}} = 12$. The estimate of the causal effect of the parenting skills class would be 8 units. If the probability of obtaining a difference of at least 8 units—assuming there really is no effect of the training skills class—is low enough (usually less than 5%), the typical researcher would conclude that the training class has a statistically significant effect on parenting skills. If a difference of 8 units is regarded as substantively significant, this finding might justify investing the resources required to provide more parents with skills training. So, in addition to making a social justice argument for investing more resources in such training, such a finding might ground an evidence-informed argument as well.

When the outcome of interest is nominal or ordinal, researchers tend to estimate causal effects by calculating differences between proportions or percentages. Suppose we're interested in the causal effect of poverty on the probability of neglecting one's child. Let Percentage$_{\text{neglect for poor parents}}$ be the percentage of those parents who are poor (the "intervention group" in this context) who've neglected their kids and Percentage$_{\text{neglect for non-poor parents}}$ be that same percentage for those parents who aren't poor. The difference Percentage$_{\text{neglect for poor parents}}$ − Percentage$_{\text{neglect for non-poor parents}}$ would be the estimate of the causal effect of poverty on probability of neglect.

Suppose Percentage$_{\text{neglect for poor parents}}$ = 10% and Percentage$_{\text{neglect for non-poor parents}}$ = 1%. Then the difference Percentage$_{\text{neglect for poor parents}}$ − Percentage$_{\text{neglect for non-poor parents}}$ = 10% − 1% = 9 percentage points. This difference would be the estimate of the causal effect of poverty on chance of neglect, assuming all concerns about confounding have been addressed. If a 9 percentage point difference is regarded as statistically and, more importantly, substantively significant, we might be able to buttress a social justice argument for addressing poverty reduction among adults by highlighting it as part of a strategy for promoting the well-being of our children as well.

I think I've now arrived at the point where enough has been said about basic statistics. My intention, obviously, hasn't been to turn readers into statisticians. Instead, I've attempted to provide an overview of statistical reasoning, as well as how probability theory enters into that reasoning. Having done so, I can now turn to the topic of the next, and final, chapter of this book: the mathematics of political and social decisions.

NOTES

1. When I use the term "measurement" in this chapter, I'll have in mind the representational theory of measurement. See Chapter 3 for an overview of this conception of measurement.

2. There are techniques which have been developed for probability samples that aren't random samples, but I won't cover those in this book. If you're interested, any book on sampling theory will cover them.

3. See Westfall and Henning (2013).

4. I'm assuming here what statisticians call a *two-tailed* hypothesis test. So, when I say "at least as extreme as" I mean at least as extreme as in terms of absolute value. Thus, if I were to obtain a test statistic p value of −2.00, everything I've said earlier would still apply because the absolute value of −2.00 is 2.00.

5. Some of the details regarding how this translation is carried out can be found in advanced statistics texts such as Westfall and Henning (2013).

6. Here "or" is being used in its exclusive sense. That is, it means "one or the other but not both."

7. The "4.3% ± Error" notation is actually a variation on the "Measured value – Error" expression from Chapter 3, where "4.3" is playing the role of "Measured value" and "Error" is playing the role of "Error." The Error being referred to in the "Measured value – Error" expression can be positive or negative. If it's negative, we'd get Measured value – (–Error) = Measured value + Error, which would correspond to 4.3% + Error. If it's positive, we'd get Measured value – Error, which would correspond to 4.3% –Error.

8. This isn't the same as type I or II error, concepts I said I'd come back to later.

9. This perspective on causality is also called the *potential outcomes* view because $Outcome_i(Int = 1)$ and $Outcome_i(Int = 0)$ are the outcomes that could potentially be observed depending on the intervention i is exposed to.

10. From an ethical point of view, it's better for members of the control group to receive the best available intervention other than the one being studied.

11. See Cancian et al., *The Effect of Family Income on Risk of Child Matreatment*.

12. See Vanderwheele (2015).

13. See Chapter 5 for a discussion of marginal tax rates.

14. Since I'm assuming a two-tailed test, the alternative hypothesis states that there is a difference between the two averages. It's silent about the direction of that difference (whether one mean is larger or smaller than the other).

9

THE MATHEMATICS OF POLITICAL AND SOCIAL DECISIONS

AT THIS WRITING, Donald Trump is President of the United States, after winning a controversial and bitterly contested election against Hillary Rodham Clinton. Yet, even though Trump won the election, Clinton won more votes than he did. This sounds like a contradiction, but if you understand the mathematics of how the United States elects its presidents, you'll know it isn't one at all.

Also at the time of this writing, the United States is about 3 years from the point when another constitutionally required census of its entire population must be conducted. From a political point of view, the census is extremely important because it helps determine the number of congressional seats a given state will receive in the US House of Representatives. What you may not know is that some fairly involved mathematics goes into determining such a number.

Redistricting is the political process in which states draw the lines of voting districts that will elect members of the US House of Representatives. A perennial issue regarding these districts is whether they're unconstitutionally drawn in such a way that they disadvantage voters of a specific political party, a phenomenon known as *gerrymandering*. What you may not be aware of is the fact that a measure called *the efficiency gap*, which we'll discuss in this chapter, is at the heart of this issue. You can think of the efficiency gap as a measure of when the drawing of a Congressional district has gone too far in disadvantaging a political party.

You're aware, no doubt, about the problem of global climate change. The average temperature of the Earth has been warming for some time now, and the overwhelming majority of climate scientists believe this is due to increased carbon emissions from human activities. There are a number of things we can do to address this problem, although they involve some difficult political and social decisions. What you may not be aware of is the fact that a branch of mathematics called *game theory*, the quantitative aspects of social decision-making, can help illuminate the nature of these political and social choices.

This chapter will explore the mathematics of situations like these. We'll start with how the United States chooses its president.

HOW THE UNITED STATES CHOOSES A PRESIDENT

As I said earlier, Donald Trump became President of the United States after a bitterly contested election. He won 306 electoral votes to Clinton's 232. Yet Clinton won almost 66 million popular votes to Trump's almost 63 million.[1] So, in a sense, Clinton won the election even though she lost it. What's going on here? The answer has to do with the mathematics of how the United States chooses a president. The first step in understanding this is understanding what *electoral votes* are.

The United States is made up of 50 states plus the District of Columbia (or Washington, DC). According to the US Constitution, each state is awarded a number of electoral votes in presidential elections, which depends, in part, on how many members of the US House of Representatives (the House) a state has. And the number of members a state has in the House depends on that state's overall population. More populous states have more members representing them in the House and, therefore, are entitled to more electoral votes. Even though Washington, DC, isn't a state, the United States doesn't want to completely disenfranchise its residents; so it's allotted three electoral votes. This system of electoral voting is called the *Electoral College*.

The total number of electoral votes allotted to the 50 states plus Washington, DC, is 538. In order to become president, a candidate must receive a majority of these 538 electoral votes. Since half of 538 is 269, a candidate needs at least 270 electoral votes to become president. Since Trump received 306 electoral votes, he won the presidency by a pretty comfortable margin.

I said earlier that the number of electoral votes a state receives depends, *in part*, on the number of members it has in the House because a state is also allotted two electoral votes for the two members it has in the US Senate. This is thought to address the fact that allocating electoral votes solely on the basis of the number of members a state has in the House would disadvantage less populous states.

How does the popular vote play into all this? When a US presidential election occurs, it isn't really one national election, although that's often how it's portrayed; instead, it's 50 state elections and one Washington, DC, election. In all states except Maine and Nebraska, this is how these elections work.

In each state, the winner of most of the popular votes in that state gets to receive *all* that state's electoral votes; this is known as a *winner-take-all* system. For example, Hilary Clinton received more popular votes in New York than did Donald Trump, but he received more popular votes in Alabama than she did. New York is allotted 29 electoral votes, while Alabama is allotted 9 of them.[2] So, Clinton received all 29 of New York's electoral votes, contributing to her total of 232, while Trump received all 9 of Alabama's, contributing to his total of 306. So, even though popular vote totals don't directly decide presidential elections since only the number of electoral votes received does, popular votes do have an indirect effect on the outcomes of such elections because they do affect electoral vote totals.[3]

You might be wondering at this point how Clinton could win the popular vote but lose the election. This has only happened a few times in US history, most recently (before the Trump–Clinton adventure) during the 2000 election between George W. Bush and Al Gore. *Electoral vote–popular vote splits*, which is what these episodes are sometimes called, tend to happen in very close elections, as was the case in Trump versus Clinton. Also, Clinton tended to do well in populous states, like New York and California, while Trump tended to do better in less populous ones in the South and Midwest. So, when Clinton won a big state like California or gained a lot of popular votes in a big one she lost, like Texas, this tended to run up her popular vote total. But, because of the winner-take-all system of electoral votes, all Trump had to do to offset Clinton's popular vote advantage was win enough popular votes in enough relatively small states to win *all* those states' electoral votes. And that's exactly what he did.

A number of people have called for the abolition of the Electoral College and want to see it replaced with popular vote elections of US presidents. One of the main reasons for this opposition is what we've already been discussing—it's possible for someone to win the presidency even though they received fewer popular votes. This is sometimes referred to as the problem of electing a *minority president*. A minority president is one who won the office even though they didn't receive a majority of the popular votes cast in the election.

A president assuming office even though they received fewer popular votes than the loser isn't the only way the United States could end up with a minority president. Another way this could happen is when there are more than two candidates running for president.

During the presidential election of 2017, there were actually four candidates: Donald Trump, Hillary Clinton, Jill Stein, and Gary Johnson. Neither Stein nor Johnson received enough popular votes to win the electoral votes of a state (remember that most states have winner-take-all systems), so neither was really a factor in the Electoral College math. But, in theory, there could be a race with three or more candidates in which each one of them received enough popular votes to win several states' electoral votes, but no candidate received a majority of the popular or electoral votes cast. If this were to happen, then, according to the provisions of the 12th Amendment to the US Constitution, the US House of Representatives would choose the president from among the three candidates who received the largest number of electoral votes.[4] This would automatically mean we'd end up with a minority president.

A third way the United States could end up with a minority president is if there were three or more candidates and one of them won enough states to receive at least the required 270 electoral votes, although they didn't received a majority of the overall popular votes cast. This is how Bill Clinton won the presidency in 1992 against George H. W. Bush and Ross Perot when he received only 43% of the popular vote but 370 electoral votes.[5]

Another criticism of the Electoral College focuses squarely on the winner-take-all aspects of the system. The contention is that this disadvantages "third-party" candidates because, even though a significant number of voters in a given state might vote for such a candidate, those votes would be wasted if, due to the winner-take-all system, that candidate didn't receive any electoral votes from that state. This, the criticism goes, effectively disenfranchises the supporters of third-party candidates.

In order for the Electoral College to be abolished, the US Constitution would have to be changed. And this can be done in only two ways. One is by at least two-thirds of state legislatures calling for a Constitutional Convention. States would send representatives to this convention, and they would hammer out some new method of electing US presidents. The other way the Constitution can be changed is itself a two-step process. First, at least two-thirds of the House as well as the Senate must vote in favor of the proposed amendment. Second, at least three-quarters of state legislatures must ratify this congressional vote. Notice that both methods for amending the US Constitution involve states in the process. And this raises a problem for those who want to get rid of the Electoral College.

If the US elected presidents by popular vote, then the advantage of states with larger populations would grow. In fact, presidential candidates might decide to ignore small rural areas entirely, focusing instead on winning votes in states with densely populated areas like New York and California. Supporters of the Electoral College argue that this wouldn't be fair to less populous states. Yet opponents of the Electoral College rebut by arguing that it already gives smaller states too much voting power. To understand what they mean, consider an (updated) example discussed in Bennett and Briggs's (2008) book on applications of mathematics.

California has a population of about 39,000,000 people and it's been allotted 55 electoral votes.[6] Wyoming has a population of about 585,500 and it has 3 electoral votes.[7] Bennett and Briggs measure the electoral power of a state by dividing its population by the number of electoral votes it has. So, California's electoral power would be

$$\frac{35,000,000}{55} = 636,364$$

And Wyoming's would be

$$\frac{585,500}{3} = 195,167$$

So each electoral vote in California represents about 636,000 people and each one in Wyoming represents about 195,000 persons. Since in California one electoral vote has to be "spread" over more people than is the case in Wyoming, the power of voters in California is more "diluted" than is the case in Wyoming. That is, each voter, on a voting resident per electoral vote basis, has more power in Wyoming than in California.

A supporter of the Electoral College could respond that measuring electoral power this way is misleading. They might argue that what matters isn't the number of voters represented by each electoral vote but the probability that a state will be decisive in determining the outcome of a presidential election. And this depends on the number of electoral votes a state has divided by the total number of electoral votes. California's 55 electoral votes make up about 10% of all such votes (55/538 = .10, which is 10% when multiplied by 100) while Wyoming's 3 make up about .6% of the total of 538 electoral votes (3/538 = .006, which is .6% when multiplied by 100). So, in a close election, California appears to have a better chance, with its 10% of electoral votes, in swinging the election its way than Wyoming does with its 3.

The point of this book isn't to convince you that the United States should keep or scrap the Electoral College. Just notice all the math involved. As I write these lines, Donald Trump is a very controversial president. Clinton argued that Trump was unfit to serve, and many agreed with her, although, of course, his supporters didn't. But regardless of what was said before the election, he's now in office because of some mathematics the Founding Fathers came up with more than 200 years ago.

DEMOCRACY AND MAJORITY RULE

The United States is often called a *representative democracy*. This is a system where people vote for others to represent them in legislative bodies, such as the Senate, House of Representatives, the City Council, and the like. The folks who make up these bodies are the one who directly enact laws and policies, instead of the citizens who voted for them. If you're a US voter, you don't have to consider federal budget proposals and vote on them when they come before the Senate. You leave that to your Senator, although you might decide to lobby your representative every now and then.

Another form of democracy is *direct democracy*. This is a system in which people do consider public policies, as well as vote on them, instead of having representatives do it for them. Even though the United States is considered a representative democracy, there are instances of direct democracy as well. For example, California has been known for its system of propositions where residents can vote directly on policy questions. One of its most famous such votes was back in 1978. This was when almost two-thirds of voters supported Proposition 13, a plan to substantially decrease California's property tax rates.

But whether we're talking about representative or direct democracy, people often associate democracy with *simple majority rule*. Simple majority rule means that candidates can win an election as long as they receive more than 50% of the votes cast. When US citizens elect senators and members of the House, or state and city residents elect their public officials, those who win these elections usually receive a simple majority of the votes cast, at least if we're talking about general elections as opposed to primaries. But democracies don't have to be based on simple majority rule.

For example, we saw already that one way to amend the US Constitution requires at least two-thirds of the votes in both the House and Senate, as well as ratification by at least three-quarters of the states. For many acts of the House and Senate, it takes a simple majority to send a bill to the President. But if the President vetoes it, at least two-thirds of each chamber of Congress is required to override it. Two-thirds is about 66%, so it takes more than a simple majority (slightly more than

50%) to override a president's veto. When it takes more than a simple majority to win something, we say that winning requires a *super majority*.

Another variation on democracy, which doesn't involve majority rule, is called *plurality voting*. In plurality voting, the winner is the one who receives the most votes, even if they don't receive a majority of the votes cast. For example, consider a local community organization which is holding an election to see who'll become its president. Three people are running: Buffy, Angel, and Willow. Suppose Buffy receives 30% of the vote, Angel also receives 30%, and Willow receives 40%. If the rules of the election stipulate that all a candidate needs to win is a plurality of the votes cast, then Willow would become president, since she received a higher percentage and, therefore, a higher absolute number, of the votes cast.

Parliamentary systems depart even more from simple majorities. These are systems in which people vote for parties instead of candidates, even though candidates represent parties. The proportion of seats in a legislative body that the party gets to fill depends on the proportion of overall votes that party received in the election.

Consider Buffy, Angel, and Willow again. This time they're representing their parties in an election for seats in parliament. Since Buffy and Angel each received 30% of the vote, their parties would each be granted 30% of the seats in parliament. Willow's party would be granted 40% of the seats. You don't hear much about proportional representation in the United States, but there are those who think such a system would be more democratic than the current US system. The reasoning here is that proportional representation "makes more room" for third, fourth, fifth parties.

Under proportional representation, political parties that receive a relatively small proportion of the overall votes cast are still entitled to representation in the legislative body. But if a Democrat, Republican, Socialist, and Libertarian from a given state were running for the US Senate, and the Democrat received 51% of the vote, the Republican 40%, the Libertarian 5%, and the Socialist 4%, the Democrat would win the seat, while the other three parties would gain no seats. So supporters of these three parties would have no representation in the Senate except to the extent that the Democrat chose to represent them.

I've spent a fair amount of time in this section discussing how voting works in the US Congress. What I haven't said much about is how members of Congress, particularly members of the House, get there in the first place. I'm not talking about the fact that voters must elect them. I'm talking, instead, about how it is that voters, in a given state, get the right to send a certain number of members to the House of Representatives. This is the topic of *apportionment*.

APPORTIONMENT

Article I, Section 2, Clause 3 of the US Constitution reads as follows:

> Representatives and direct taxes shall be apportioned among the several states which may be included within this Union, according to their respective Numbers, which shall be determined by adding to the whole number of free Persons, including those bound to service for a Term of Years, and excluding Indians not taxed, three fifths of all other Persons. The actual Enumeration shall be made within three Years after the first Meeting of the Congress of the United States, and within every subsequent Term of ten Years, in such Manner as they shall by Law direct. The Number of Representatives shall not exceed one for every thirty Thousand, but each State shall have at least one Representative. . . .[8]

In an attempt to translate this bit of eighteenth-century English, the provision is saying that states are granted the right to send members to the US House of Representatives. The number of members each state is allowed to send depends a state's population, and states' populations will be counted every 10 years. An enslaved person, however, would only be counted as three-fifths of a person, and an Indian wouldn't be counted at all. Thankfully, things have changed since then, with slavery being illegal; blacks being regarded, "on paper at least," as full persons; and "Indians" being fully counted. This decennial count of state populations is called a *census*.

The provision of the US Constitution referred to here contains two important constraints. It stipulates that each state must get least one seat in the House, but also that it can get no more than one seat for every 30,000 state residents. The task of allocating seats in the House to all states, depending on their populations, so that the allocation in question meets these constraints is called *apportionment*.

Although the US Constitution is clear that apportionment must occur, it leaves out something very important: how should it be done? It was left to the Founding Fathers, as well as others, to fill this vacuum, and, over the course of the nation's history, several methods have been proposed. Going through a couple of these is instructive because it clearly shows another link between mathematics and political power.

From a mathematical point of view, apportionment "is the problem of dividing up a fixed number of things among groups of different sizes."[9] Any apportionment process is governed by the following rules:

1. The items being divided can only occur in whole numbers.
2. All of the items being divided must be used up in the process.
3. Each group must receive at least one of the items being divided.

4. The number of items allocated to each group depends on a group's population, in the sense that the larger the population, the larger the number of items allocated to that group

Applying all this to the apportionment problem for the US House of Representatives, we get the following:

1. The fixed whole number of items allocated is 435.
2. All 435 seats must be apportioned in some way.
3. Each state must receive at least one seat.
4. The larger a state's population, the greater the number of seats it receives.

One of the earlier methods of apportionment used in the United States was Alexander Hamilton's (the one who's the subject of a very popular Broadway play). Hamilton's method requires the following steps:

1. Divide the total population of all the states by the total number of representatives in the House (435 these days). The result is called the *divisor*.
2. Divide each state's population by the divisor. The number you end up with is called the state's *quota*.
3. Drop the numbers to the right of the decimal point for any quota which isn't a whole number.
4. Calculate the sum of the whole numbers left after the numbers to the right of their decimal points have been removed (this sum will always be less than or equal to the total number of seats).
5. If the sum from step 4 is less than the required number of seats, assign one seat each to those states whose numbers to the right of their decimal points were biggest.

To see how Hamilton's method works in practice, let's apply it to a fictional country with just three states. These states appear in the table, along with their corresponding populations:

State	Population	Quotas	Whole Number Versions of Quotas
Sunnydale	160,417	8.664295	8
Stars Hollow	565,302	30.532571	30
Bedrock	200,017	10.803134	10
Totals	925,736		48

Suppose that the House of Representatives in this country has 50 seats. Following step 1 of Hamilton's method, we'd divide 925,736 by 50, obtaining 18,514.72. This result is our divisor. If we divide the populations of each state by the divisor (step 2), we get the quotas in column three of the table. If we follow Hamilton's step 3 and drop the decimal parts of the quotas, we get the first three entries in the last column of the table. Following step 4 of Hamilton's method gives us the total in the column.

So, Sunnydale would start out with 8 seats, Stars Hollow would get 30, and Bedrock would get 10. Since this only comes out to 48, there are two seats left to assign. Sunnydale and Bedrock have the two largest numbers after the decimal points in their quotas, so they each get assigned another seat (step 5 of Hamilton's method). Therefore, Sunnydale ends up with 9 seats, Stars Hollow with 30, and Bedrock with 11.

Hamilton's method used to be one of choice in the United States, but it isn't any longer. The main reason is that it's subject to the so-called *apportionment paradoxes*. One such paradox is the *Alabama paradox*.

The Alabama paradox occurs when (1) there is an increase in the number of seats apportioned, (2) there is no change in the overall population, and (3) at least one state loses at least one seat. This happened to Rhode Island after the 1870 census and to Alabama after the 1880 one.

The Alabama paradox isn't the only one Hamilton's method is vulnerable to. Another is the *population paradox*. When more House seats, due to population growth, are allocated among states, faster growing populations ought to be the ones to gain seats at the cost of slower growing ones; at least, this is what most in the business regard as fair. Yet, under Hamilton's method, it's possible for slower growing states to gain seats at the cost of faster growing ones. This is the population paradox.

The current method of apportionment used in the United States is called the *Huntington-Hill method*, named after statistician Joseph Hill and mathematician Edward Huntington. The steps involved in the Huntington-Hill method are similar, in some ways, to those in Hamilton's. The main difference has to do with how Huntington-Hill addresses the problem of ending up with quotas that aren't whole numbers. Unlike Hamilton, they address this by drawing on the *geometric means* of states' quotas (after the numbers to the right of the decimal points of these quotas have been dropped).

Suppose the whole number version of a state's quota were n. Then the geometric mean of that's state's quota would $\sqrt{n} * (n + 1)$. So, if a state's quota were 10, then the geometric mean for that state would be $\sqrt{10} * (11)$, which is about 10.5.

I've been talking so far about how the United States decides the number of seats a state gets in the House of Representatives. I haven't said much about how members of the House are voted into office. This, too, involves math, and not just because it involves counting votes. In order for states to elect representatives to the House, they first have to draw the lines of state Congressional districts. This is because people who run for the House have to be elected by the voters in these districts. The problem of how to draw them is a source of bitter legal and political battles. As I write these lines, a fair amount of mathematics has entered those battles.

THE MATH OF GERRYMANDERING

In the previous section, the focus was on the apportionment of seats in the House. When people run for the House, voters in specific districts within their states must elect them. After every decennial US census, states must redraw the lines or boundaries of their districts. This process is called *redistricting*, and it is controlled by elected officials in a given state. So, if elected officials in a state are heavily Democrat or Republican, then the Democrats or Republican officials in that state will control the redistricting process. This makes that process very political. Perhaps the biggest political issue raised by redistricting is *gerrymandering*.

Gerrymandering occurs when elected officials in a state from a particular party use their control of the process to draw district boundaries which disadvantage members of the other party. This can be done pretty easily because there is so much data on the demographic composition of neighborhoods, as well as voting patterns by race, ethnicity, education level, and the like. So, all a party has to do is draw district boundaries to dilute or concentrate certain demographic groups in such a way that the opposing party is disadvantaged. For example, black voters tend to vote for Democrats. So Republican Party officials in a given state might draw districts in such a way that black voters are concentrated in a few districts. This might almost assure that Democrats will win these districts, but the bulk of the state's districts, made up of more white voters, are more likely to be won by Republican candidates. If Democrats were in power, they could do the same to disadvantage Republican candidates.

The game of drawing districts to advantage one party or the other is perfectly legal up to a point. The question, one US courts have been addressing for some time, is where's that point? This is where math enters the picture.

The math I have in mind is a measure called the *efficiency gap*, developed by Nicholas Stephanopoulos and Eric McGhee.[10] It measures how votes wasted by those supporting one party compare to those wasted by those supporting another one. In the form of an equation, the efficiency gap is

$$\text{Efficiency Gap} = \frac{\textit{Total \# Democratic votes wasted} - \textit{Total \# of Republican votes wasted}}{\textit{Total \# of votes cast}}$$

To calculate this, you first take the difference between Democratic and Republican votes wasted in each district. You next take the sum of these differences. Finally, you divide this sum by the total number of votes cast.

You might be wondering what a wasted vote is. According to Nicholas Stephanopoulos and Eric McGhee, a vote can be wasted in two ways: (1) it's expended on a losing candidate, and (2) it exceeds the number of votes a candidate needs to win. To understand these two conditions, considering the following example.

Instead of using real US districts, which would require dealing with some pretty big numbers, I'll use a smaller scale example that will simulate what goes on in the real world. Suppose Buffy, a Democrat, and Faith, a Republican, are running for office; there are five districts in a given state; and 100 voters in each district.[11] The following table contains the numbers we'll need to calculate the efficiency gap for this state:

District	Buffy Votes	Faith Votes	Buffy Votes Wasted	Faith Votes Wasted	Total # Democratic votes wasted – Total # of Republican votes wasted = $(135 - 110) = 25$
1	60	40	9	40	Efficiency Gap = 25/500 = .05
2	60	40	9	40	
3	41	59	41	8	
4	30	70	30	19	
5	46	54	46	3	
Total	237	263	135	110	

Take a look at the first line of the table. In District 1, Buffy receives 60 votes and Faith receives 40. So, Buffy wins the district, and, since she'd only have needed 51 votes to win, 9 votes are wasted on her; this is why 9 appears in the fourth column. Since Faith lost in this district, all 40 votes expended on her are wasted; this is why 40 appears in column five.

In columns 4 and 5 of the row labeled "Total," we see the total number of Democratic (column 4) and Republican (column 5) votes wasted. In column 6 of that row we see that the Democratic candidate wasted 25 more votes than the Republican candidate. Right beneath that difference, we see the efficiency gap of .05. How do we interpret this quantity?

If there were no, or a small, efficiency gap, the number of votes wasted by Democrats would equal, or be close to, the number wasted by Republicans. This means the numerator of the efficiency gap would be 0 or close to it, and, therefore, so would the efficiency gap. According to its developers, the bigger the gap, the stronger the case for gerrymandering. This is because the bigger the gap, the more votes being wasted by Democrats compared to Republicans. When Democrats are either almost all bunched into Democratic districts where many of their votes won't be needed for the Democrat to win (wasted votes) or in districts where they're small minorities competing against Republican majorities (more wasted votes), there will be a large efficiency gap.

Now here's a question: is a gap of .05 big or small? That is, how much of a gap must there be before there is unconstitutional gerrymandering? These are questions US courts will answer as cases come before them where the efficiency gap figures prominently. In the meantime, you can appreciate the role played by mathematics regarding another social issue.

SOME PROBLEMS OF DEMOCRACY

The World War II British leader Winston Churchill is claimed to have said that "democracy is the worse form of government except for all those other forms that have been tried from time to time." Mathematicians, along with quantitative social scientists, have found that the current practice of democracy in much of the United States does have its problems.

One that has received a fair amount of attention by economists is that, by focusing on how many people vote for a candidate, democracy takes no account of the intensity of preference for or against a candidate. Consider the following example.

Suppose Niklaus Michalson is running for the US House of Representatives and ends up winning with 54% of the popular vote. The 46% of voters who cast their ballots against Michalson absolutely despise him. The 54% who voted for him don't despise him, but they don't love him either. In fact, they're pretty lukewarm toward Michalson but think he'd be a little better in office than his opponent would be. Just counting votes to determine who wins an election only accounts for direction of preference; it completely ignores the strength of voters' preferences.

Part of the reason intensity of voting preference is ignored is, no doubt, because how much or little someone likes someone else is not that easy to observe. We could ask people about this, but, depending on the incentives they face for telling the truth, they might misrepresent their true preferences. One way to allow voters to express the intensity of their preferences, at least to some degree, is through the use of *cumulative voting*.

Brams and Taylor (1996) define cumulative voting as a "system in which each voter is given a fixed number of votes to distribute among one or more candidates." Suppose, in a given election, this fixed number is 8 votes and there are 12 candidates running for office. A voter would be allowed to divide their 8 votes among the 12 candidates in any way they wanted to. So, the more a voter preferred a candidate, the more of their 8 votes they could "spend" on that candidate. If we were talking about an election for 8 seats in the House, then the candidates who received the 8 highest numbers of votes would win those 8 seats. In general, if there were *n* seats (where *n* can be any integer greater than or equal to 1), the candidates (or candidate) with the highest *n* numbers (or number) of votes would win those seats (or that seat).

GAME THEORY AND SOCIAL DECISIONS

Social workers are, in a sense, experts in social interaction. We interact with people in order to help them in various ways—at least that's what we tell ourselves. We also try to understand the nature of social interactions because we think doing so will make us better helpers. What we don't hear much about in social work, though, is the fact that mathematicians and economists have come up with a way of representing social interactions which can illuminate a number of issues facing us as a society. That way is called *game theory*.

Game theory can be thought of as a branch of applied mathematics that's used for modeling how human beings interact with one another when those interactions take place under certain conditions.[12] It focuses specifically on how people make decisions when their goal is to get what they want, the degree to which they're able to get what they want depends on what at least one other person does, they're aware of this dependence, and this dependence influences what they ultimately decide to do.

Game theory can be used to understand why governments finance child protection services, why it's so hard to address global climate change, and a host of other social issues. In game theory, there are paradigmatic models of social interaction called *games*. The ones we'll meet later are the *tragedy of the commons, the assurance game*, and *the prisoner's dilemma*. In order to understand the "setup" of a given game, there are four things we need to know about that game.

First, who are the decision-makers in the game? Second, what courses of actions are available to them? What are the payoffs in the game? What information is available to the game's players (Heap Hollis, et al., 1992)? I should say bit more about the third and fourth questions.

Regarding the third one, the players in any game will have outcomes they want to attain and some they'd rather avoid. Think of the outcomes they want to attain as *benefits* and those they'd like to avoid as *costs*. You can think of these costs and benefits as having the appropriate units of measurement associated with them depending on the nature of the game in question. The net benefit of a decision would be the difference between benefits and costs or

Net benefit = benefit − cost

Let's assume that both benefits and costs can be any number greater than or equal to 0. This would mean the net benefit could be positive, negative, or 0, depending on whether benefits exceeded costs, were less than costs, or equaled costs, respectively. Having said this, you can think of a player's payoff from a given decision in a given game as the net benefit to that player which results from that decision combined with those made by the game's other players. I'll assume, as is typically done in game theory, that a player will choose that course of action associated with the largest payoff.

When it comes to the fourth condition, the games we'll discuss assume *each* player is informed about the possible actions that *all* other players can choose from. To be a bit more precise about this, let's use some set theory.

Suppose a game has two players, player 1 and 2. Suppose S_1 is the set of actions that player one can choose from, and S_2 is the set player 2 can choose from. When it comes to the fourth assumption, as applied to this game, we're saying that players 1 and 2 are both aware of the elements (that is, possible actions) in S_1 and S_2. All of this should become clear as we discuss some examples of games. Let's begin by discussing a concept related to game theory called *collective action problems*.

GAME THEORY AND COLLECTIVE ACTION PROBLEMS

The games we'll discuss in this section have one thing in common: they all represent situations where players are driven to behave in ways that seem to be the best courses of action from their individual points of view but which end up being pretty bad for the set of players as a whole. These types of situations are referred to as *collective action problems*. The first one we'll discuss is the *prisoner's dilemma*.

Suppose two men suspected of having been involved in a serious crime are being questioned separately by the police. The police tell each man that they know both of them were involved in the serious crime but don't have enough evidence to convict them. They also tell both suspects that they know the two of them were involved in a less serious crime and that they do have enough evidence to convict each of them of this minor infraction. Each suspect is offered the following deal.

If one of them confesses but the other doesn't, the one who confesses will be freed, while the one who didn't will be sentenced to 10 years in prison. If neither of them confesses, both will do 1 year in prison for the minor offense. If both of them confess to the more serious crime, they will each do 3 years, as opposed to 10, as a reward for their cooperation. Assuming each of the two men would rather do less time in prison than more time, they'd both be better off if they both kept quiet. What we'll find out, however, is that each man is under tremendous pressure to confess. To see this, take a look at the following table:

		Suspect 2's possible actions	
		Confess	Don't Confess
Suspect 1's possible actions	Confess	3, 3	0, 10
	Don't Confess	10, 0	1, 1

Tables like this appear frequently in the game theory literature. They clearly show the players, their possible courses of action, and the payoffs associated with those actions. Suspect 1's payoffs are listed first, suspect 2's second. And remember, we're assuming that each player in this game is informed about the set of possible actions available to the other player. Let's consider the table from suspect 1's point of view.

Suppose suspect 2 confesses. If suspect 1 confesses, too, they'll both end up in prison for 3 years. But if suspect 1 doesn't confess, he'll end up doing 10 years, while suspect 2 will do no time at all. So, if suspect 2 confesses, suspect 1 will be better off be confessing as well.

Now suppose suspect 2 doesn't confess. If suspect 1 confesses, he'll end up a free man, but, if he doesn't confess, he'll end up doing a year in prison. So, if suspect 2 doesn't confess, suspect 1 is still better off confessing. In other words, no matter what suspect 2 does, suspect 1 is better off confessing than not.

It can be shown that suspect 2 faces the same situation as suspect 1. That is, no matter what suspect 1 does, suspect 2 is better off confessing. We see from the table that if both suspects confess, they each get 3 years in prison. But if each man could have kept his mouth shut, each one would have gotten only a year in prison. So we have a situation where each person doing what's in their best interest *from their individual points of view* results in an outcome which is worse for both of them. Many social scientists think the prisoners' dilemma is a pretty good model for representing a number of real-world interactions.

One of the hallmarks of societies, as well as collective projects of various kinds, is that those involved in them must cooperate with one another. What's meant by "cooperate" will vary depending on the nature of the project in question. What the prisoners' dilemma game forces us to think about is the possibility that the incentive structure regarding some collective project may mean that each person involved in the project is under tremendous pressure not to cooperate, no matter what others involved do. To take an example, consider child welfare.

As you may know, efforts to protect the welfare of children, other than what parents and private citizens do, are typically financed by governments, usually state or local governments. Governments may contract with private organizations to have them directly provide child welfare services, but, in these arrangements, governments are still the ones "coughing up the cash." Why is this the case? Perhaps the prisoners' dilemma provides the answer.

Imagine the government in a given locality decided not to finance child protection services. Instead, it decided this should be left to "the free market." A company, Child Protection Inc., comes along and says that it will protect all the locality's children, as long as each resident pays a monthly fee to the company. This fee would be used to hire workers, purchase other materials required to protect children, rent office space, and the like. The fee would also be high enough to provide the company with a profit for doing this important work. Now here's the question: assuming all residents of this area prefer that children be protected from harm, do you think all or most of them would willingly pay the fee? A game theorist might answer "no." Here's why.

From the point of view of *each* resident, they're like one of the prisoners in the prisoner's dilemma. If everyone else pays the fee (what "cooperation" means in this setting), but a given resident doesn't, that resident can benefit from knowing child protection will be provided even though they didn't have to pay for it. If everyone else doesn't pay the fee, this resident is better of not paying, too, assuming they don't want to be a "loser" and end up paying the fee when no one else does. So, no matter what everyone else does, this resident is better off not paying the fee.

I'll refer to not paying the fee as the *free rider* move. But here's the problem: if everyone (or almost everyone) reasons like this resident does, no one (or almost no one) will pay the fee. And if too few people pay the fee, Child Protection Inc. won't be able to get the resources it needs to do its work, and, if it can't get those resources, that work won't get done. So, even though everyone, or almost everyone, wants children protected, there is a powerful incentive for them to choose a course of action which results in this not happening.

Notice the similarity between this situation and the prisoner's dilemma. As I said earlier, an individual resident is like one of the prisoners. Everyone else plays the role of the other prisoner. Paying the fee is like refusing to confess, while not paying the fee is like confessing. If everyone pays, they get to receive child protection services; this is like both prisoners refusing to confess and, as result, each getting only 1 year in prison. Everyone refusing to pay is like both prisoners confessing and each getting 3 years instead of 1.

One way to get around this outcome is for the government not to leave child protection to the so-called free market. It could finance such provision and force people to pay for it by taxing them. And this is precisely what states and localities typically do.

Another version of the prisoners' dilemma, one that's relevant to environmental problems, is called the *tragedy of the commons*. This was discussed in an article by scientist Garrett Hardin.[13] Hardin's concern was the overuse of commonly owed natural resources. By "commonly owned natural resources" I mean those which aren't owned privately but are available to all who want access to them. When a resource is commonly owned, according to Hardin, individual actors are driven to use it for their own purposes, without much regard for how their use of the resource affects others. The "tragedy" is that when all those with "free" access to the resource behave this way, it's at increasing risk of being significantly degraded or depleted.

Some scientists interested in global warming think of this as, largely, a problem of the tragedy of the commons. The Earth's atmosphere is a commonly owned natural resource. Many of us, through driving and other activities, use this natural resource for the emission of greenhouse gases. And we may do this without much regard for how our emissions affect the natural environment. But when billions of us all over the world do this, the result is global climate change as well as the negative outcomes many climate scientists think are caused by such change (more powerful tropical storms, sea level rise accompanied by more coastal flooding, etc.).

As I'm sure you've heard, there are many people urging us to change our behaviors so the threat of global climate change is averted. We should drive less, drive hybrid or electric cars, use solar and wind energy, turn off the lights in our homes when we aren't using them, unplug appliances when we aren't using them, and so forth. And nations around the world have negotiated deals to address global climate change. The problem that all such efforts face is captured by another model called the *assurance game*.

This game is similar to the prisoners' dilemma in one respect. To see how, think of "don't confess" as cooperating in some sense with the other player and think of "confess" as not cooperating. So, as in the prisoner's dilemma, if player 2 in the assurance game doesn't cooperate, then player 1 is better off not cooperating as well. But, unlike the prisoners' dilemma, if player 2 does cooperates, then player 1 is better off cooperating, too. A similar situation faces player 2 when it comes to their payoffs depending on what player 1 does. We can see this situation in tabular form below:

		Player 2's possible actions	
		Don't Cooperate	Cooperate
Player 1's possible actions	Don't Cooperate	3, 3	10, 0
	Cooperate	0, 10	20, 20

We see clearly that if both players could find some way to cooperate, it would result in their highest payoffs.

The problem that players face in this game is that each of them has to decide what to do without knowing what the other will do. Again, they each know what the other player *could* do but not what they *will* do. This uncertainty results in a strong tendency for each player not to cooperate. Each one worries that they'll cooperate while the other player won't, with the result that they'll end up with their worst possible payoff, one of 0 units. But if both fail to cooperate, each gets a payoff of 3 units when they could've got one of 20 units had they just found some way to work things out. Let's see how the assurance game relates to global climate change.

We mentioned earlier that nations around the world have engaged in efforts to address the problem of global climate change, the most recent one, as I write these lines, being the Paris Climate Accord. In the hopes of preventing dangerous increases in the average global temperature, these efforts typically include agreements among nations regarding what they'll do to decrease greenhouse gas emissions. Yet, without a world government in place, it may be that such agreements lack real enforcement mechanisms. I'm no expert on international climate agreements, but if enforcement is a problem, this renders them quite vulnerable to a real-world version of the assurance game.

Each nation may be better off if it, along with all the rest, acts in accordance with the agreement (the cooperate decision). Yet a given nation can't be sure if others will do their share and may fear that it will follow through on its obligations only to later find that no other nation, or very few of them, followed through on theirs. This may make it difficult to resist the temptation to renege on the agreement. But if all, or too many, nations take this approach, the climate agreement may not amount to much.

Individual residents throughout the world face a similar problem. We get the biggest payoff from others joining us when we drive hybrids, turn off our lights, buy solar panels, and the like. But we have no way of being assured that others will join us. So we may decide to forgo the inconvenience and expense of changing our lifestyles to address global climate change because we're worried others won't do their fair share of inconvenience and expense. This climate change collective action problem may be the most challenging one the world has ever seen. I hope we can find some way to address it—the future state of humanity seems to depend on it.

MATHEMATICS AND FAIRNESS

The National Association of Social Workers (NASW) Code of Ethics (the Code) states that social workers "should promote social, economic, political, and cultural values and institutions that are compatible with the realization of social justice."[14] This isn't the only place in the Code where the terms "equity" or "social justice" are used. Yet nowhere in the document do we find a definition of "equity" or "social justice." We also don't find much guidance regarding how best to promote these two values.

Theologians and philosophers have spent a lot of time thinking about equity and social justice. What may surprise you is that mathematicians and quantitative social scientists have thought about this a bit, too. To get a sense of what they've tried to offer, let's start by considering what they call an *allocation* or *distribution problem*.

The mathematician H. Peyton Young defines an allocation problem as a situation which "arises whenever a bundle of resources, rights, burdens, or costs is temporarily held in common by a group of individuals and must be allotted to them individually."[15] Young defines an allocation as "an assignment of the objects to specific individuals."[16]

Entire books have been written on the topic math and fairness. So I obviously can't cover everything here. Instead, just to give you a taste of how mathematics comes up in such discussions, I'll focus on a few examples involving the allocation of an *indivisible resource*. An indivisible resource is one which must be allocated as a whole object; that is, there is no way to split it up so that parts of it can be allocated.

An example of an indivisible resource is a child. I know thinking of a child as a resource sounds kind of yucky, but, within the context of a discussion about mathematics and fairness, a child is just as much a resource as is a spot in the incoming class of a university. To see why, consider a child custody battle. The judge in such a trial faces an allocation problem—how to distribute the child between the two parents, assuming only two parents are involved. The judge couldn't cut the child in two and give half a child to each parent. Well, technically, the judge could do that but doing so would be murder. Also, half a dead child wouldn't have much value for either of the two parents.

A common way judges use to get around this problem, of course, is to order shared custody between the parents. That is, although the child can't be split in half, the time parents get to spend with the child can be. If a judge doesn't think a 50/50 split of time is fair, they could order some other one.

Although child custody battles do come up in discussions about the mathematics of fairness, I won't say any more about that topic here. Instead, I'll turn to one which has been a source of controversy in the United States for more than three decades: *affirmative action*.

For the purposes of this discussion, affirmative action is the granting of preferential treatment to members of a group that is thought to have historically faced discrimination or to be currently facing it. It began under President Lyndon Johnson and has been extensively implemented in employment and education. Almost from the beginning, the policy has been a source of bitter dispute.

Proponents of affirmative action contend that it's a fair way of righting historical and current wrongs. Some also argue that diversity, including diverse points of view, is something to be valued. Since diversity is something of value, and racial, ethnic, and gender differences are associated with different points of view, these proponents argue that affirmative action assures that this value will be realized.

Opponents of affirmative action contend that the policy, although well-meaning perhaps, amounts to reverse discrimination. That is, in trying to address discrimination against blacks and others, the policy fosters discrimination especially against white men. This is seen as patently unfair. Instead of making hiring and college admissions decisions on the basis of race, only qualifications should matter. What counts as qualified for a given job will depend, of course, on the nature of the job. What counts as qualified for college, at least according to many people, has to do with a person's pre-college grades, as well as their scores on a standardized test, such as the Scholastic Aptitude Test (SAT).

As I suspect many readers know, the SAT is an exam that many US colleges and universities require applicants to take as part of the admissions process. The idea is that students' scores on this test predict how well they'll do in college. However, there are those who dispute this claim. Although it's been found that SAT scores *overall* are pretty good predictors of performance in college, it's also been found that SAT scores aren't such good predictors when it comes to performance at *some* schools.[17]

You might be wondering at this point "what on earth does mathematics have to say about the affirmative action debate?" Well, the first thing to be said is that mathematics can't settle it. It may be useful, though, when it comes to developing proposals intended to address the concerns of affirmative action's supporters while also taking into account its opponents' objections. This is precisely the intention of a proposal put forth by Norman Matloff.

Matloff is a statistician and member of the computer science department at the University of California. He's written about an alternative to affirmative action which he argues could be used in college/university admissions processes.[18] The basics of his proposal are as follows.

Some minimum score on the SAT would be determined. All applicants to a university who scored above that minimum would be eligible for admission. The purpose of the minimum is to weed out those who have little chance of doing well in the program. This, again, brings up the question of the predictive power of the SAT; but let's assume, for the sake of discussion, that the SAT is a good predictor of college performance. If the number of people who scored above the minimum exceeded the number of available slots for admission, then some random selection mechanism would be used to select from the eligible pool of applicants. Matloff argues that the random selection mechanism would be a way of promoting diversity in admissions, but, at the same time, it would meet some of the concerns of opponents of affirmative action. This is why it might be regarded as fair to both sides of the debate.

Political scientist Bernard Grofman and mathematician Samuel Merrill wrote a paper in which they examine some of the statistical issues related to Matloff's proposal.[19] To discuss their analysis, I'll use the following notation:

1. $Minority_{mean}$ is the mean SAT score for members of the minority group.
2. $Majority_{mean}$ is the mean SAT score for members of the majority group.

3. T is the minimum SAT score an applicant must attain in order to be eligible for admission.
4. $Success_{min}$ is the success rate for members of the minority group.
5. $Success_{maj}$ is the success rate for members of the majority group.

I suspect $Minority_{mean}$, $Majority_{maj}$, and T are pretty clear. $Success_{min}$ is simply the number of those in the minority group who scored above T divided by the total number of people in the minority group. $Success_{maj}$ is defined similarly.

The terms "minority" and "majority group" have been chosen to keep the discussion general, but you can think of them as referring to blacks and whites, Latinos and whites, women and men, or whichever other two groups you have in mind. The reason I'll focus only on two-group comparisons is because that's what Grofman and Merrill do.

If you were to read the Matloff's article, you'd see that he thinks the idea of admitting people with the highest SAT scores, regardless of race or any other factor, may be placing too much emphasis on SATs as a criterion of admission. However, by still allowing SAT scores to play a role in his random selection scheme, he apparently thinks they have some value in admissions decisions. So, let's assume that T, using Matloff's scheme, would be less than T used in a race, gender, or the like "blind" admissions process. To make the distinction clearer, we'll call the T used in Matloff's proposal T_{random} and the T used in a race, gender, and the like blind admissions process $T_{highest}$.

What Grofman and Merrill show is that using T_{random} in conjunction with random selection to make final admission decisions would result in a higher proportion of those accepted being members of the minority group than would be the case under the $T_{highest}$ admissions process. This might satisfy proponents of affirmative action, while it might upset opponents of it. However, Grofman and Merrill show something else which might satisfy opponents of affirmative action but upset those who support it.

They show that if T_{random} in conjunction with random selection is used, if $Majority_{mean}$ exceeds $Minority_{mean}$, and $Success_{maj}$ exceeds $Success_{min}$, then the proportion of those accepted who are members of the majority group might be greater than the proportion accepted who are minority group members. In an example used in their article, the proportion of majority group members accepted under these conditions is four times that of minority group members.

The intuition here is that lowering the threshold from $T_{highest}$ to T_{random} gives an advantage to members of the minority group who wouldn't have gotten in under the $T_{highest}$ threshold. But it also gives an advantage to members of the majority group who are in the same situation, especially if the proportion of majority group members who can make the T_{random} cut greatly exceeds the proportion of minority group members who can do so.

Affirmative action remains highly contested. Mathematics has received far less attention in this debate than politics, economics, and the fairness of allocating resources on the basis of race and gender. What Matloff's proposal, as well as Grofman and Merrill's analysis of it, suggests is that mathematics may have something to contribute to this discussion as well.[20]

This affirmative action example raises an important conceptual question about fairness—what exactly do we mean when we call a process for allocating spots in college "fair?" The following definition seems to be implicit in Mattlof's proposal: a procedure for allocating college/university spots is fair if (1) only those qualified for a spot are eligible for admission, and, (2) among those eligible, no one should be preferred over any other candidate.

Determining if the qualification condition is met seems to require assessing an applicant's SAT score. But, as I said earlier, some worry that the SAT score may not be a good predictor of college performance. Even if you think a person's SAT score is a good predictor of performance, you may not think it's the only thing colleges should look at. Perhaps a person's high school grade point average (GPA) should be added to the mix.

This discussion about SAT scores and GPA raises an issue I highlighted in Chapter 3. Recall that, in that chapter, we discussed the concepts of the reliability and validity of measurement. The thing we're trying to measure here is whether an applicant is qualified for admission into college. So the question is whether SAT scores and GPAs are valid and reliable measures of qualification. That is, do these measures actually assess the degree to which someone is qualified for college-level work (validity), and do they do so consistently (reliability)? The concerns about predictability notwithstanding, the SAT is a *standardized test*. One of the features of such tests is that they undergo a very involved process of validity and reliability assessment using the tools of a branch of psychology called *psychometrics*.

Psychometrics is an area of study that uses tools from mathematics and statistics to design tests such as the SAT, as well as to evaluate the reliability and validity of such tests. To my knowledge, student GPAs haven't been subjected to the same type of examination. This doesn't mean that GPA is an invalid and unreliable measure of qualification. But it does mean that we know less about how reliable and valid the GPA is than we do about the SAT. I should add, however, that there is research which suggests that even though the GPA hasn't been subjected to the psychometric evaluations that the SAT has, it's a better predictor of college performance than the SAT.[21] This question of how the reliability and validity of GPA and the SAT compare is important because of an issue called *weighting*.

When the term "weighting" is used in mathematics, it refers to the use of numbers to indicate how important something is. Let's apply this idea to the current example.

As I've been saying, we might think that both SAT score and GPA are useful when it comes to predicting how qualified a college applicant is. Thus, we might be interested in using Matloff's procedure, but we might also want to modify it to include GPA. Suppose we've developed a measure which takes the following form:

Qualification = SAT*a + GPA*b

"SAT" stands for a student's percentile rank on the SAT, while "GPA" stands for their GPA rank.[22] The letters "a" and "b" stand for real numbers, each of which can be no smaller than 0 and no larger than 1. We choose a and b on the basis of what we've decided about the relative importance of the SAT versus GPA. And we might determine relative importance on the basis of how we think the SAT and GPA compare when it comes to reliability and validity.

As an example, suppose we've decided that a person's qualification score has to be at least 90 in order for them to be included in the lottery which will ultimately determine whether they're admitted. Also, suppose we've decided to weight SAT and GPA equally in the qualification equation by assigning a = 1 and b = 1. Finally, suppose a candidate's SAT score was at the 75th *percentile* and their GPA was at the 95th one. Being at the 75th percentile means that this person did at least as well as 75% of the students who took the SAT. Being at the 95th percentile means that this person's GPA is at least as high as 95% of the other students' GPA's. Now let's apply the qualification equation:

75*1 + 95*1 = 170

This equation tells us that a student at the 75th percentile for the SAT and the 95th for GPA is well above 90. So they'd clearly be eligible for the admissions lottery. But some might see a problem here. The 75 in the equation is in reference to a US sample of students who took the SAT. There are US data on student GPAs, so it's conceivable that the 95 in the equation could be in reference to a national sample as well.[23] But because of what I said earlier about the assessments of the reliability of the SAT versus the GPA, some might doubt that the GPA is as credible a predictor of school performance as the SAT. Those who hold his view might use the following version of the equation:

75*75 + 95*.25 = 80

Notice that the SAT and GPA scores haven't changed. But now a = .75 and b = .25. That is, the SAT score has a higher weight in determining if this person makes the cut. And since 80 is less than 90, they wouldn't.

Someone who thinks that the GPA is a better predictor than the SAT might reverse the weights and use the equation

$$75*.25 + 95*.75 = 90$$

With these weights in place, the person would just barely make the cut but would get a chance to win a spot in the college.

Questions of fairness, of course, go well beyond college/university admissions. They come up regarding tax policy, social welfare spending, government spending in general, and a host of other areas. Let's consider a few other issues.

The NASW Code of Ethics states the following: "social workers should engage in social and political action that seeks to ensure . . . *equal access to* the resources . . . and *opportunities* they require to meet their basic human needs" (emphasis added).[24] The phrase "equal access to opportunities" sounds like the widely held "*equality of opportunity*" principle of fairness.

Equality of opportunity is usually contrasted with "*equality of outcome*." Equality of outcome, of course, means that some relevant set of people (for example, the set residing in the United States) are to end up with absolutely equal shares of some resource. One question is what resource—money, wealth, or what? For the sake of discussion, let's assume that we want folks to end up with equal amounts of money. So, if N people make up the population, $X must be allocated, and X exceeds N, then the amount of money each person would get would be $X divided by N.

At this writing, the US population is around 300,000,000 people, while the US total personal income (a rough measure of the total amount of money in the nation) is about $16,000,000,000,000.[25] If we divide $16,000,000,000,000 by 300,000,000, we end up with about $53,000. So this is about the amount of money each resident of the United States would get if we were applying the principle of absolute equality. But all US residents clearly don't have the same $53,000 stock of money. In order to ensure that they did, someone, presumably the government, would have to enact policies to maintain an equal distribution of money holdings, *no matter what people did*. That is, people's behavior (how much they worked, invested, how much formal schooling they'd attended, etc.) would have no impact on how much money they ended up with.

This insensitivity of the equality of outcome principle to behavior is why some turn away from it and toward equality of opportunity. One question raised by the equality of opportunity principle is opportunity to do what? Do we want to equalize opportunity to make a high wage or salary, and, if so, what level of wage or salary constitutes a high one? Do we want to equalize the opportunity to attend school, and, if so, how far? Community college? A 4-year college? Graduate school? Or what?

A second question has to do with how we measure opportunity. This is important because if we're going to equalize opportunity, it seems we need some way of knowing how much opportunity people have in order to determine if they have equal amounts of it. And would we measure the opportunity to make a high wage the same way we would the opportunity to attend school?

Some might suggest that we could approach the issue of equality of opportunity a little differently. They might contend that making a sharp distinction between outcomes and opportunities to attain outcomes is misguided—this is because outcomes shape opportunities. A society where there is extreme income and wealth inequality is one where there isn't equality of opportunity. Thus, to equalize opportunity, we have to prevent income and wealth inequality from getting too high. And this raises two more questions.

One is how should we measure income or wealth inequality? To see a common way of doing so, let's focus on wealth.[26] This is often measured using the following steps:

1. Estimate the total net wealth of some population of people.
2. Rank members of the population (or, more likely, a sample of them) from the person with the lowest net wealth to the person with the highest net wealth.
3. Divide this ranked distribution of people into the highest 20%, the next highest 20%, etc., all the way down to the lowest 20% (these 20% groupings are called *quintiles*).
4. For each quintile, add up the net wealth of each person in it to get the total net wealth for the each of the quintiles.
5. Divide the total net wealth for each quintile by the estimated total net wealth for the overall population.

The result of steps 1 through 5 will be the proportion of overall net wealth owned by each quantile. If the distribution is equal, then these proportions should be the same. The degree to which they're not is the degree to which there is inequality. Based on the latest data I could find at the time of this writing, the top 20% of the US population was estimated to own about 89% of the wealth.[27] This quintile method isn't the only one used to measure inequality, but it may be the most commonly referred to one in public discussions and debates about the "wealth gap."

Once we agree on how to measure inequality, another question arises—assuming we don't want there to be too much inequality, how much is too much? If the top 20% of the population owns about 89% of the wealth, then the other 80% of the population owns only about 11% of it. That is, the top 20% owns about 8 times more wealth than the bottom 80% (89 divided by 11 is equal to about 8). Is that too much inequality? If so, where do we draw the line? Would a difference of 6 times instead of 8 times be too much? What about 5 times? How about 4 times?

You might be wondering why I've spent so much time discussing mathematics and fairness. The reason is that this is a great way of making a crucial point. Social workers have a reputation for claiming that we're not "numbers people." Instead, we often regard ourselves as "people people." That is, other than those of us who specialize in quantitative research, we're more interested in helping people than we are in mathematical pursuits. At the same time, we also often think of ourselves as having a special regard for fairness and "social justice."

What this fairness discussion shows is that questions of social justice and quantitative matters aren't so easily divorced from one another. The moment we tried to get clear on what a fair allocation is, we saw mathematical issues come to the fore. The issues we've raised here are just the "tip of the iceberg." There is actually an entire branch of mathematics, called *fair division*, that is all about the mathematics of equitably allocating divisible and indivisible resources.

This discussion about fairness and mathematics marks the end of our journey. I've tried in this book to give you an appreciation for the importance of mathematics to issues of concern to social workers. Along the way, I've also tried to teach you or, more likely, reteach you some basic mathematics. Many in our profession express a distaste for math. I've even heard some say that quantitative work is "mere technical stuff" and that it's far less relevant to our profession than, say, human behavior theory, the acquisition of intervention skills, and our "values base" in the pursuit of social justice. If you've read this far, I hope you're unpersuaded by this latter point of view. If so, then one of the goals I set for myself in writing this book has been accomplished.

NOTES

1. See CNN Politics, *Presidential Results*.
2. See List of State Electoral Votes for 2016.
3. Things are actually a bit more complicated than this. For example, in theory, a Republican candidate could win all the popular votes in a state, other than Maine or Nebraska, yet all that state's electoral votes could still go to the Democratic candidate. But this is more about raw politics than the mathematics of politics, which is what part of this chapter is about.

4. See Ragone (2004).

5. See Procon.org, *1992 and 1996 US Presidential Election Results Maps*.

6. See World Population Review, *California Population*.

7. See US Census Bureau, *Quick Facts Wyoming*.

8. See Ragone (2004, p. 273).

9. See Lippman (2013, p. 75).

10. See Stephanopoulos and McGhee (2014).

11. This is a modification of an example found in Petry (2017), *How the Efficiency Gap Works*.

12. Biologists also use game theory to model interactions among nonhuman organisms.

13. See Hardin (1968), "The Tragedy of the Commons."

14. See National Association of Social Workers, *Code of Ethics*.

15. See Young (1994, p. 7).

16. Ibid.

17. See Jaschik, "Faulty Predictions."

18. See Mattloff, *Why Not a Lottery to Get into UC?*

19. See Grofman and Merril (2004).

20. This section first appeared in an article I wrote (Lewis, 2014).

21. SeeNiu Tienda, "Test Scores, Class Rank, and College Performance: Lessons for Broadening Access an Promoting Success."

22. For the sake of discussion, I'm assuming we have data on students' GPA rankings.

23. See US Department of Education, *The Nation's Report Card*.

24. See National Association of Social Workers, *Code of Ethics*.

25. See Statistica, *Personal Income in the United States from 1990 to 2016*.

26. What I say about wealth here also applies to income.

27. See Desilver, *The Many Ways to Measure Economic Inequality*.

References

Arias, Elizabeth. "United States Life Tables," *National Vital Statistics Reports*, Volume 63, Number 7, November 2014. http://www.cdc.gov/nchs/data/nvsr/nvsr63/nvsr63_07.pdf.

Bennett, Jeffrey, and Briggs, William. (2008). *Using and Understanding Mathematics: A Quantitative Reasoning Approach*. New York: Pearson Education, Inc.

Blau, Joel, and Abramovitz, Mimi. (2014). *The Dynamics of Social Welfare Policy*. New York: Oxford University Press.

Brams, Steven and Taylor, Alan. (1996). *Fair Division: From Cake Cutting to Dispute Resolution*. New York: Cambridge University Press.

Cancian, Maria, Slack, Kristen Shook, and Yang, Mi Youn. (2010). *The Effect of Family Income on Risk of Child Matreatment*. https://www.irp.wisc.edu/publications/dps/pdfs/dp138510.pdf.

Centers for Disease Control and Prevention. *Child Abuse and Neglect: Risk and Protective Factors*. https://www.cdc.gov/violenceprevention/childmaltreatment/riskprotectivefactors.html.

Central Intelligence Agency. *The World Fact Book*. https://www.cia.gov/library/publications/the-world-factbook/rankorder/2091rank.html.

Center on Budget and Policy Priorities. *Where Do Our Federal Dollars Go?* https://www.cbpp.org/research/federal-budget/policy-basics-where-do-our-federal-tax-dollars-go.

CNN Politics. *Presidential Results*. http://www.cnn.com/election/results/president.

DeNavas-Watt, Carmen, and Proctor, Bernadette, D. *Income and Poverty in the United States: 2013*. http://www.census.gov/content/dam/Census/library/publications/2014/demo/p60-249.pdf.

Desilver, Drew. *The Many Ways to Measure Economic Inequality*, September 2015. http://www.pewresearch.org/fact-tank/2015/09/22/the-many-ways-to-measure-economic-inequality/.

Drake, Pamela Peterson. *Calculating Interest Rates*. http://educ.jmu.edu//~drakepp/principles/module3/interestrates.pdf.

Ellis, Erle C. "Overpopulation Is Not the Problem," *The New York Times*, September 2013. https://my.vanderbilt.edu/greencities/files/2014/08/overpopulation-is-not.pdf.

Falk, Gale. *Individual Development Accounts (IDAs): Background on Federal Grant Programs to Help Low-Income Families Save*, July 2013. https://fas.org/sgp/crs/misc/RS22185.pdf.

Frankel, Max. *2016 Estate Tax Rates*. https://www.fool.com/retirement/general/2015/12/18/2016-estate-tax-rates.aspx.

Garman, E. Thomas, and Forgue, Raymond E. (2008). *Personal Finance*. Mason, OH: South-Western Cengage Publishing.

Grofman, Bernard, and Merril, Samuel (2004 December). "Anticipating Likely Consequences of Lotter Based Affirmative Action," *Social Science Quarterly*, 85(5), 1447-1468.

Hand, David. (2004). *Measurement and Practice*. New York: Arnold Publishers.

Hardin, Garret. (1968). "The Tragedy of the Commons," *Science*. http://science.sciencemag.org/content/162/3859/1243.full.

Hasssett, Matthew J., and Stewart, Donald G. (1999). *Probability and Risk Management*. New Hartford, CT: Actex Publications.

Heap, Shaun; Lyons, Bruce; Hollis, Martin; Sugden, Robert; and Albert Weale. (1992). *The Theory of Choice: A Critical Guide*. New Jersey: Wiley-Blackwell.

Hedden, Sarra L., Kennet, Joel, Lipari, Rachel, Medley, Grace, Tice, Peter, Copello, Elizabeth, and Kroutil, Larry A. *Behavioral Health Trends in the United States; Results from the 2014 National Survey on Drug Use and Health*. http://www.samhsa.gov/data/sites/default/files/NSDUH-FRR1-2014/NSDUH-FRR1-2014.htmidtextanchor074.

Internal Revenue Service. *Estate Tax*. https://www.irs.gov/businesses/small-businesses-self-employed/estate-tax.

Internal Revenue Service. *Topic 409-Capital Gains and Losses*. https://www.irs.gov/taxtopics/tc409.html?_ga=1.172080224.279361225.1475119144.

Jackson, Brooks. *Who Holds Our Debt*. http://www.factcheck.org/2013/11/who-holds-our-debt/.

Jaschik, Scott. "Faulty Predictions," *Inside Higher Ed*, January 2016. https://www.insidehighered.com/news/2016/01/26/new-research-suggests-sat-under-or-overpredicts-first-year-grades-hundreds-thousands.

Knoema. *Wealth of the World's Richest People vs. GDP of Countries*. http://knoema.com/wqezguc/world-s-billionaires-wealth-vs-countries-gdp.

Lewis, Michael A. "Should Affirmative Action Be Replaced with Random Selection?" *Significance*, May 2014. https://www.statslife.org.uk/social-sciences/1395-should-affirmative-action-be-replaced-with-random-selection.

Lippman, David. (2013). *Math in Society*. http://www.opentextbookstore.com/mathinsociety/2.4/mathinsociety.pdf.

List of State Electoral Votes for 2016. http://state.1keydata.com/state-electoral-votes.php.

Mahajan, Sanjay. (2010). *Street Fighting Mathematics: The Art of Educated Guessing and Opportunistic Problem Solving*. Cambridge, MA: MIT Press.

Masters, Jonathan. *US Gun Policy: Global Comparisons*. http://www.cfr.org/society-and-culture/us-gun-policy-global-comparisons/p29735.

Mattloff, Norman. *Why Not a Lottery to Get into UC?* January 1995. http://heather.cs.ucdavis.edu/pub/AffirmativeAction/LAT.NM.html.

McLaughlin, Thomas A. (2009). *Financial Basics for Nonprofit Managers*. Hoboken, NJ: John Wiley and Sons, Inc.

Mook, Delo E., and Vargush, Thomas. (1987). *Inside Relativity*. Princeton: Princeton University Press.

Morgan, Stephen L., and Winship, Christopher. (2015). *Counterfactuals and Causal Inference: Methods and Principles for Social Research*. New York: Cambridge University Press.

Murray, Charles, and Hernstein, Richard. (1994). *The Bell Curve: Intelligence and Class in American Life*. New York: The Free Press.

National Association of Social Workers. *Code of Ethics*. https://www.socialworkers.org/About/Ethics/Code-of-Ethics/Code-of-Ethics-English.

National Center for Health Statistics. *Marriage and Divorce*. www.cdc.gov/nchs/fastats/marriage-divorce.htm.

Niu, Sunny X., and Tienda, Marta. "Test Scores, Class Rank, and College Performance: Lessons for Broadening Access an Promoting Success," *Rassegna Italiana di Sociologia*, April 2012. https://www.ncbi.nlm.nih.gov/pmc/articles/PMC3685191/.

Pearl, Judea. (2009). *Causality*. New York: Cambridge University Press.

Petry, Eric. (2017). *How the Efficiency Gap Works*. https://www.brennancenter.org/sites/default/files/legal-work/How_the_Efficiency_Gap_Standard_Works.pdf.

Procon.org. *1992 and 1996 US Presidential Election Results Maps*. http://clinton.procon.org/view.resource.php?resourceID=004025.

Ragone, Nick. (2004). *The Everything American Government Book*. Avon, MA: Adams Media.

Rowland, Donald T. (2003). *Demographic Methods and Concepts*. New York: Oxford University Press.

Schmitt, John. (2013). "Why Does the Minimum Wage Have No Discernible Effect on Unemployment?" http://www.cepr.net/documents/publications/min-wage-2013-02.pdf.

Statistica. *Personal Income in the United States from 1990 to 2016 (in Billions of US dollars)*. https://www.statista.com/statistics/216756/us-personal-income/.

Stephanopoulos, Nicholas, and McGhee, Eric. (2014). "Partisan Gerrymandering and the Efficiency Gap," *Public Law and Legal Theory Working Papers*. http://chicagounbound.uchicago.edu/cgi/viewcontent.cgi?article=1946&context=public_law_and_legal_theory.

Taboga, Marco. (2010). *Lectures on Probability Theory and Mathematical Statistics*. Self Published.

Treasury Direct. *The Debt to the Penny and Who Holds It*. http://treasurydirect.gov/NP/debt/current.

US Census Bureau. (2012). *Statistical Abstract of the United States*. Washington, DC: Government Printing Office.

US Census Bureau. *Trade in Goods with China*. https://www.census.gov/foreign-trade/balance/c5700.html.

US Census Bureau, *Trade in Goods with China*. https://www.census.gov/foreign-trade/balance/c5700.html.

US Census Bureau, *Quick Facts Wyoming*. https://www.census.gov/quickfacts/fact/table/WY/EDU685215.

US Congress. *The Federal Budget in 2015*. https://www.cbo.gov/sites/default/files/114th-congress-2015-2016/graphic/51110-budget1overall.pdf.

US Congress. *H.R. 3734*. https://www.gpo.gov/fdsys/pkg/BILLS-104hr3734enr/pdf/BILLS-104hr3734enr.pdf.

US Department of Education, *The Nation's Report Card*. https://nces.ed.gov/nationsreportcard/pdf/studies/2011462.pdf.

US Inflation Calculator, *Consumer Price Index Data from 1913–2017*. http://www.usinflationcalculator.com/inflation/consumer-price-index-and-annual-percent-changes-from-1913-to-2008/.

US Tax Center, *2015 Federal Tax Rates, Personal Exemptions, and Standard Deductions*. https://www.irs.com/articles/2015-federal-tax-rates-personal-exemptions-and-standard-deductions.

Vanderwheele, Tyler. (2015). *Explanation in Causal Inference*. New York: Oxford University Press.

Westfall, Peter H., and Henning, Kevin S. S. (2013). *Understanding Advanced Statistical Methods*. Boca Raton, FL: CRC Press.

Wolfsohn, Reeta, and Michaeli, Dorlee. "Financial Social Work, *"Encyclopedia of Social Work*, February 2014. http://socialwork.oxfordre.com/view/10.1093/acrefore/9780199975839.001.0001/acrefore-9780199975839-e-923.

World Health Organization. *Crude Death and Birth Rate Data by Country*. http://apps.who.int/gho/data/node.main.CBDR107?lang=en.

World Population Review. *California Population*. http://worldpopulationreview.com/states/california-population/.

World Wide Tax Summaries. *United States Corporate-Taxes on Corporate Income*. http://taxsummaries.pwc.com/uk/taxsummaries/wwts.nsf/ID/United-States-Corporate-Taxes-on-corporate-income.

Young, H. Peyton. (1994). *Equity*. Princeton: Princeton University Press.

Index